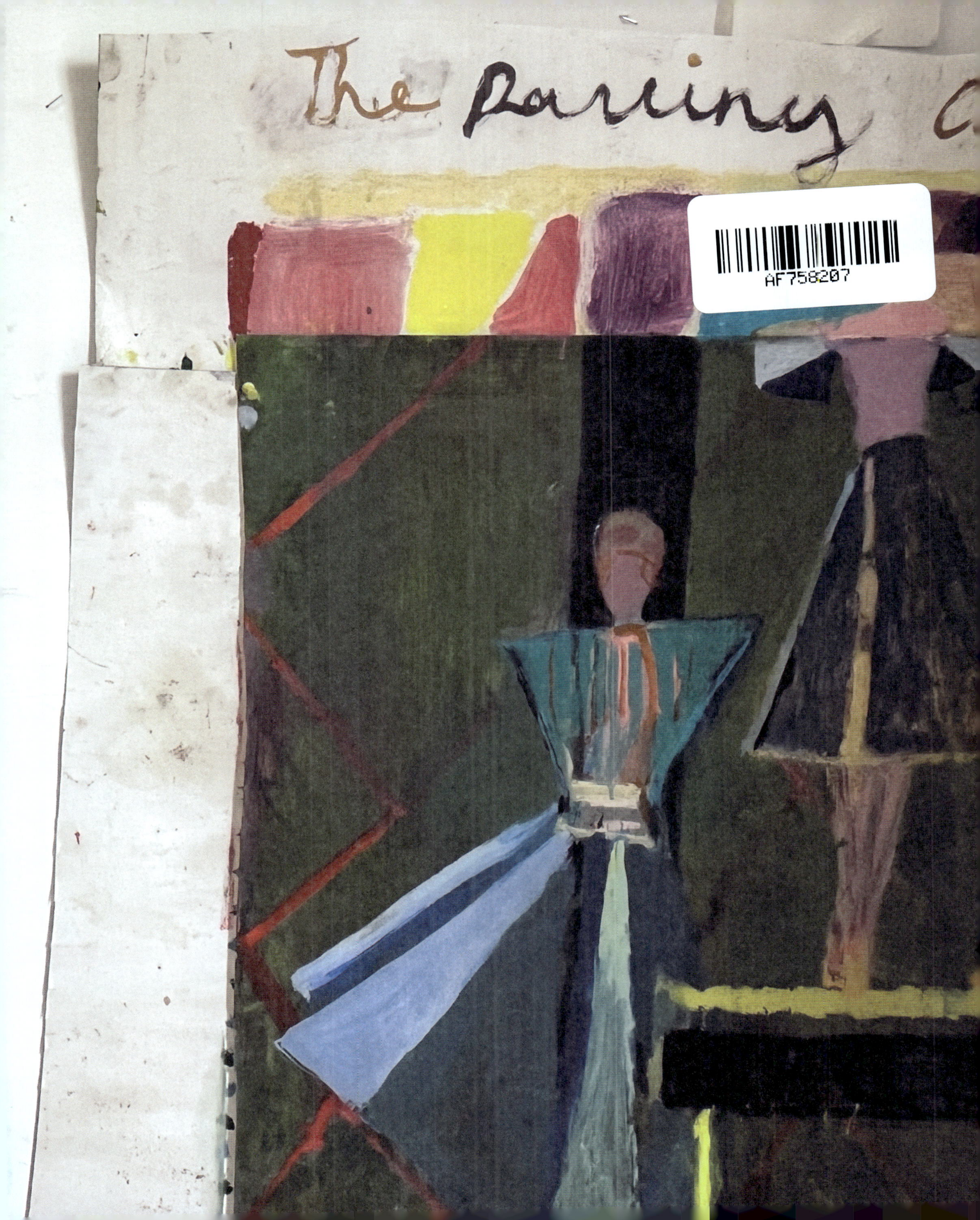


AF758207

# LORNA ROBERTSON thoughts, meals, days

LORNA ROBERTSON

# thoughts, meals, days

INGLEBY **Anomie**

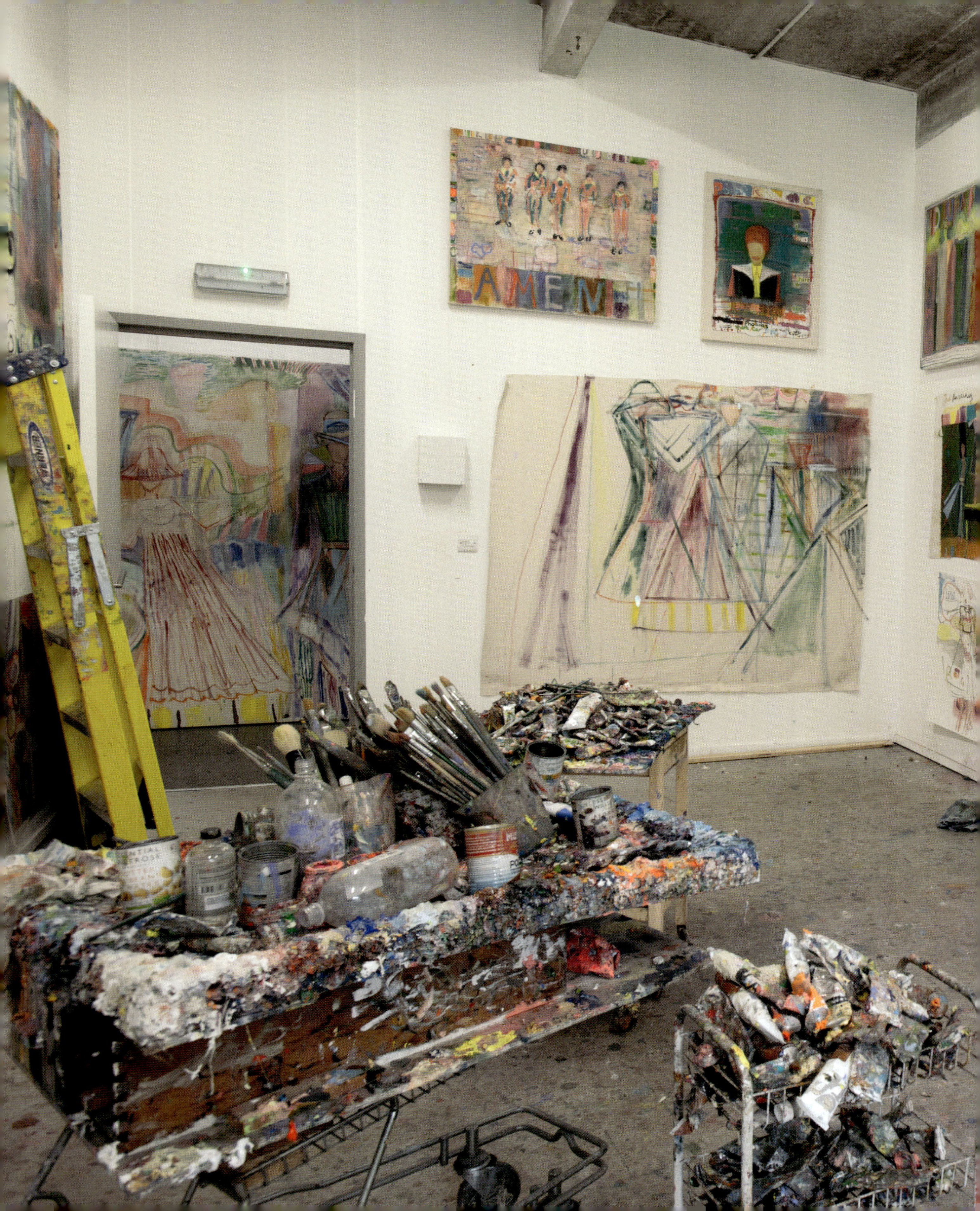
AMEN

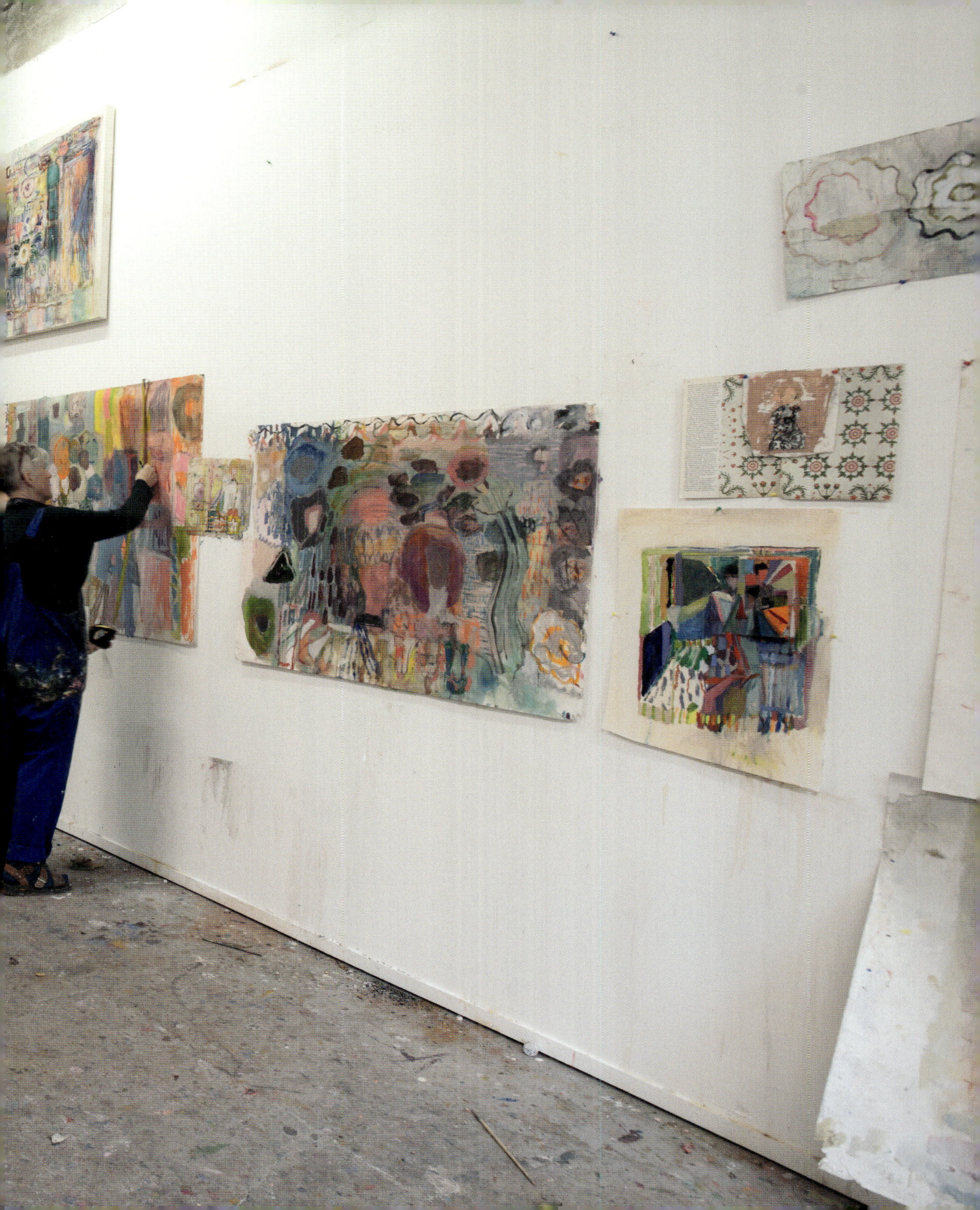

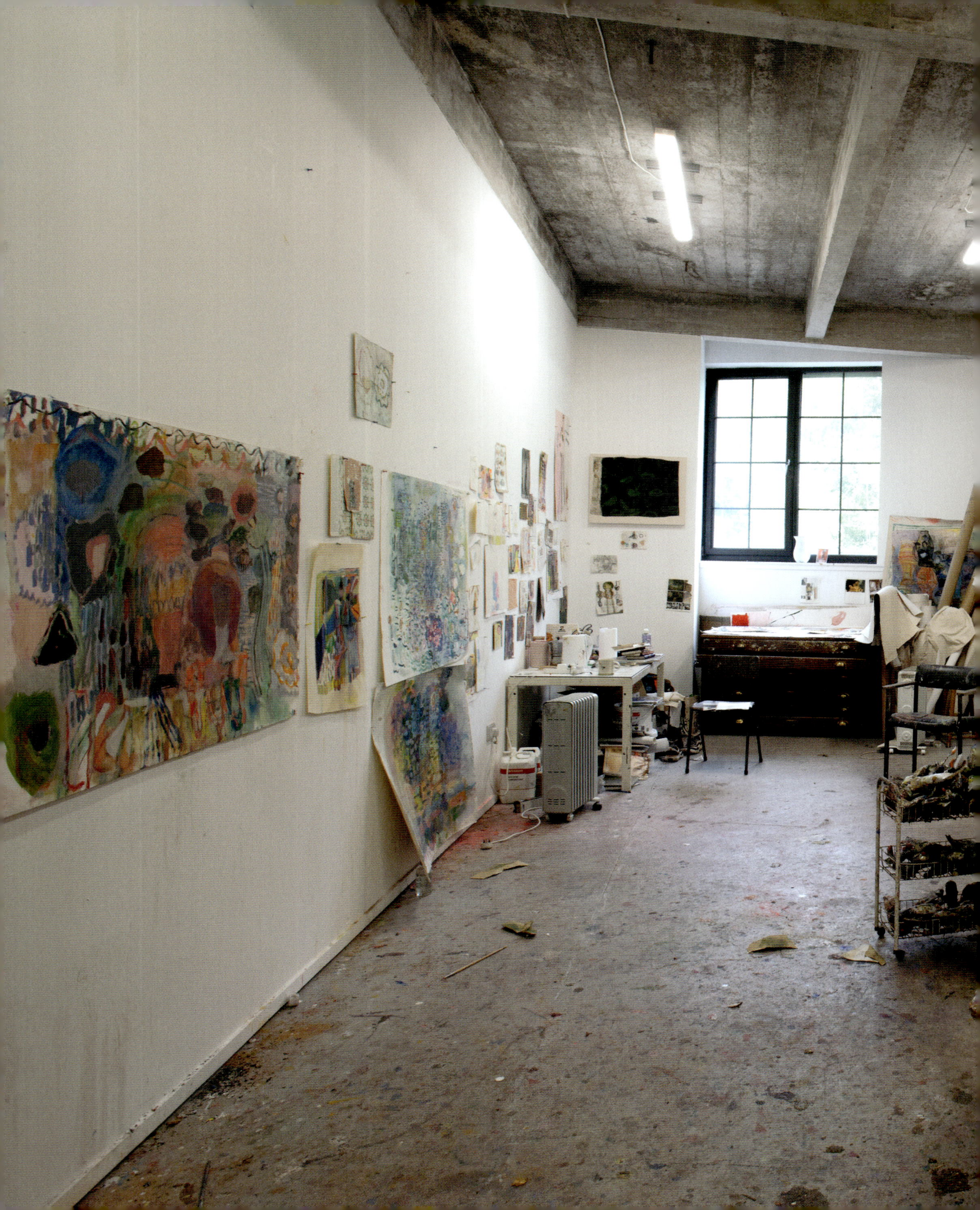

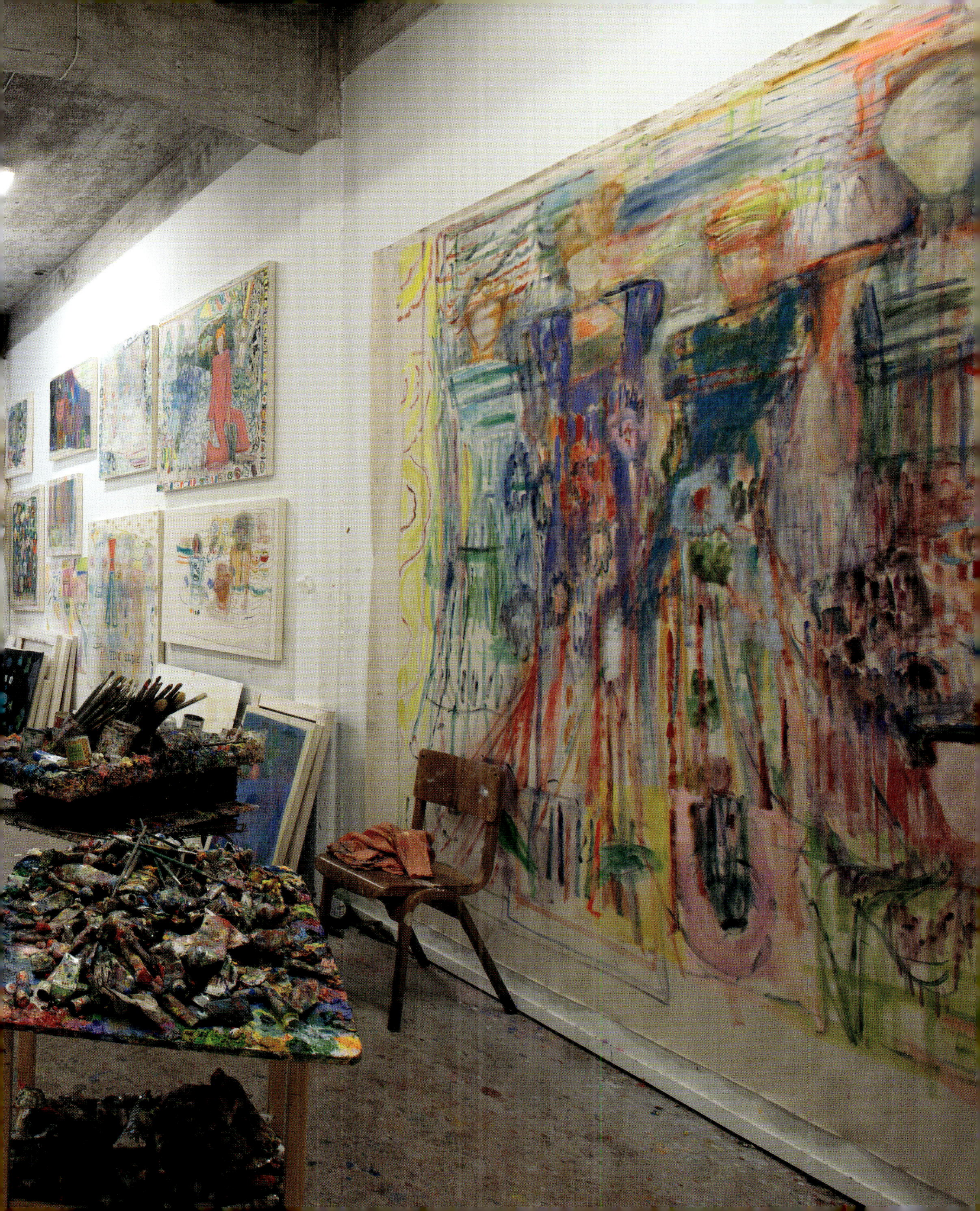

# LORNA ROBERTSON *by Hettie Judah*

*I long for the freedom to go out alone: to go, to come, to sit on a bench in the Jardin des Tuileries, and especially to go to the Luxembourg, to look at the decorated store windows, to enter churches and museums, and to stroll in the old streets in the evenings. This is what I envy. Without this freedom one cannot become a great artist.*

Marie Bashkirtseff, *I Am the Most Interesting Book of All* (1879)[1]

Lorna Robertson's paintings, with their dynamic angles and theatrical edges, make me think of how the female body is framed in the modern city. It's a body that I'd locate some time in the second half of the twentieth century – the 1970s or 80s. This is a body that is dressed to be seen in public – it is fashionable, a colourful hourglass riposte to the staid verticality of office towers. We can see it fitted into the oblong confines of magazine covers arranged on news kiosks, in the days when print still reigned. It can be found stuck, posed and dressed, behind the glass of boutique windows. It is framed, too, by garments, which squeeze it into a feminine shape that is almost architectural in its drama.

As Lauren Elkin reminds us in *Flâneuse* (2016) – in which she walks in the footsteps of women in the modern city – this is also an active body, one that is itself capable of looking. It can appraise, choose, observe, judge and gather intelligence that will assist in the telling of stories and composition of pictures. It can see itself reflected back in the glass of those same boutique windows: a phenomenon evoked in the dim warmth of jumbled figures and lettering in Robertson's painting *Train song* (2022). As Marie Bashkirtseff realised, while living in Paris in the late nineteenth century, the artist has much to gain as a watcher in the city: material details of buildings and clothes, the dynamic of streets and silhouettes, the graphic force of signage, the great circus of artificial colours.

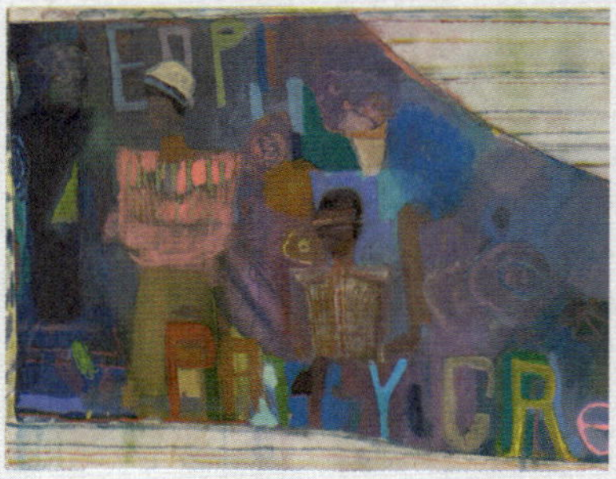

They are not women, the shapes that pattern Robertson's paintings – most have no face, and many are posed like mannequins – but they are certainly feminine, and seem to be destined for a female gaze.

 Above: Lorna Robertson, *Train song*, 2022

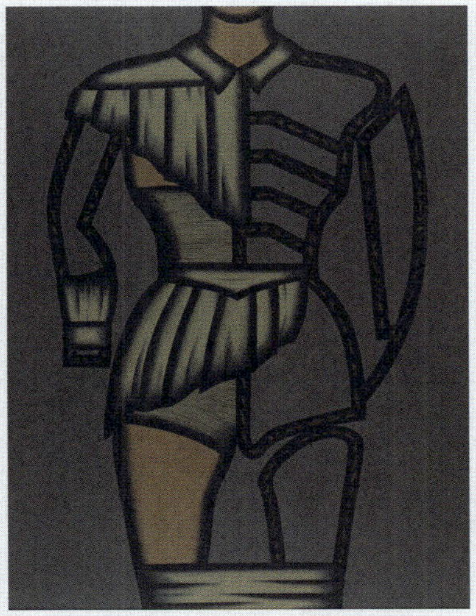

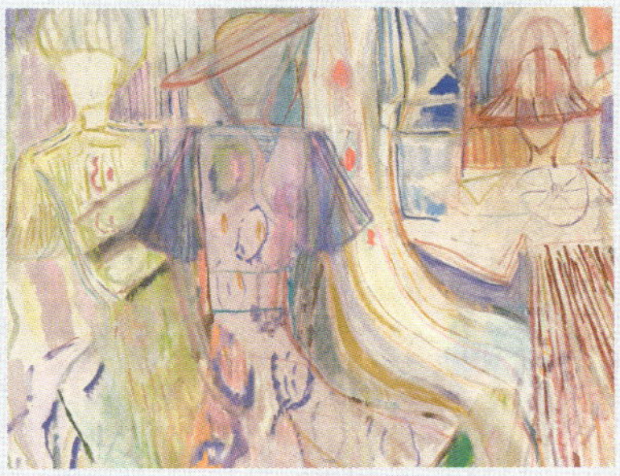

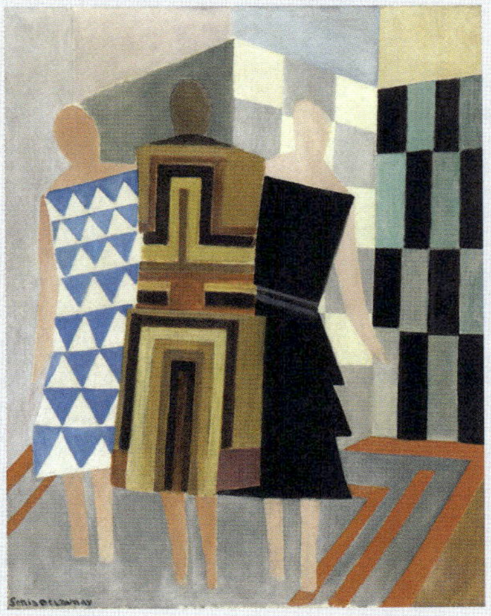

On a painting in progress, their form is reduced to a pair of abutting triangles, directing our attention towards the centre of the body, like a road junction or intersecting beams of light. As with Christina Ramberg's paintings of the mid 1970s, the ultra-feminised, cinched-waisted body becomes as one with the built environment itself. In *Words murmured* (2022) the misty layering of the painted surface suggests overlapping rows of bodies, reduced to costume and shape like dancers in a Busby Berkeley routine. The closest are bright and vividly patterned, the furthest mere ghostly silhouettes. It could be a monumental cityscape on a hazy evening, in which the bodies perform as buildings. As in Sonia Delaunay's *Simultaneous Dresses (Three Women, Forms, Colours)* (1925), Robertson constructs a city of women in which strong line and pattern bind costume to architecture.

In *Dumb* (2022) the figures are instead columnar, like caryatids on neoclassical facades: decorative, supportive, unspeaking. Robertson has inscribed that title word in coloured lettering along the top, like a sign-painter. 'Dumb', like dumb blondes, or shop dummies: either way, it's insulting. It's a reminder of how beauty comes coupled with accusations of superficiality. A body confected to be pleasing to the eye has historically been dismissed as not much of a mind. Indulging in the pleasures of colour and line comes at a cost.

Robertson's studio drawers and walls carry clippings from vintage magazines and dress patterns. She collects copies of *Vogue* and *House & Garden* from the 1970s. The exaggerated, angular silhouettes of fashion illustrations, with their nipped waists, flying skirts and tilted hats, certainly inform the abstracted figures that populate many of her canvases, but she also looks at the interplay of text and image. *Leisureline* (2015-16) evokes aspirational indolence – the tamed wilderness suggested in its composition might be taken from a magazine editorial or a commercial product range – but Robertson's lettering has none of the authority of formal graphics. The letters are multi-coloured, a little goofy: more like the hand-painted signage from a fairground than slick print or shop lettering.

Above: Christina Ramberg, *Hereditary Uncertainty*, 1977, acrylic on Masonite, 120.7 x 90.2 cm. © estate of Christina Ramberg, courtesy of Corbett vs. Dempsey, Chicago

Centre: Lorna Robertson, *Words murmured*, 2022 (detail)

Below: Sonia Delaunay, *Simultaneous Dresses (Three Women, Forms, Colours)*, 1925, oil on canvas, 146 x 114 cm. Museo Nacional Thyssen-Bornemisza, Madrid. © PRACUSA S.A

It's only rarely in her paintings that letters coalesce into actual words. *A cure* (2022) carries sense memory of a magazine cover: a head with prominent lips, fringed with fragments of text. The arrangement of letters conforms to conventions of magazine titling only in their positioning: there's nothing that you can read here. The bright painted letters are only shapes: abstract ideas of words, much as the figures are abstract ideas of women.

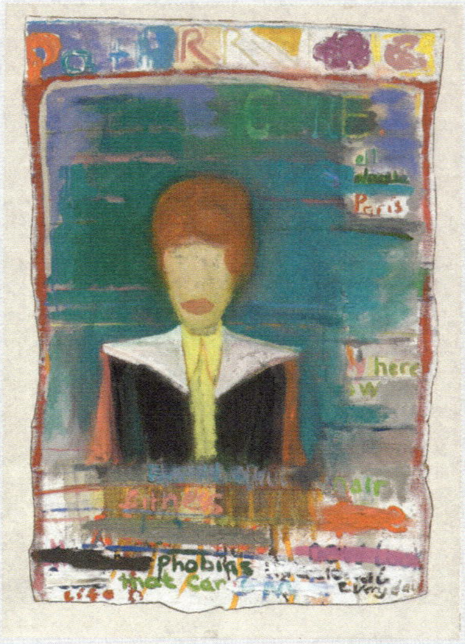

There are other types of image building that catch Robertson's eye. On her studio wall are taped various pictures of textiles and tapestries. You can see how the compositional particularities of tapestry would attract her: everything is facing front, and crammed tightly into the woven space, not a thread wasted. Like a weaver, there's often a grid structuring her work. This pictorial framework is most visible in *Try see, try say* (2022) a painting in which shapes and fragments of image are crammed together, apparently slotted into a grid structure like elements in a Modernist shelving unit infected with gaudy, flowery 1970s wallpaper and gestural drips.

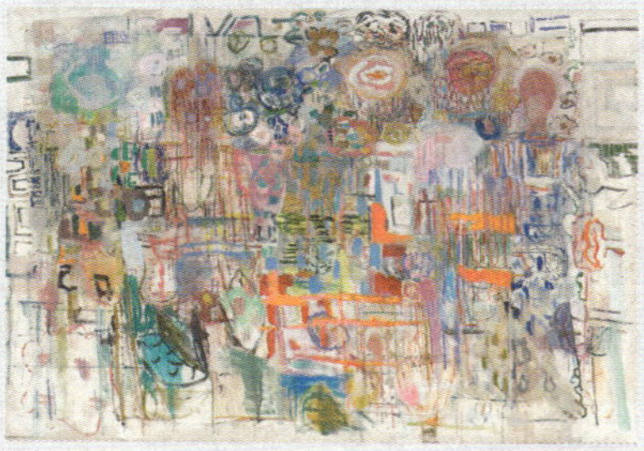

That title – *Try see, try say* – comes from Samuel Beckett's *Worstward Ho*,[2] a novella in which words are used both for their associations and for their abstract percussive qualities. There is no 'right' way to read *Worstward Ho*: its words float beyond fixed meaning. It's a useful position from which to approach Robertson's work: arrangements of familiar symbols that won't be pinned down.

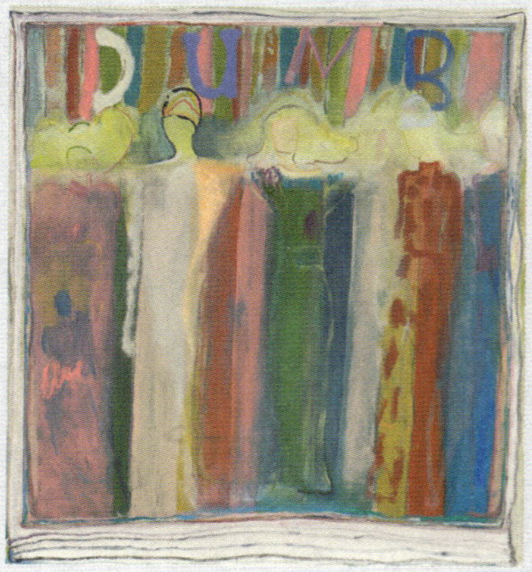

In my notes from visiting Robertson's Glasgow studio, I've boxed the phrase 'sweetness as a risk' in multiple lines of black ink. Wielding my pen to emphasise the importance of this idea, I have inadvertently adopted her compositional tactics: frames, grids, concentric lines, structures by which to organise shapes and direct the eye. Patching roughly cut canvas onto a stretched canvas support, as she has in *Dumb* and *In snow white cottages* (2022), Robertson has trailed thin lines of colour around the stuck edge, at once framing the painted panel and drawing attention to its uneven margin. *This is not a grand picture*, the uneven edging seems to say, *I'm just something she painted, then preserved, like a photo torn from a magazine pasted*

Above: Lorna Robertson, *A cure*, 2022

Centre: Lorna Robertson, *Try see, try say*, 2022

 Below: Lorna Robertson, *Dumb*, 2022

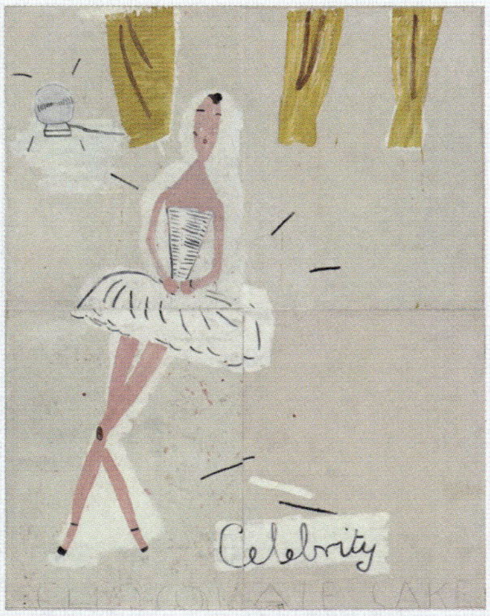


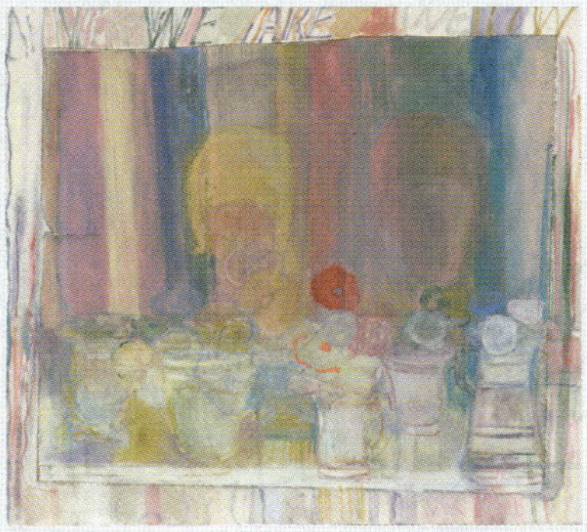

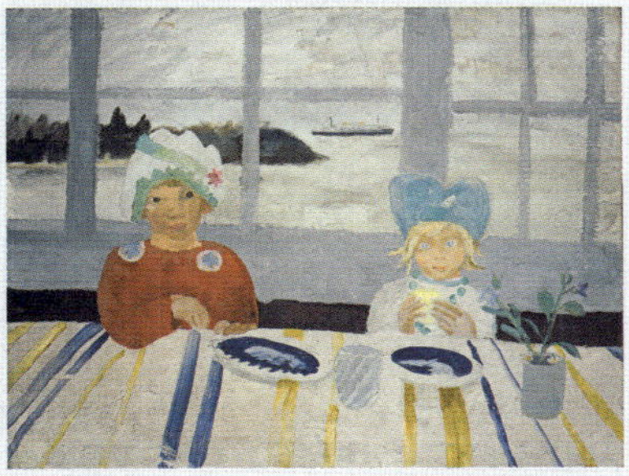

*into a scrapbook*. I wouldn't scribble over and draw boxes around the text in this essay in the way I do in my notebook: or if I did it would be to make a point about process and work in progress. Robertson's style is one of assumed informality – stuck-on scraps of canvas, lines drawn in paint – she doesn't let you relax into an image or the comfort of a slick, finished thing (a habit she shares with the painter Rose Wylie, who is likewise interested in marginalia, reduced forms and text skittering around figures.)

What do you risk with sweetness? Might you be accused of making dumb art, of being a dummy? At the centre of *Saints and liars* (2022) is a tablecloth scattered with mugs of flowers, all in the cool, sweet, chalky tones of sugared almonds. This painting, on its uneven portion of canvas, has been framed in a border of dark blue-green flowers, so roughly rendered or smeared that they are barely blooms at all. The dark, fragmenting flowers of the border mitigate the risk of the sweetness within, circling the forbidden realm of the domestic, the feminine and the appealingly decorative. The scratch dryness of the paint, which in places peters out into traces of colour caught on a rough surface, forbids us from indulging in the seductive appeal of what appears, unusually, to be a painting of a physical scene, rather than an arrangement of forms in space.

In *We are, we are* (2022) barely defined faces are seen through a jumble of vases and blooms. Robertson's composition recalls Winifred Nicholson's painting of her children, squeezed into a space between the blue and yellow stripes of the kitchen tablecloth and the firm grid of the window behind them in *Jake and Kate on the Isle of Wight* (1931). Robertson creates an even tighter, flatter pictorial space – nevertheless we are in the danger zone of decorative appeal. Just take in those stripes, all washy ultramarine and rosy pink.

When Robertson was studying at Duncan of Jordanstone College of Art in Dundee in the 1990s, a tendency toward the decorative was met with something like horror. Though perhaps unstated at the time, it carried associations with craft, beautification, the applied arts – women's stuff, by extension. Not good, big, important art, as

Above: Rose Wylie, *Celebrity*, 2006, oil on canvas, 366 x 305 cm. The Bjørnholt Collection, Norway. © Rose Wylie

Centre: Lorna Robertson, *We are, we are*, 2022

Below: Winifred Nicholson, *Jake and Kate on the Isle of Wight*, 1931, oil on canvas, 68.5 x 89 cm. Scottish National Gallery of Modern Art, Edinburgh. ©Trustees of Winifred Nicholson

made by men. This early-acquired prejudice endures in the wariness with which Robertson navigates the zone of sweetness: here is the source of the risk. She recalls the thrill, years after leaving college, on encountering the work of the Brazilian artist Beatriz Milhazes, and seeing how bold and experimental art could be in flirting with the decorative.

Filling the canvas of *In snow white cottages*, Robertson's flowers are the flowers of early Modernism: the vivid pink circles held aloft by Paula Modersohn-Becker in her *Self-Portrait with Two Flowers in Her Raised Left Hand* (1907) or the German artist's radically simplified poppies and marigolds painted in that same, final, year of her life. Here, as in many other works, there is ambiguity as to what role the flowers are performing: are they a patterned cloth? A garden? A display of cut blooms? They melt back and forth between background and foreground. In *Tomorrow* (2022) they form a simple border around a scene in which flowers cascade across the landscape, but also across the full skirt of a figure with her arms raised. All are rendered in similar pictorial shorthand – a scalloped oval indicating petals with a roundish loop at the centre.

When does a piece of canvas stop being a textile and become a painting, and vice versa? *Faint sound* (2022), with its pattern of green flora on black, could be an outsized fabric swatch. Robertson has stuck a fragment of newspaper to one edge, making the collaged scrap of canvas more object-like, as though it were something she had found rather than something she had made.

As in the floral textiles of Sonia Delaunay, Robertson's flowers spin like Catherine wheels toward geometric abstraction. Blooms are ambassadors for colour: Delaunay eventually allowed them to transform into patterns of pure coloured light in her compositions of radiant circles. Their movement across the canvas owes more to instinctive harmony and rhythm than it does to anything representational.

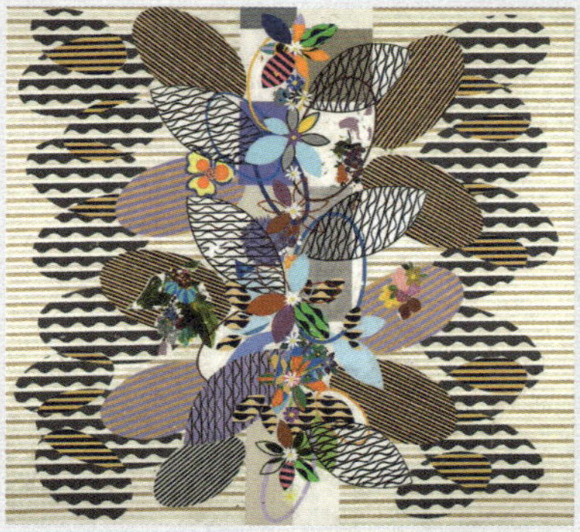

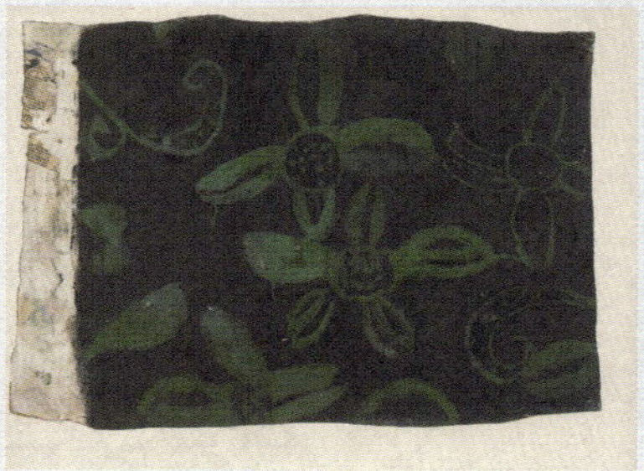

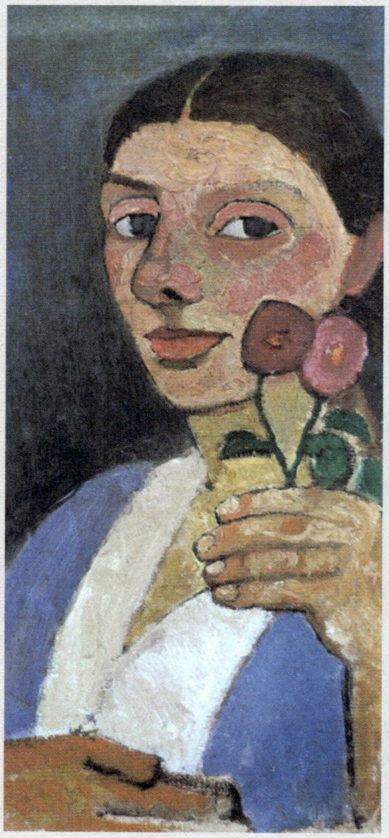

Above: Beatriz Milhazes, *Banho de Rio*, 2017, acrylic paint on canvas, 28 x 30 cm. Collection of The Tate. © Beatriz Milhazes

Centre: Lorna Robertson, *Faint sound*, 2022, oil on canvas, 56 x 75 cm

Below: Paula Modersohn-Becker, *Self-Portrait with Two Flowers in Her Raised Left Hand*, 1907, oil on canvas, 55.2 x 24.8 cm. Jointly owned by The Museum of Modern Art, New York and Neue Galerie New York

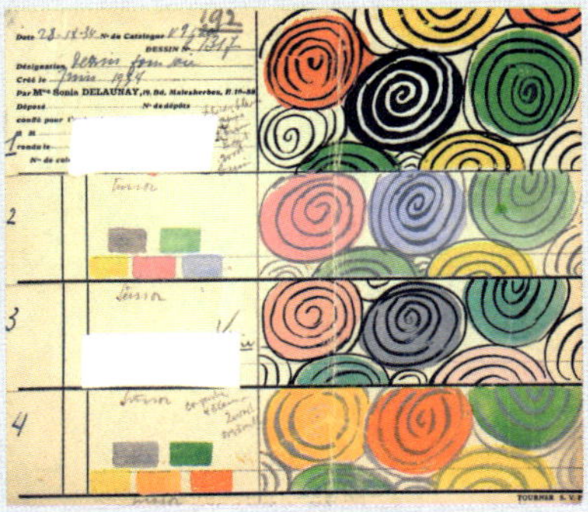

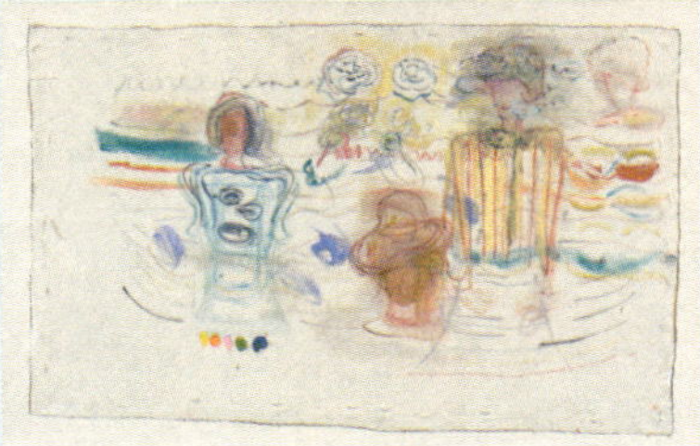

Robertson listens to music as she works, and her paintings are often composed like sound works, punctuated by returning motifs, balanced between harmony and discord, built up in many layers of different elements. The empty space in works like *If they were not* (2022) can be read like a musical pause: she's making space around the notes. Don't be fooled by the cool abstraction, there's feeling here too – memory floods in waves of colour and rhythm through these paintings. Sometimes, as in Beckett's writing, it's fugitive stuff that resists fixed form. All you can do is play, rearranging elements, until that feeling – that unfathomable sense – manifests somehow, in the spaces between words or shapes.

*Enough. Sudden enough. Sudden all far. No move and sudden all far. All least. Three pins. One pinhole. In dimmost dim. Vasts apart. At bounds of boundless void. Whence no farther. Best worse no farther. Nohow less. Nohow worse. Nohow naught. Nohow on.*

Samuel Beckett, *Worstward Ho* (1983)

[1] Quoted in Lauren Elkin, *Flâneuse: Women Walk the City in Paris, New York, Tokyo, Venice and London* (Vintage, London, 2017) p.12

[2] Samuel Beckett, *Worstward Ho* (1983), first published by Grove Press, New York, John Calder, London, 1983

Above: Sonia Delaunay, *Dessin pour soie 1317*, 1934, gouache, ink and pencil on paper, 21.4 x 24.2 cm. Private collection, © PRACUSA S.A, courtesy of Louisiana Museum of Modern Art

Below: Lorna Robertson, *If they were not*, 2022

# LARGE PAINTINGS

 *Words murmured*, 2022, oil on canvas, 217 x 253 cm

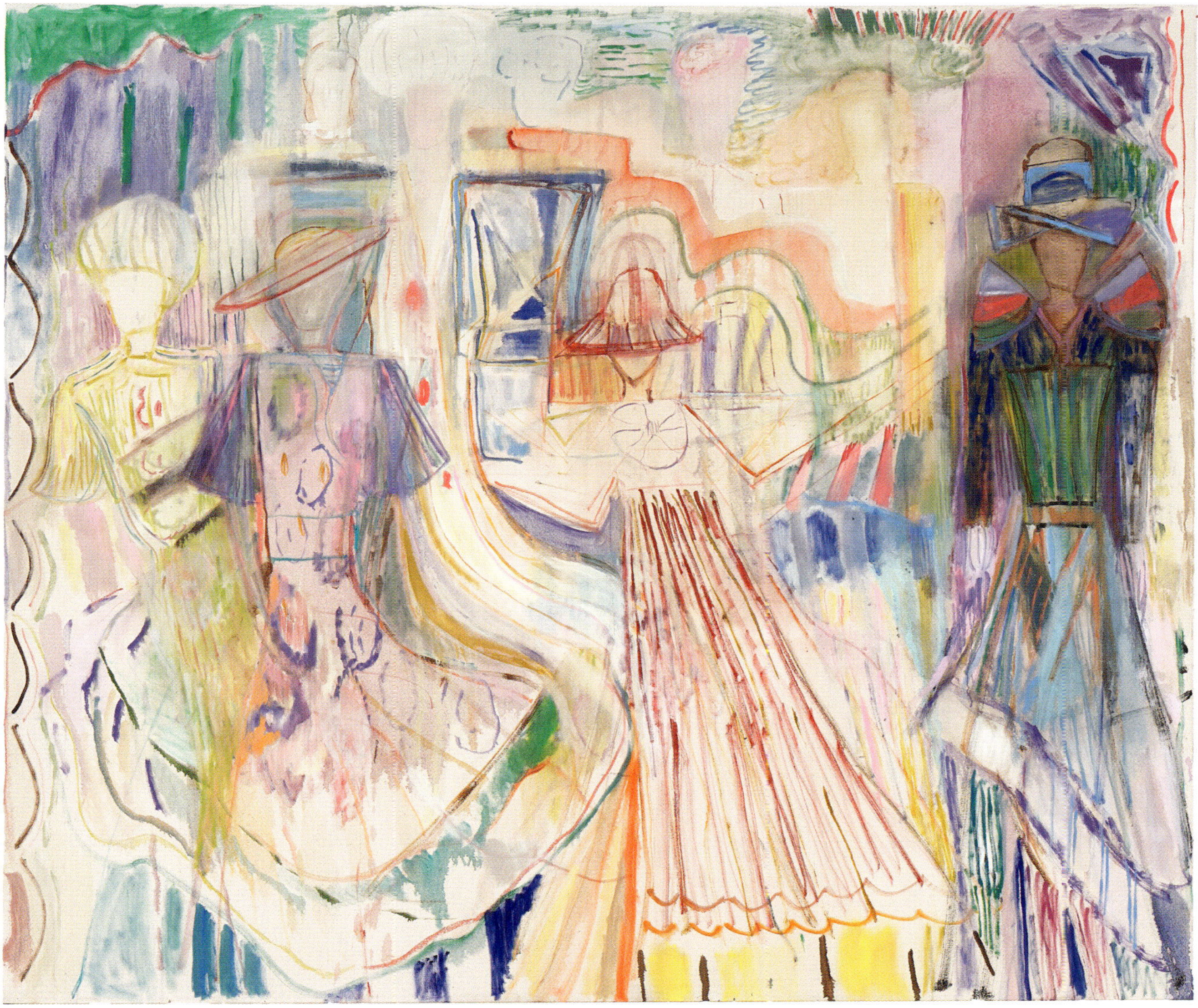

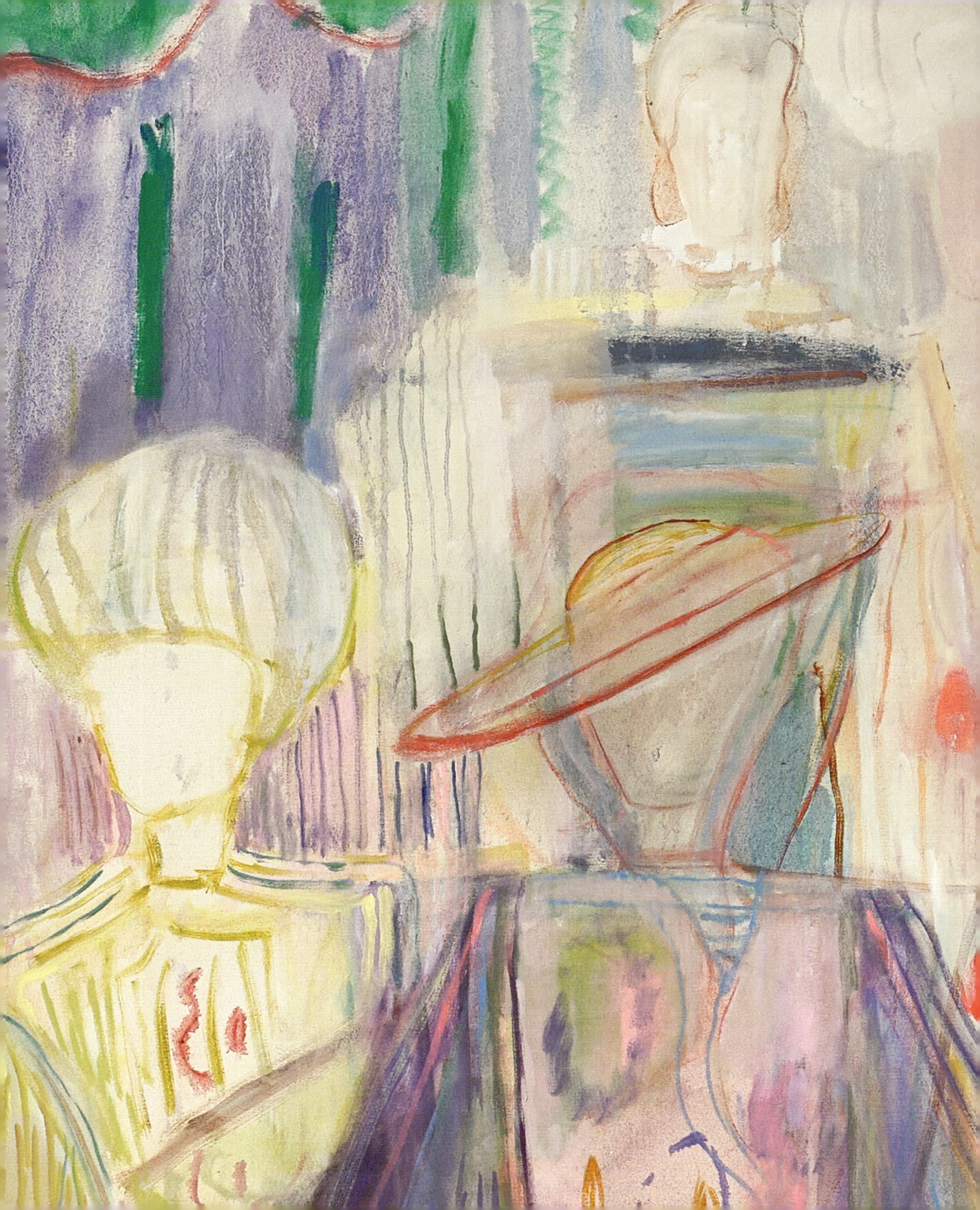

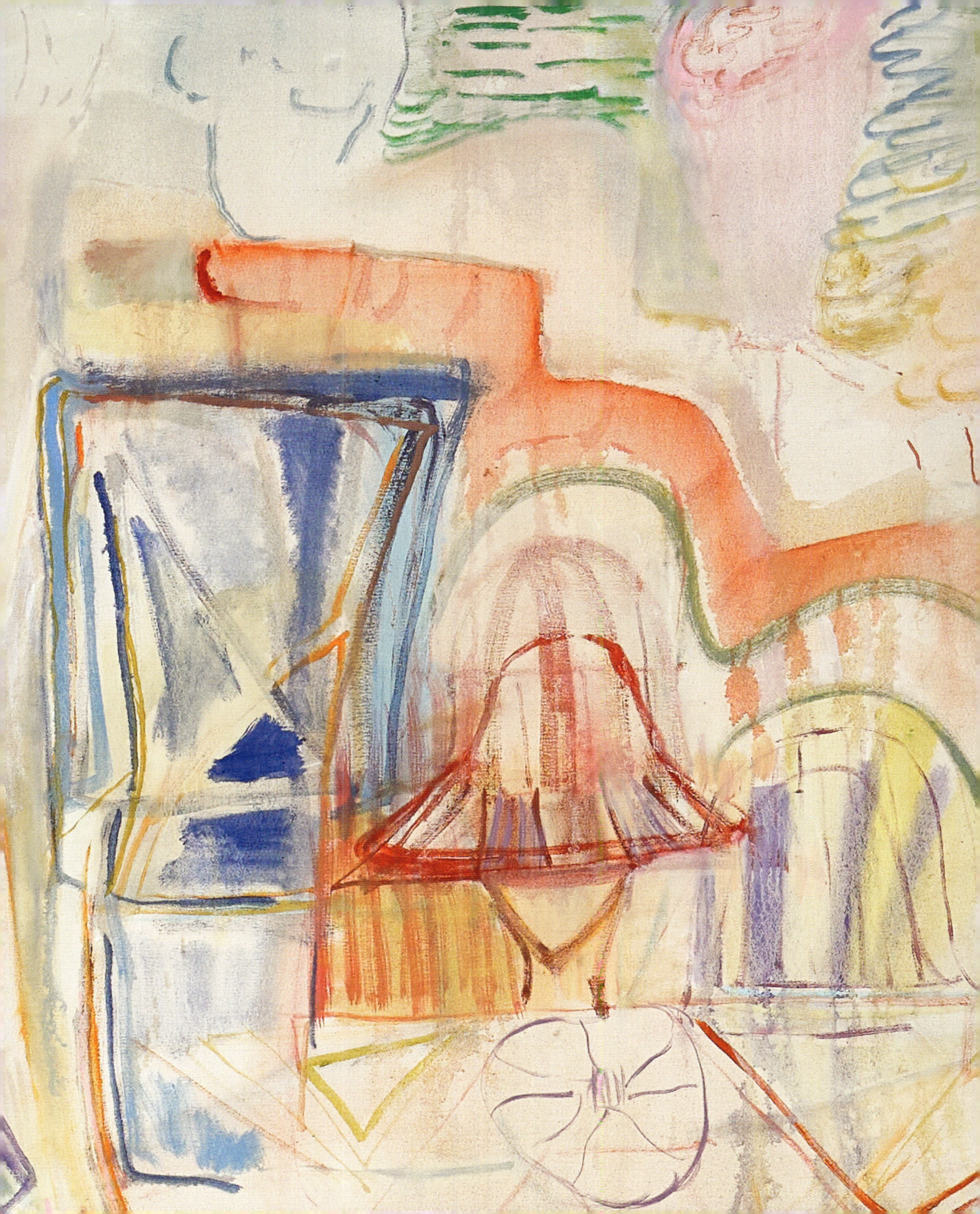

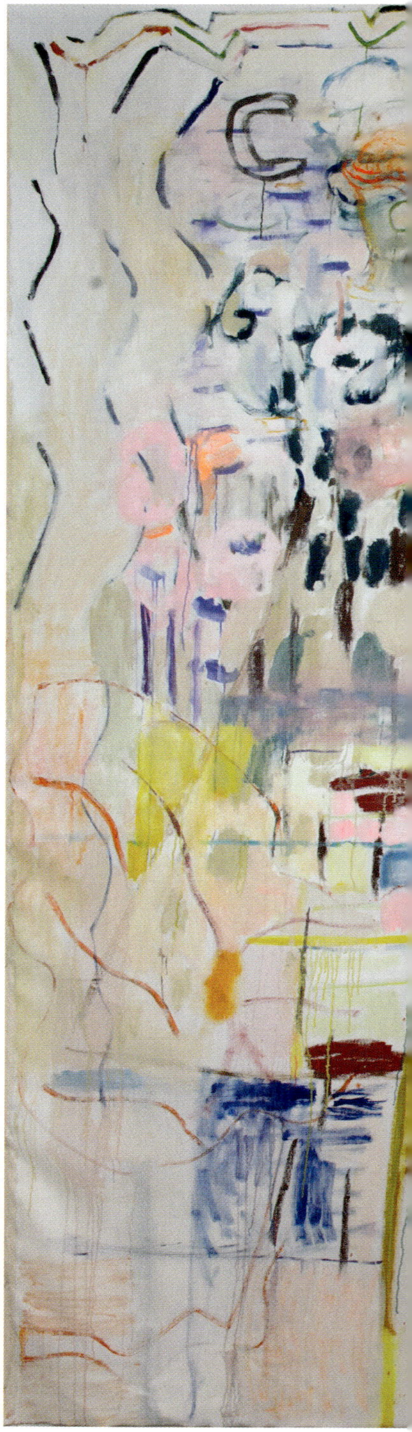

 *This is not a love song*, 2021, oil on canvas, 288 x 360 cm

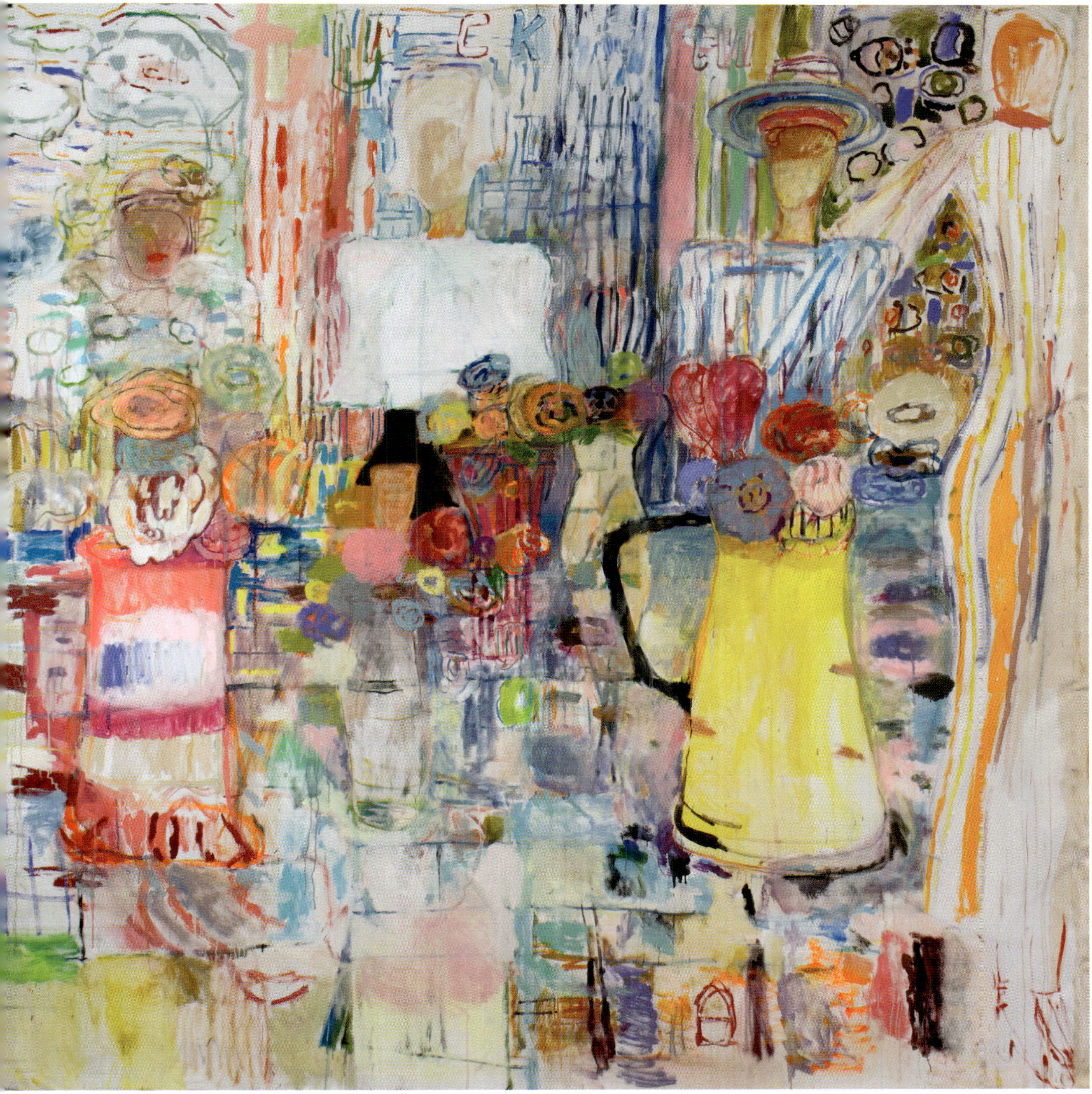

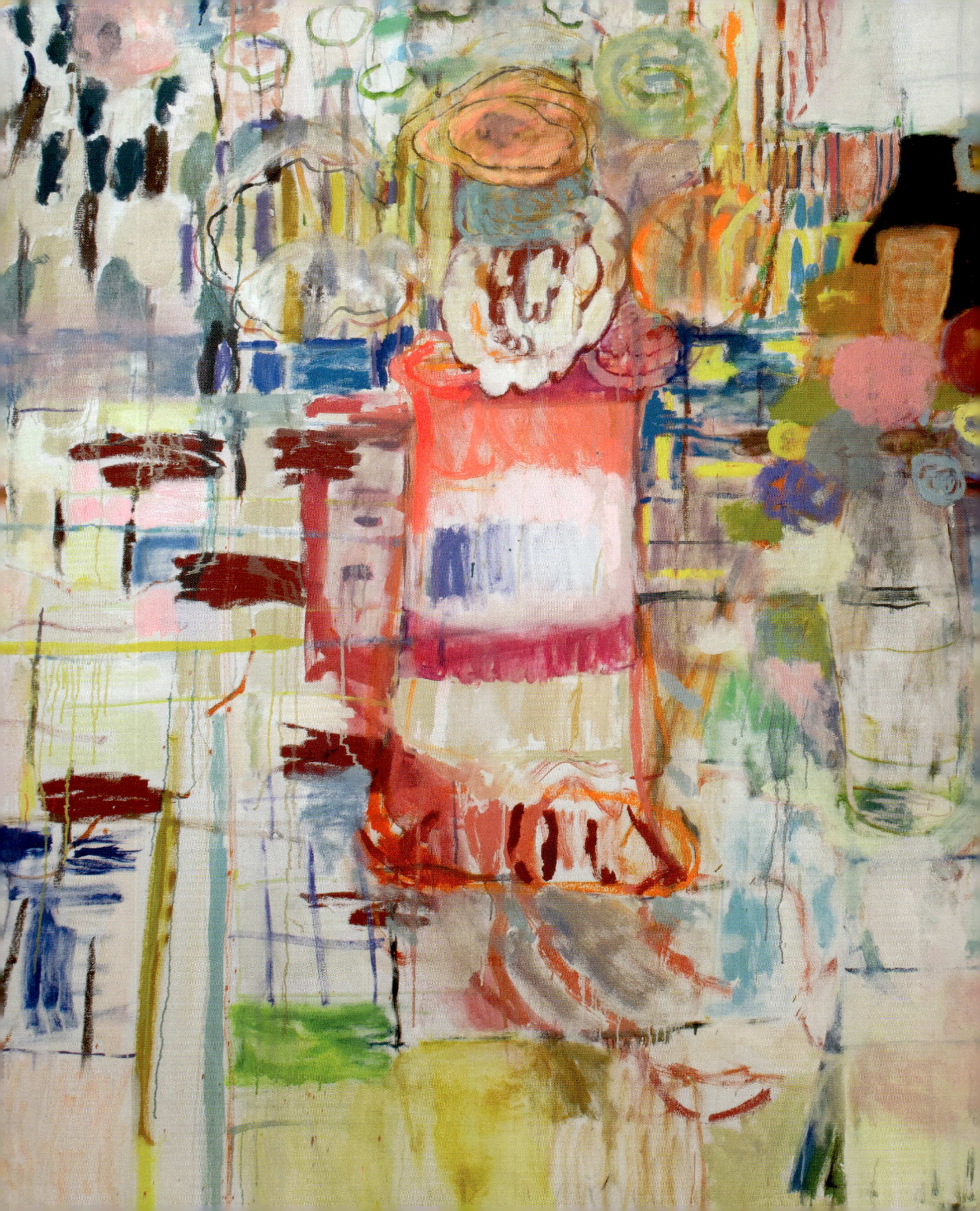

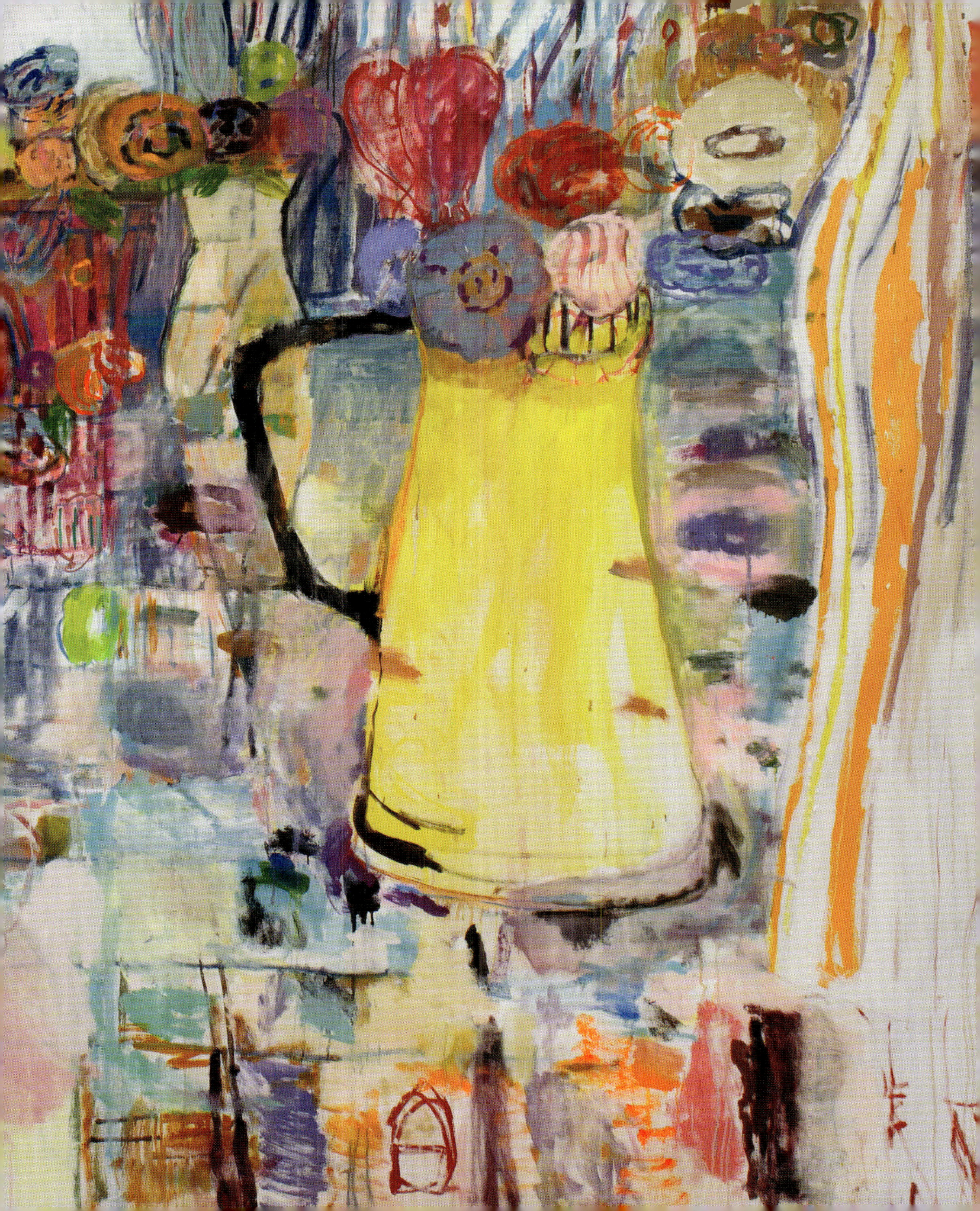

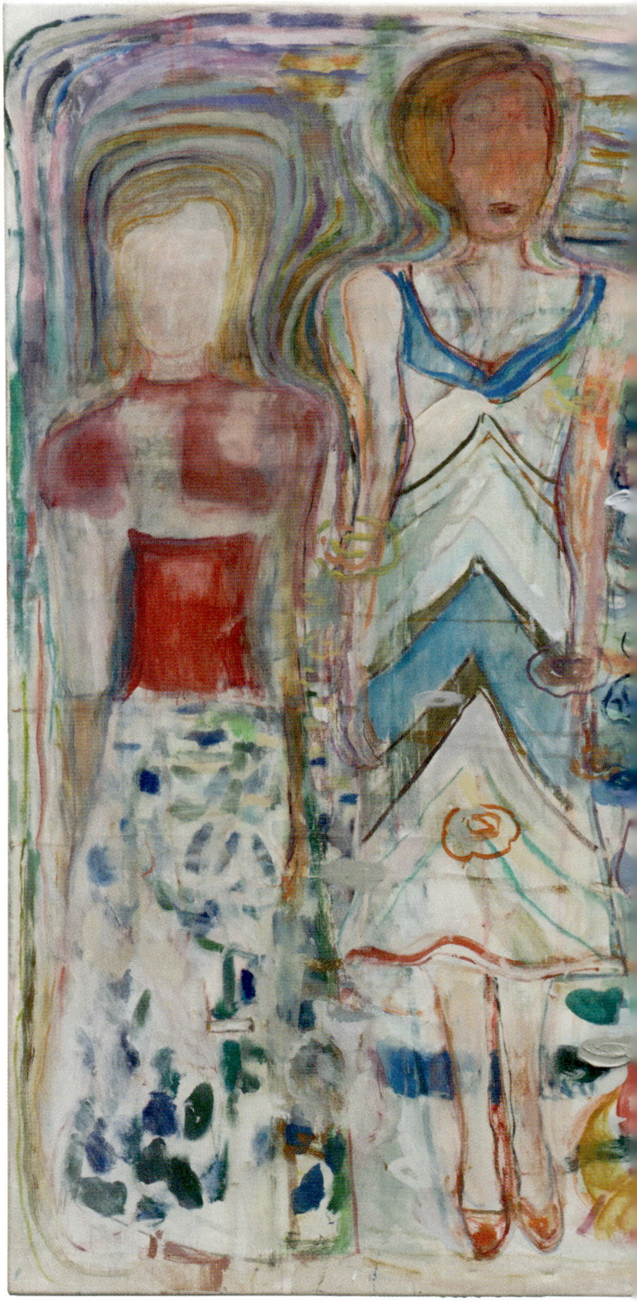

 *On a Scottish shore*, 2020, oil on canvas, 190 x 300 cm

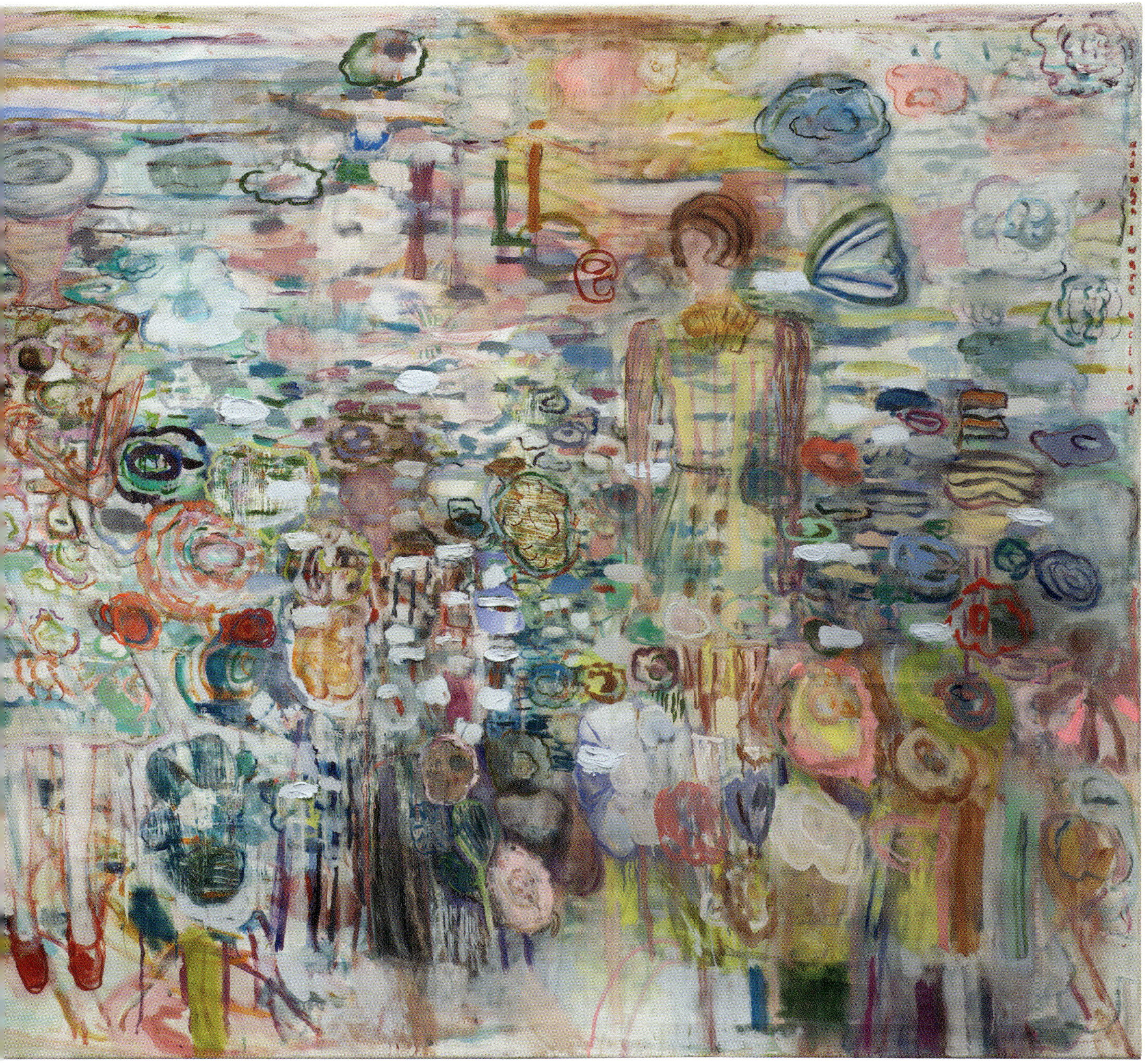

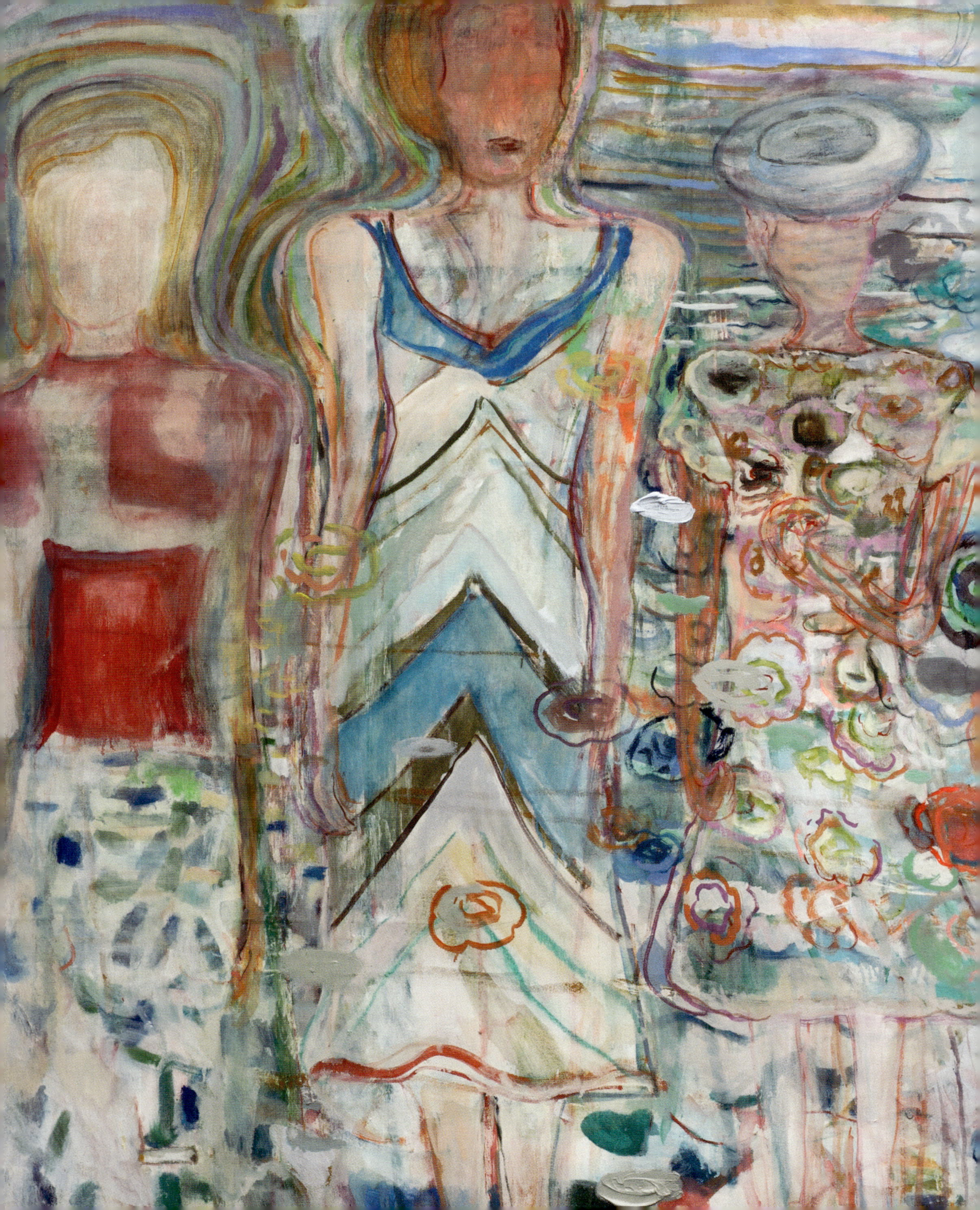

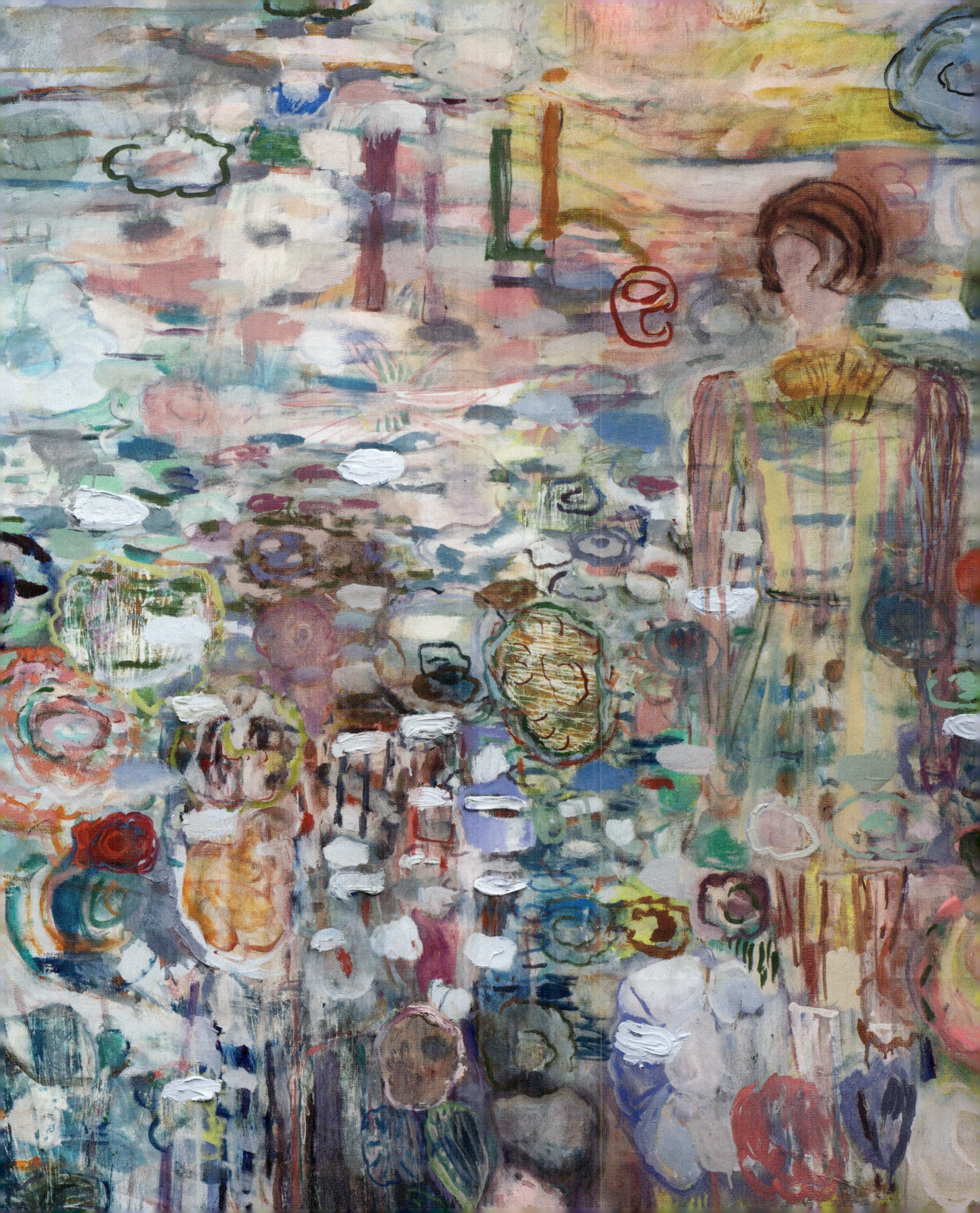

*Try see, try say*, 2022, oil on canvas, 184 x 262 cm

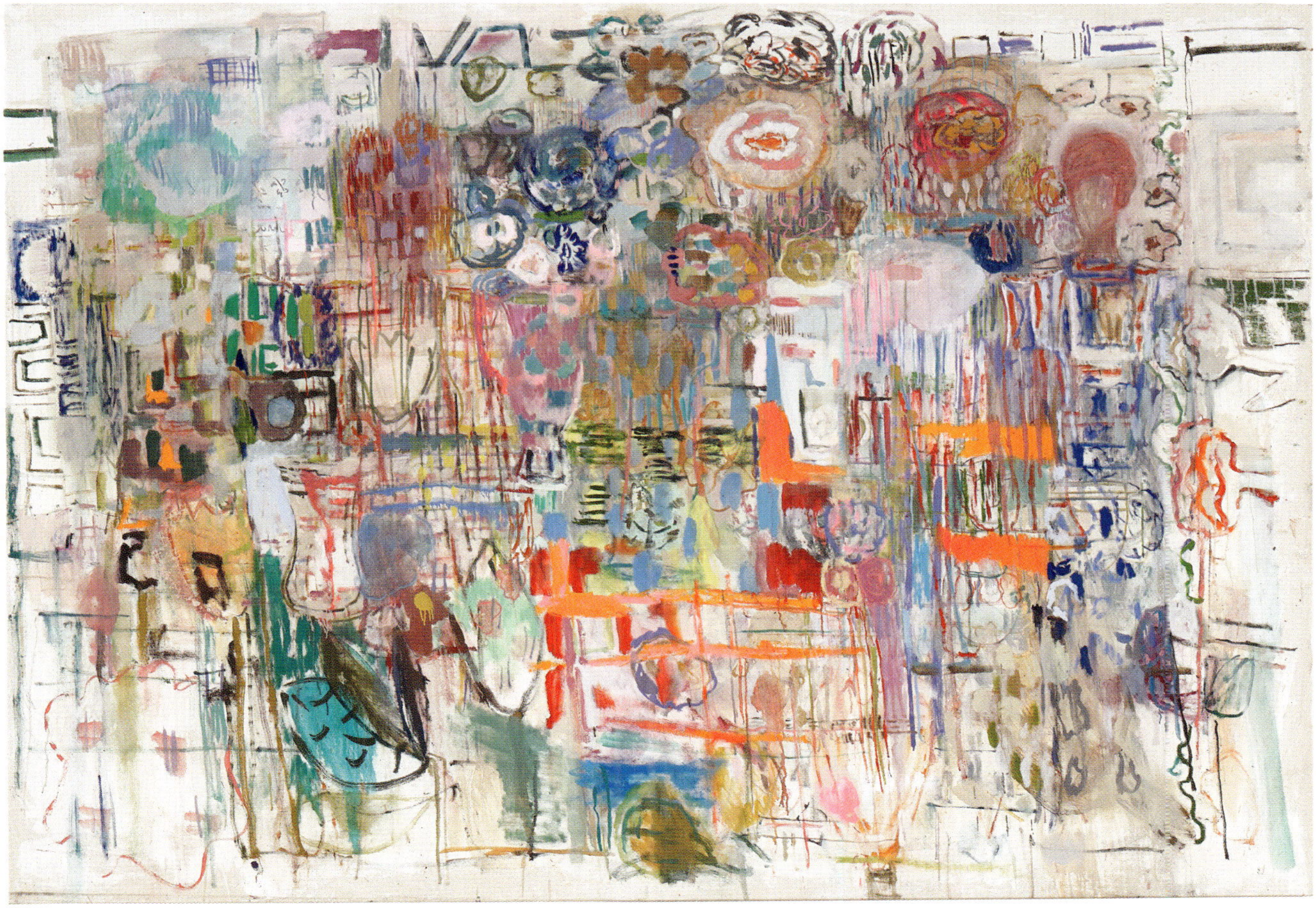

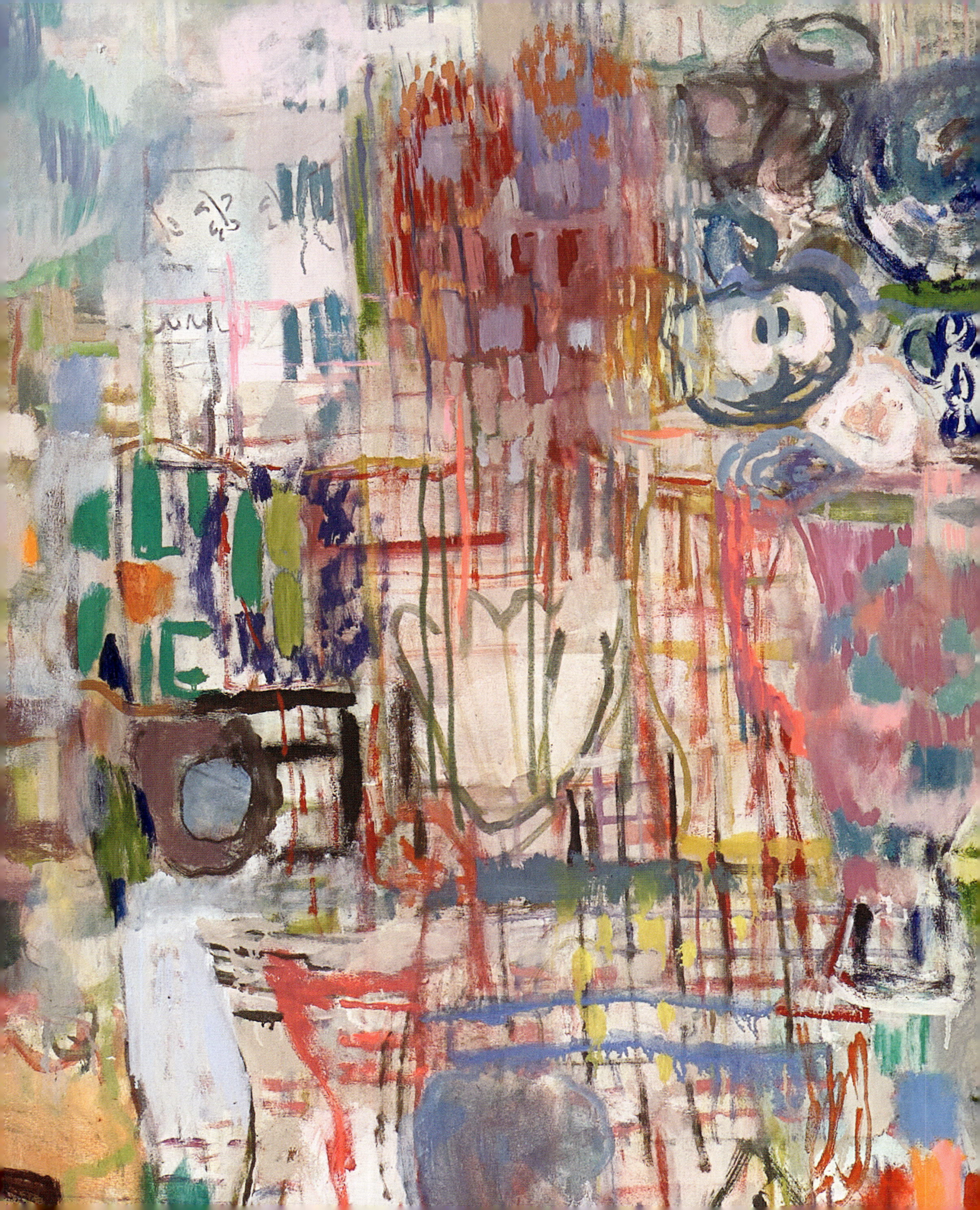

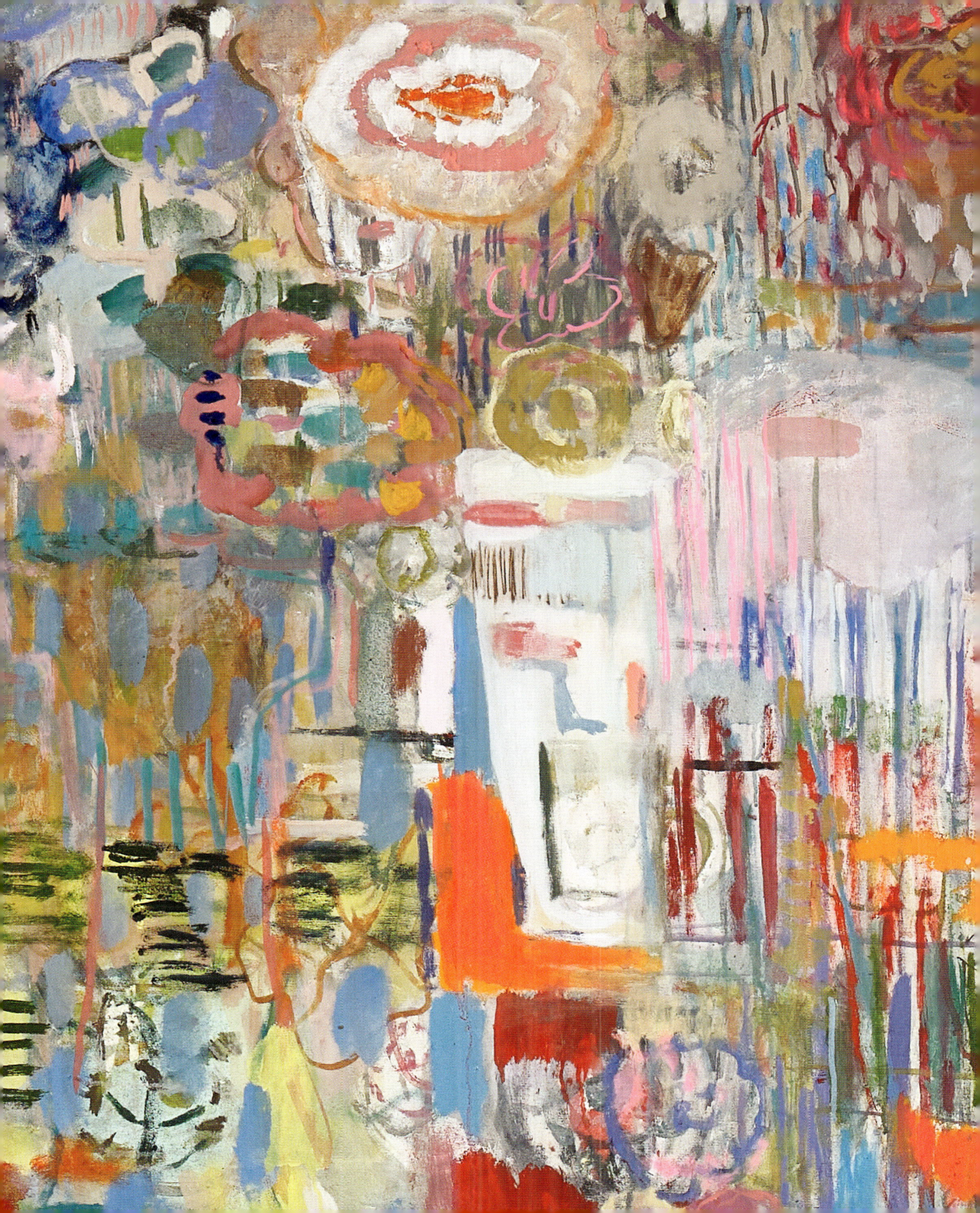

 *Play piece*, 2021, oil on canvas, 217 x 253 cm

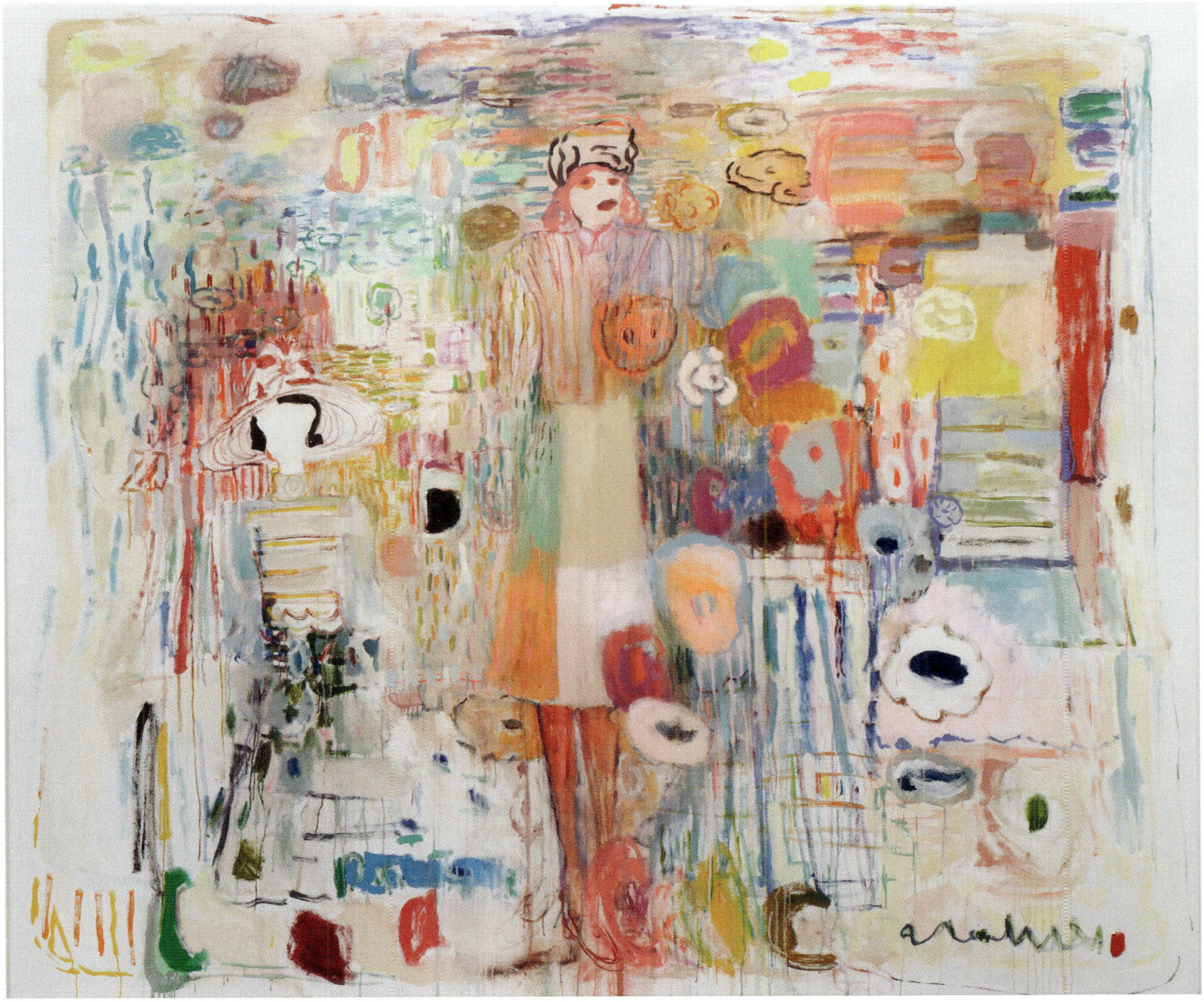

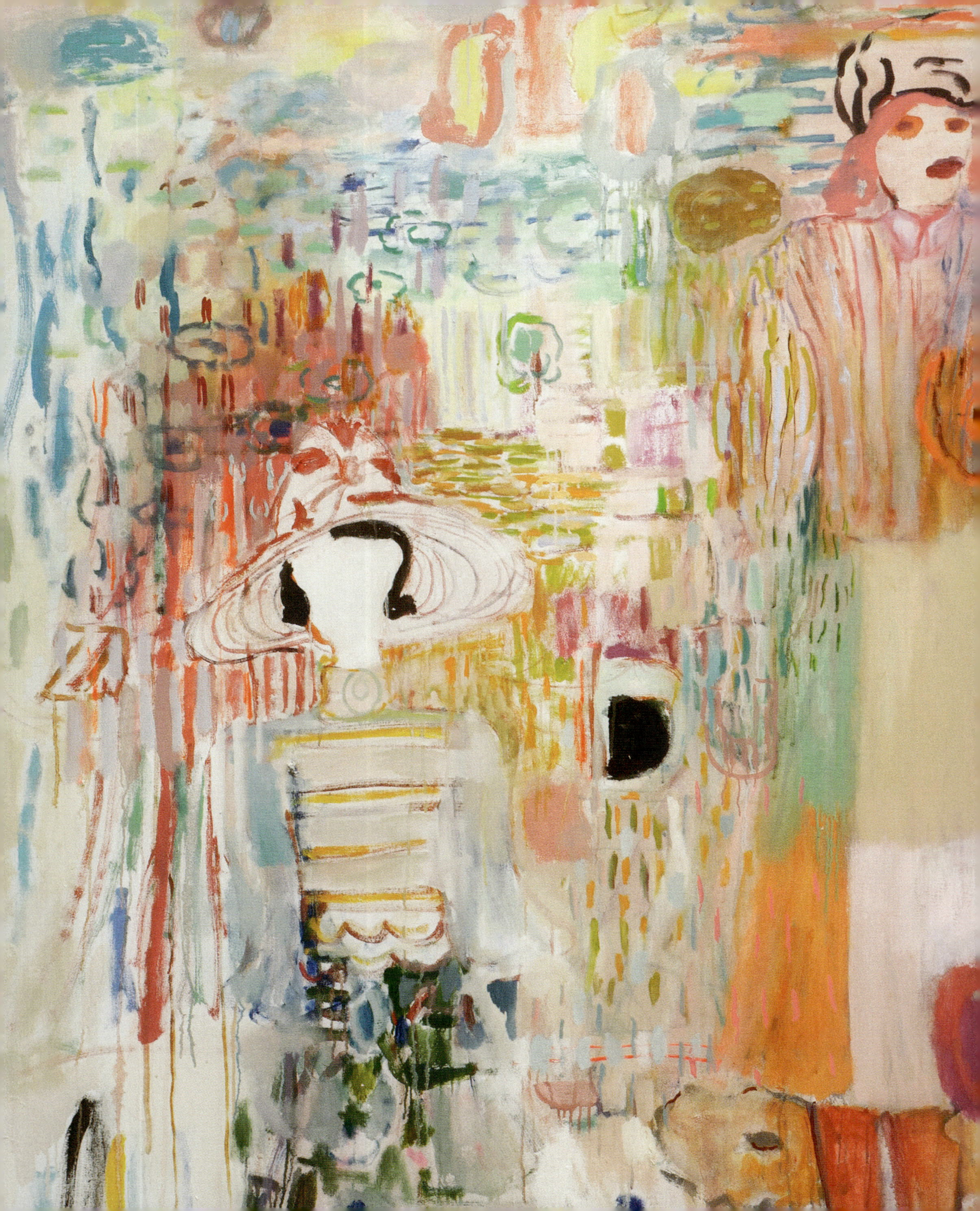

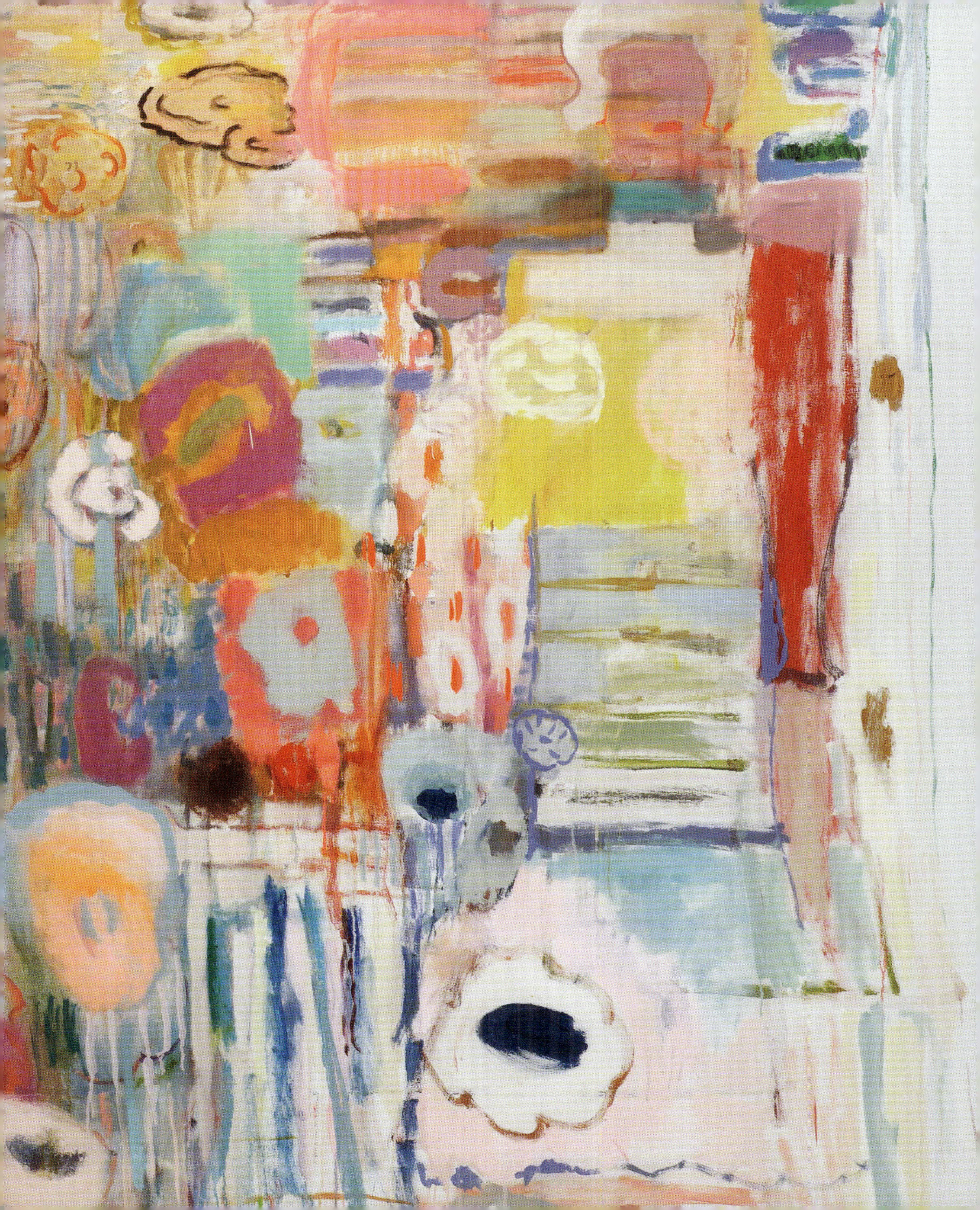

38 *Chimacum rain*, 2021, oil on canvas, 163 x 220 cm

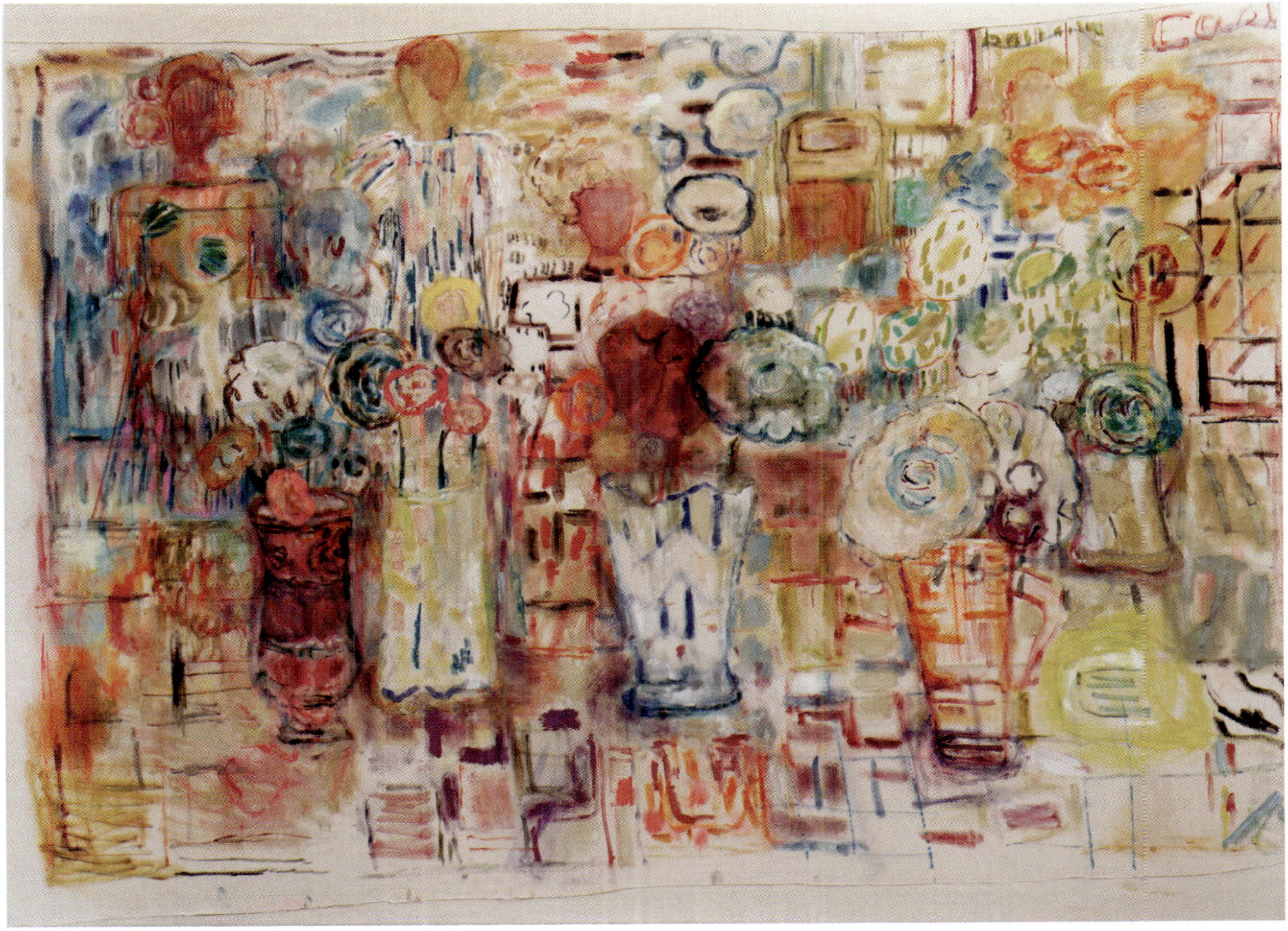

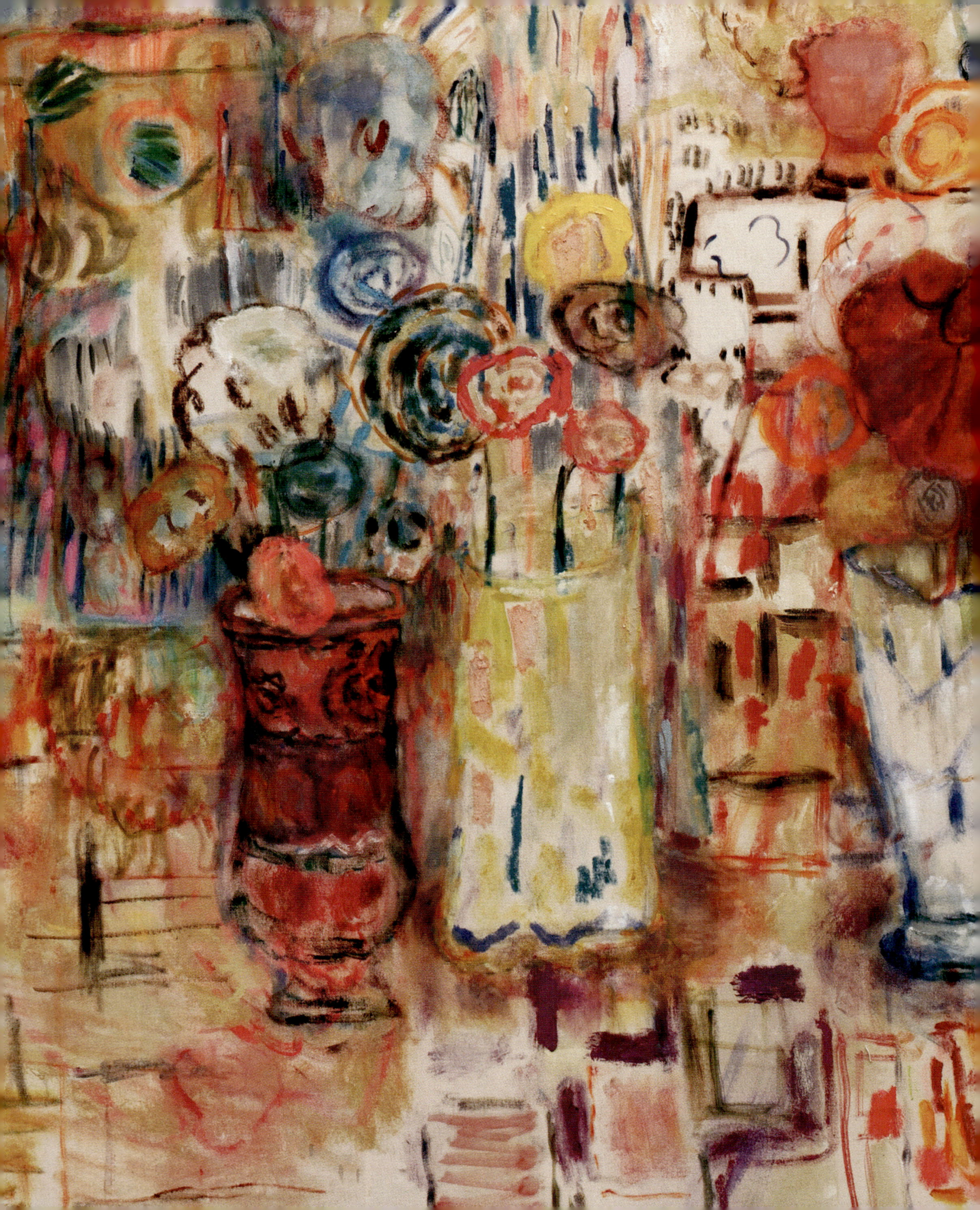

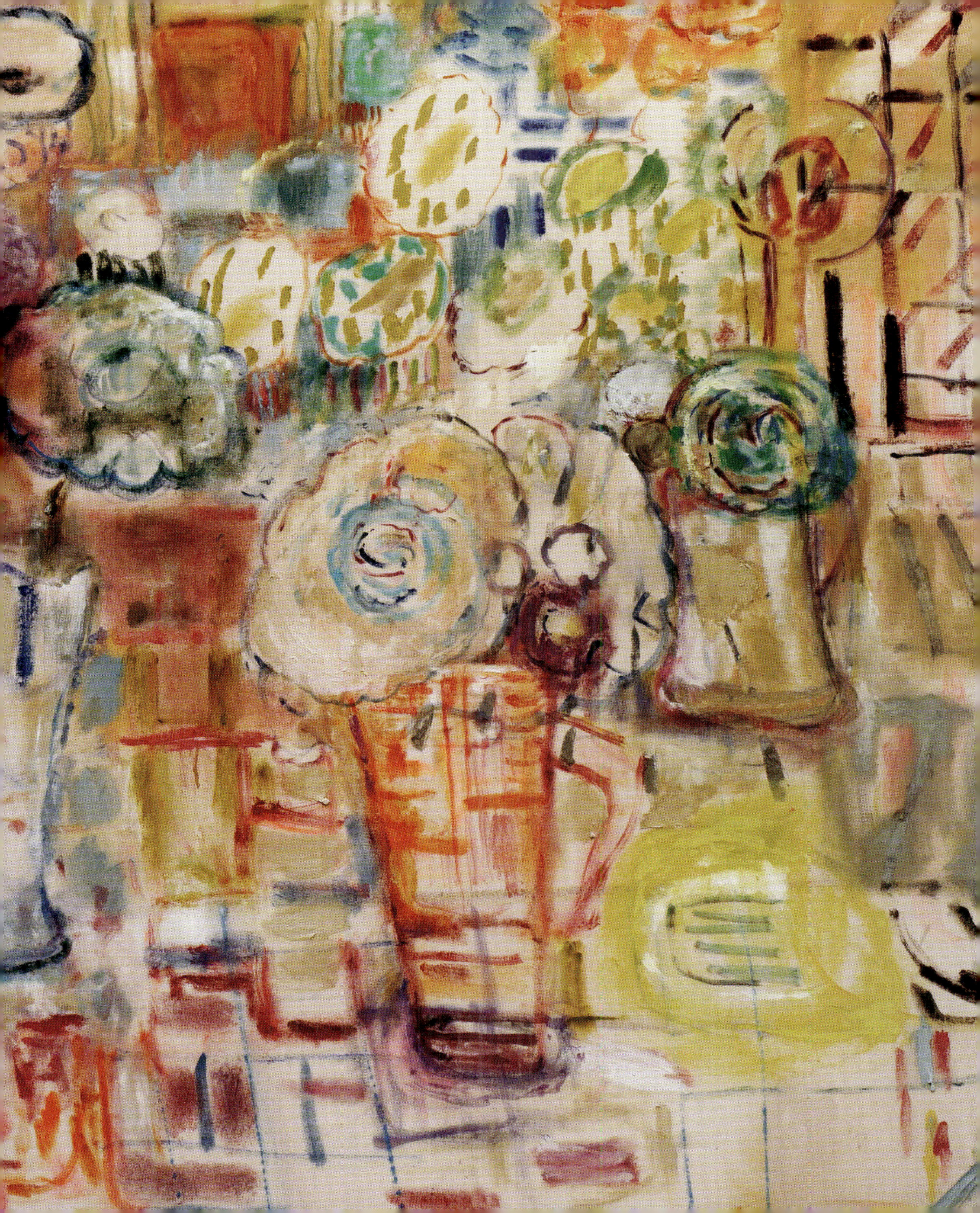

 *We are the robots*, 2022, oil on canvas, 256 x 246 cm

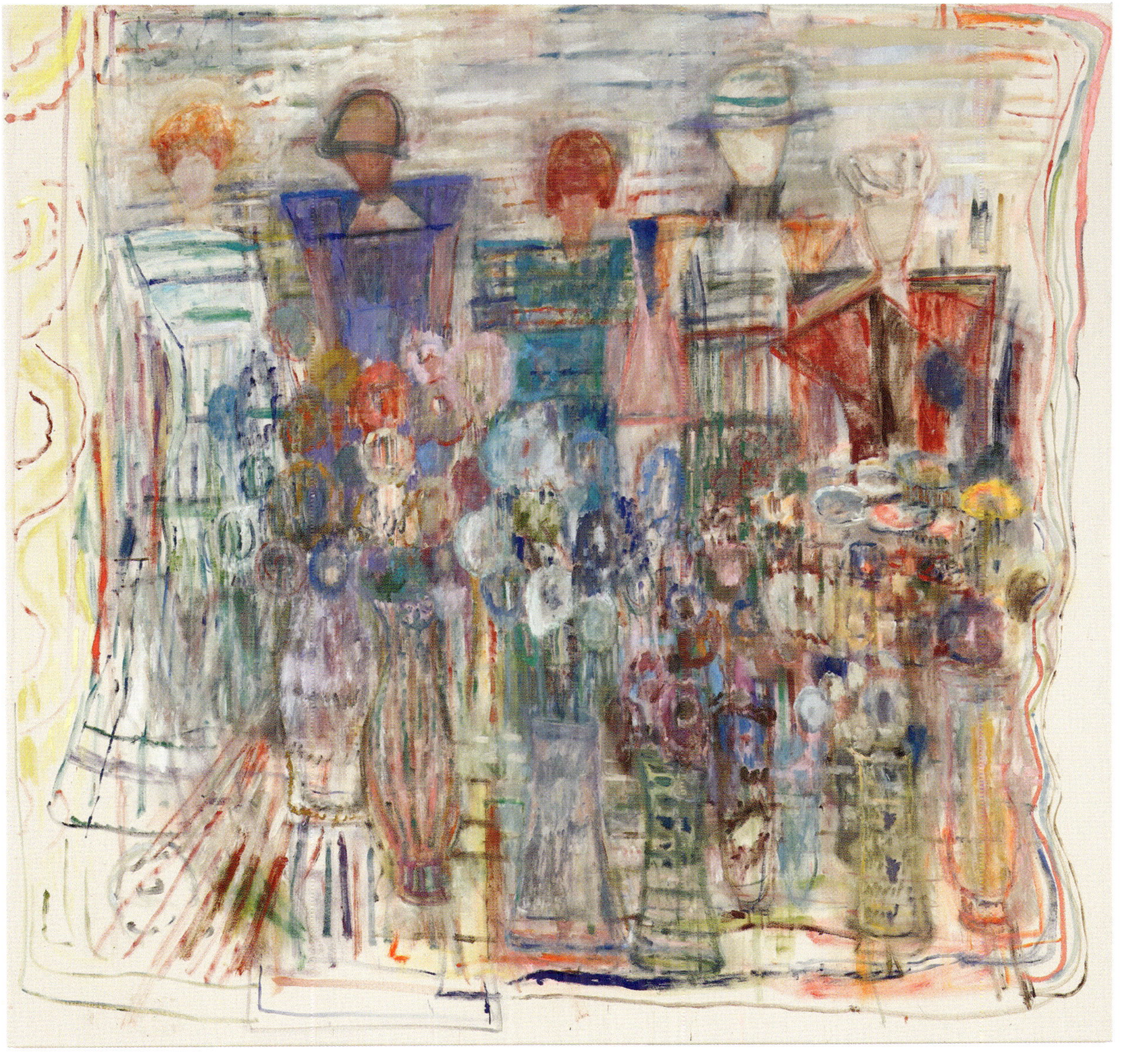

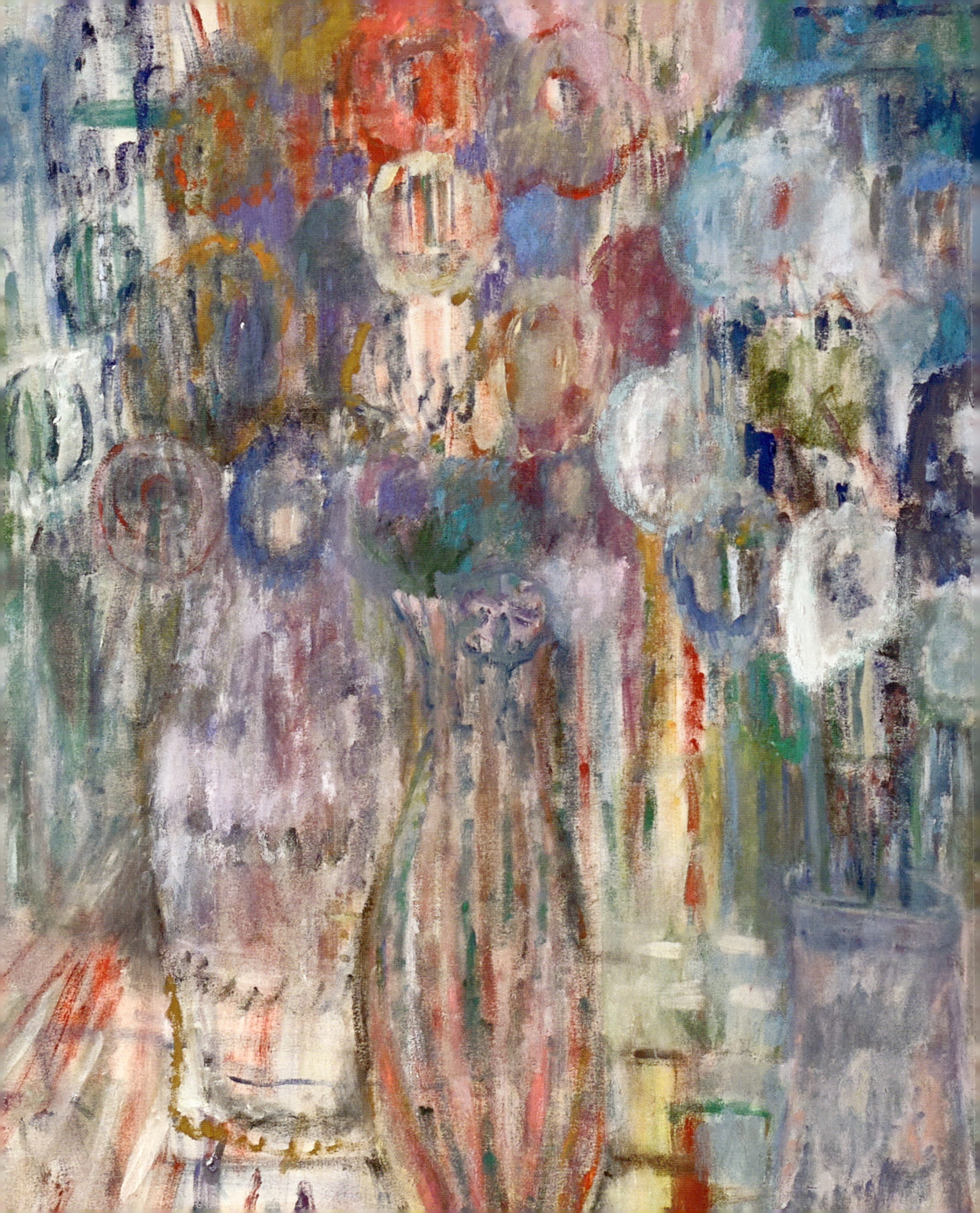

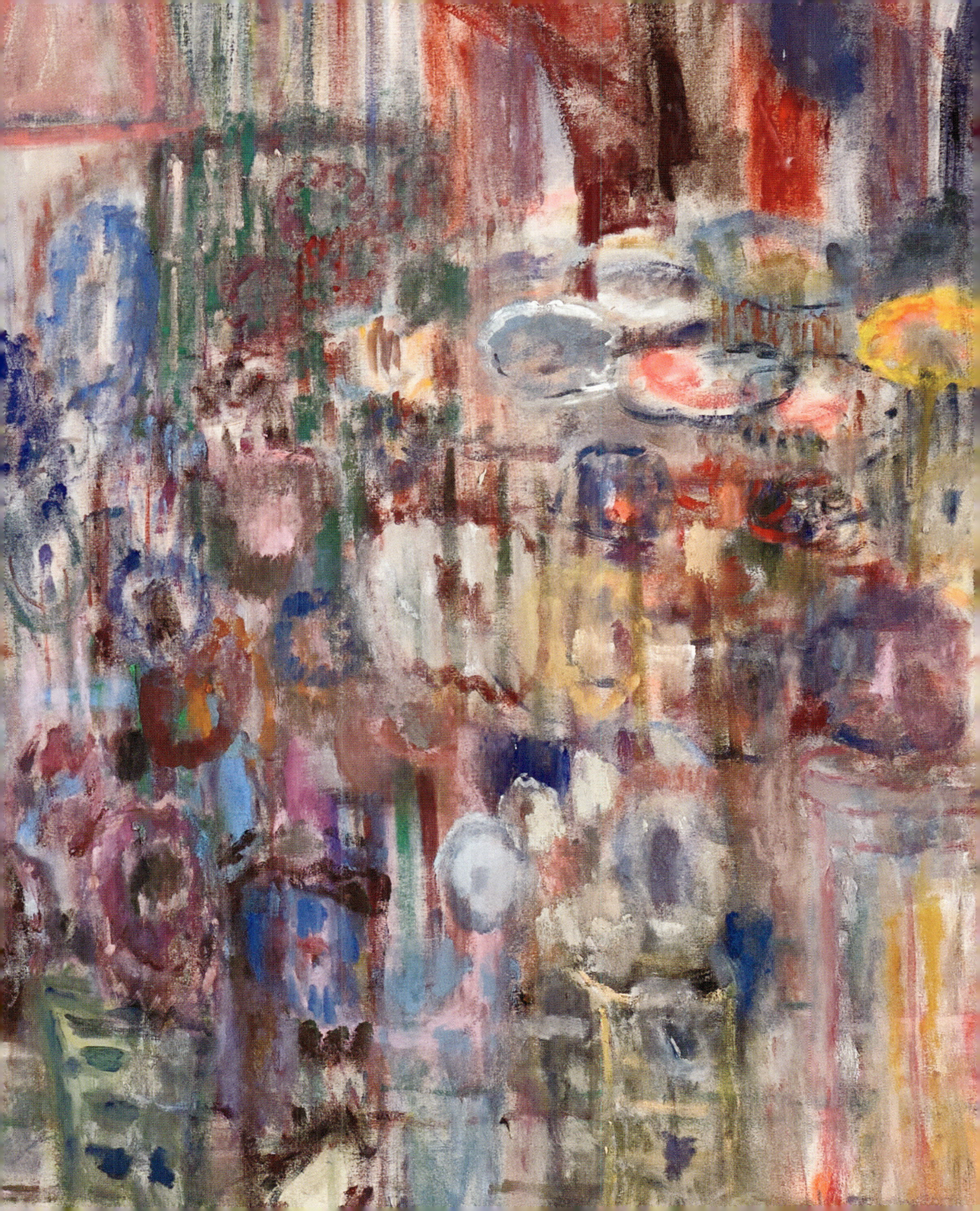

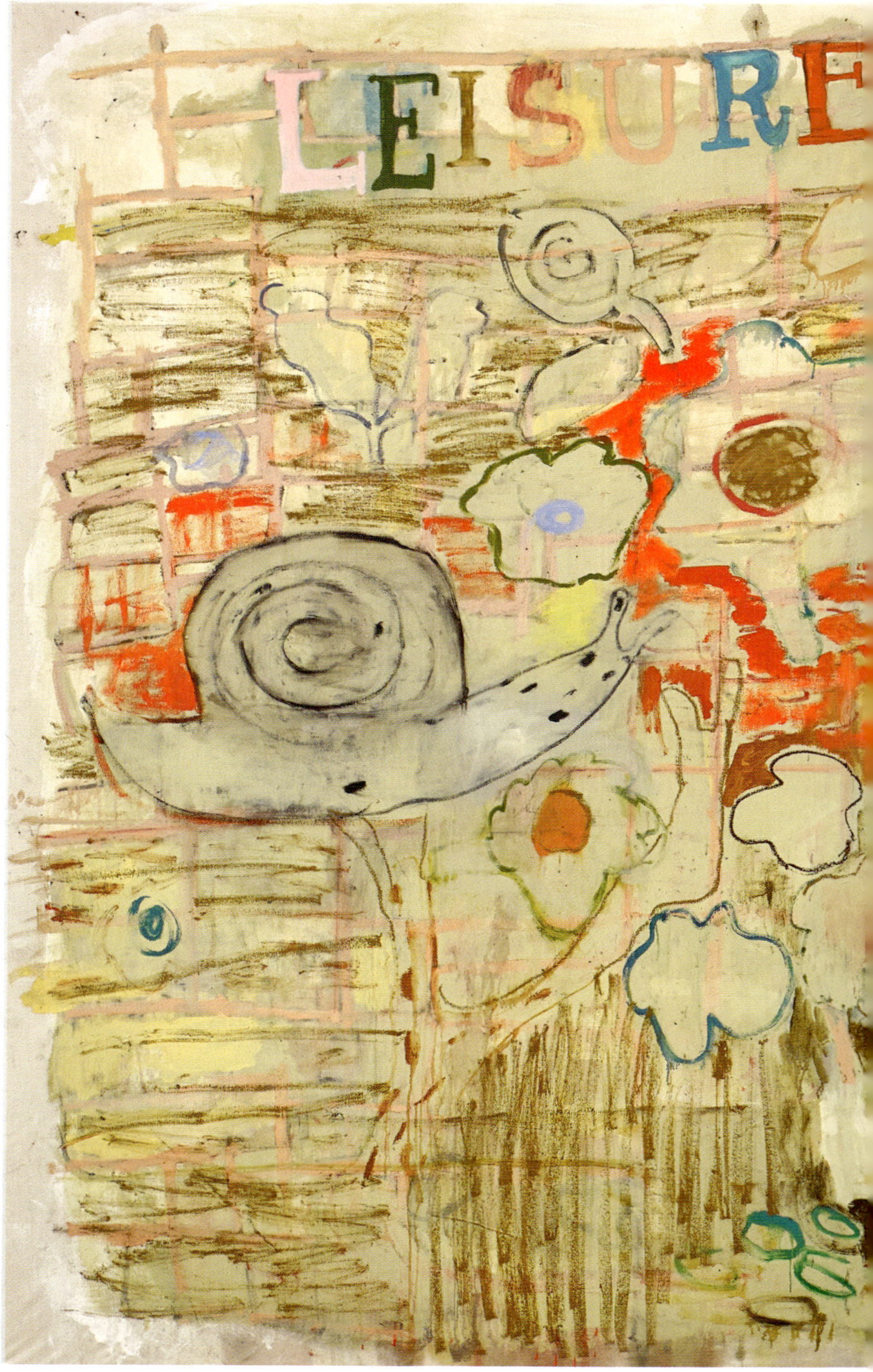


 *Leisureline*, oil on canvas, 2015-16, 250.5 x 417.5 cm

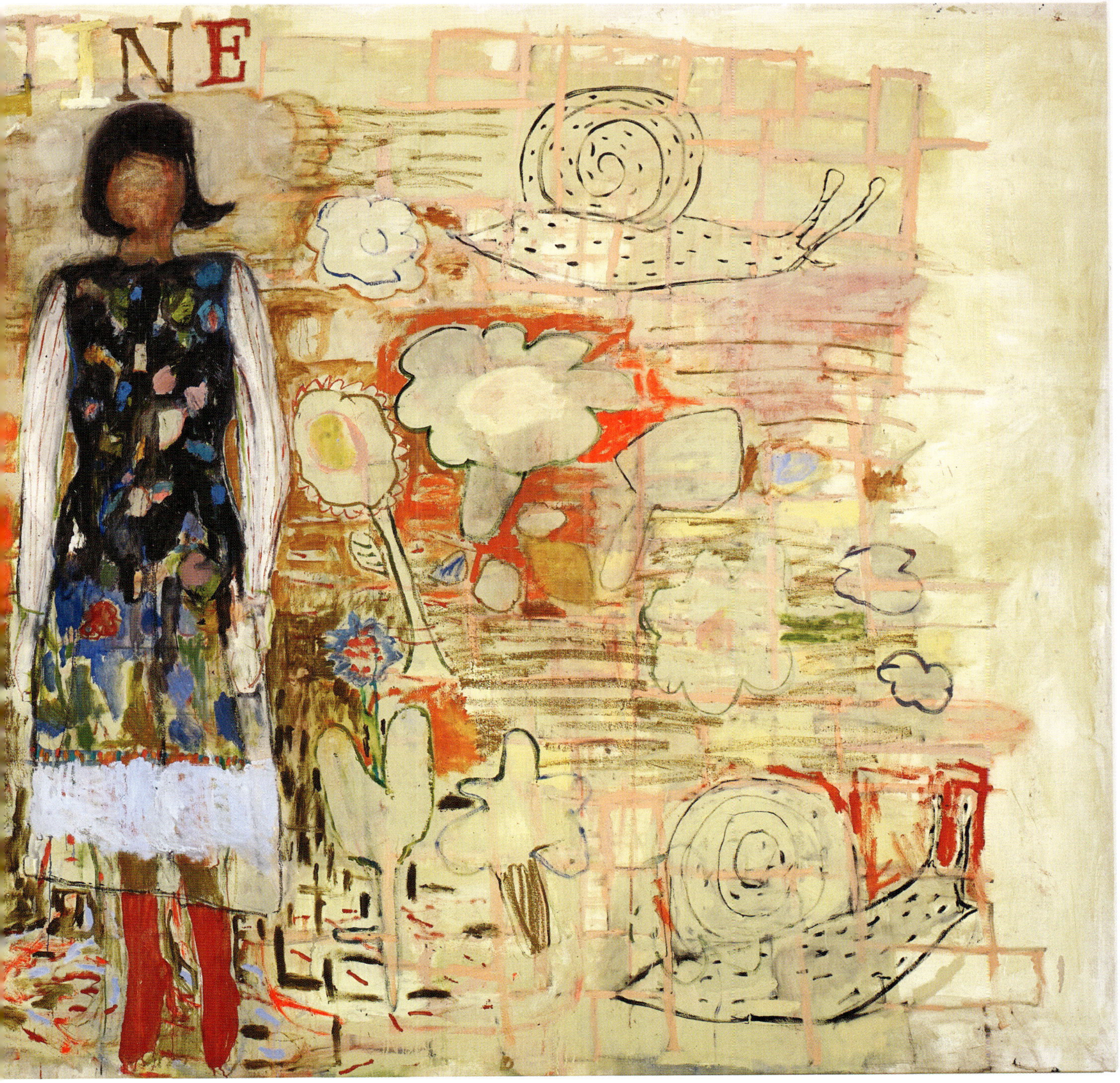
INE

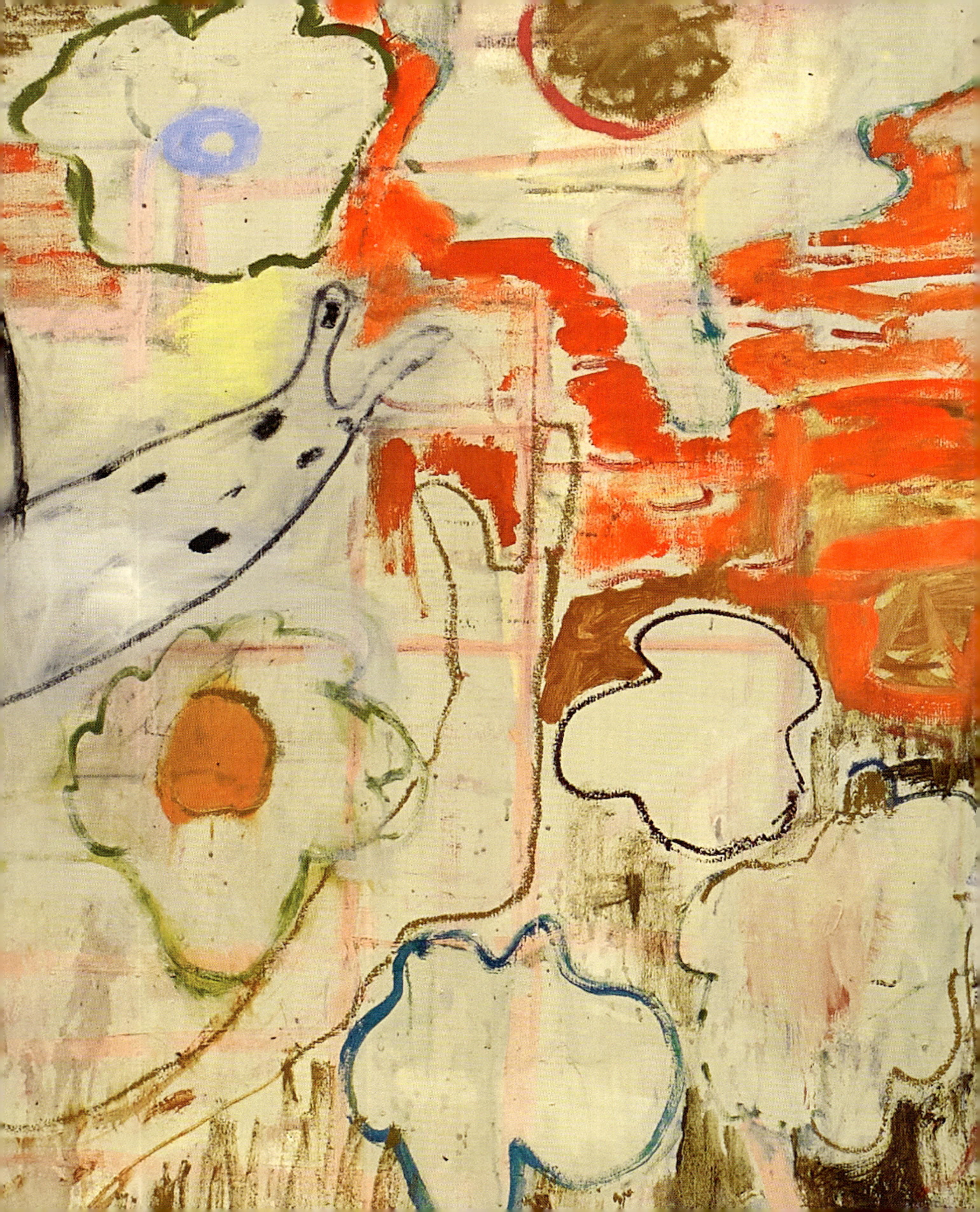

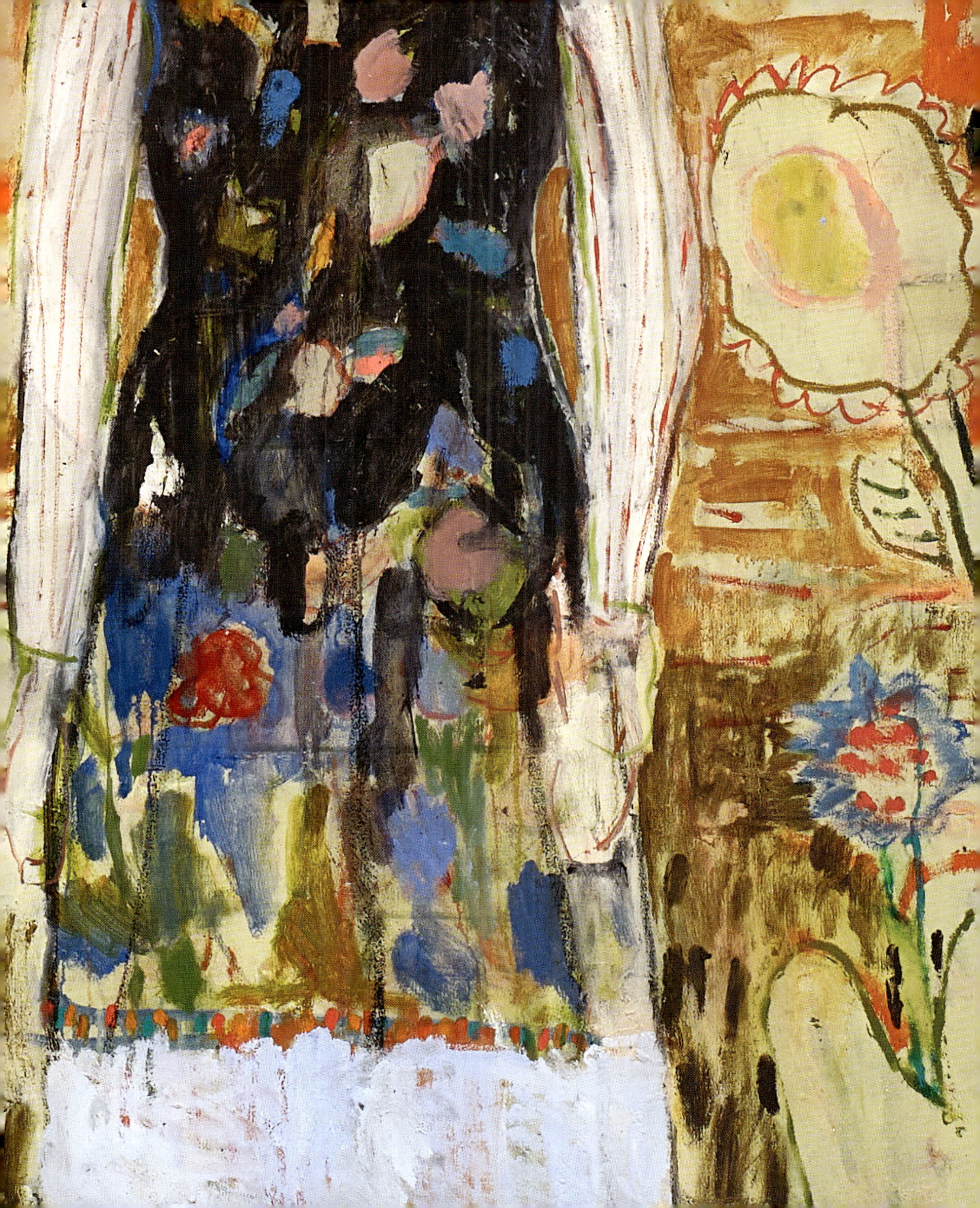

# SMALLER PAINTINGS

 *Tomorrow*, 2022, oil on canvas, 101 x 103.5 cm

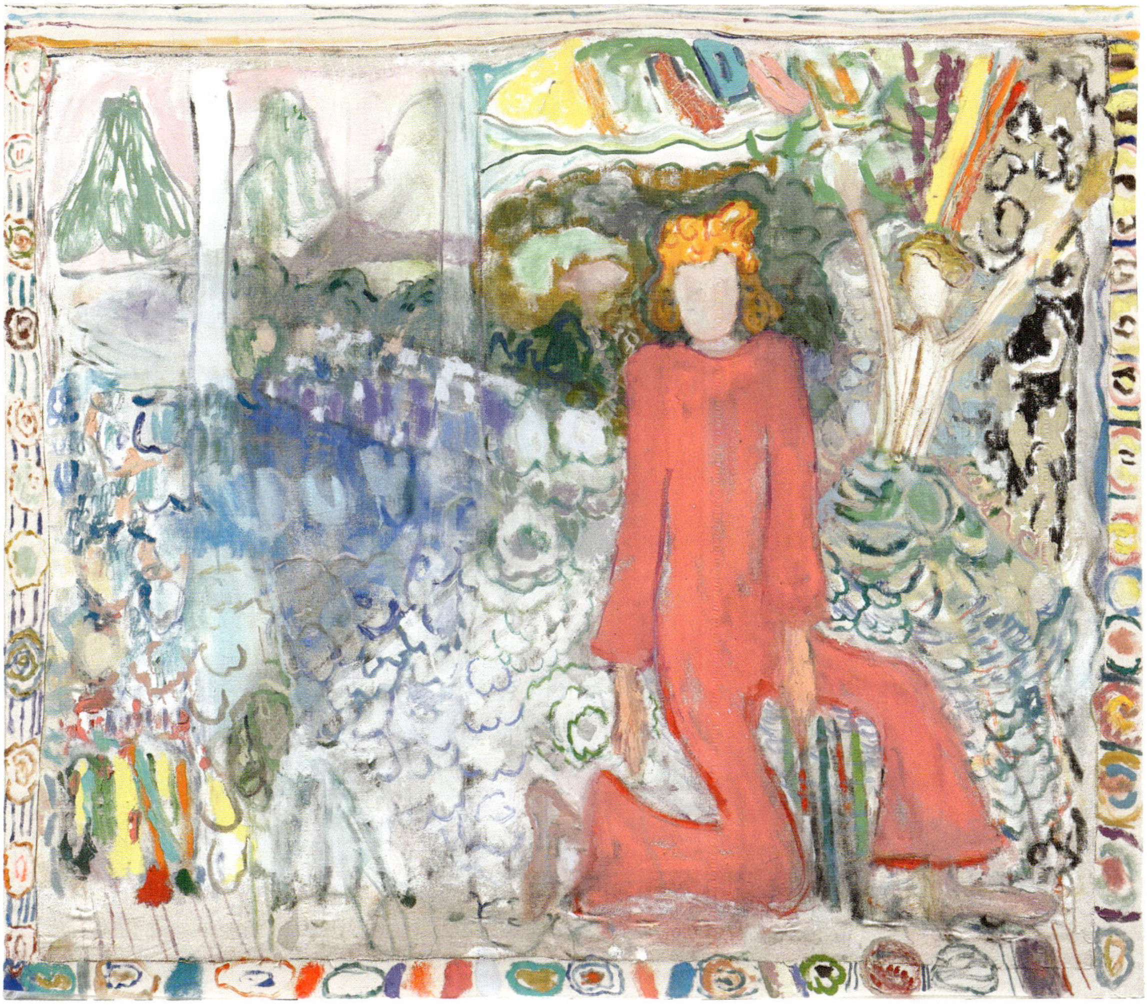

 *Saints and liars*, 2022, oil on canvas, 85 x 81.5 cm

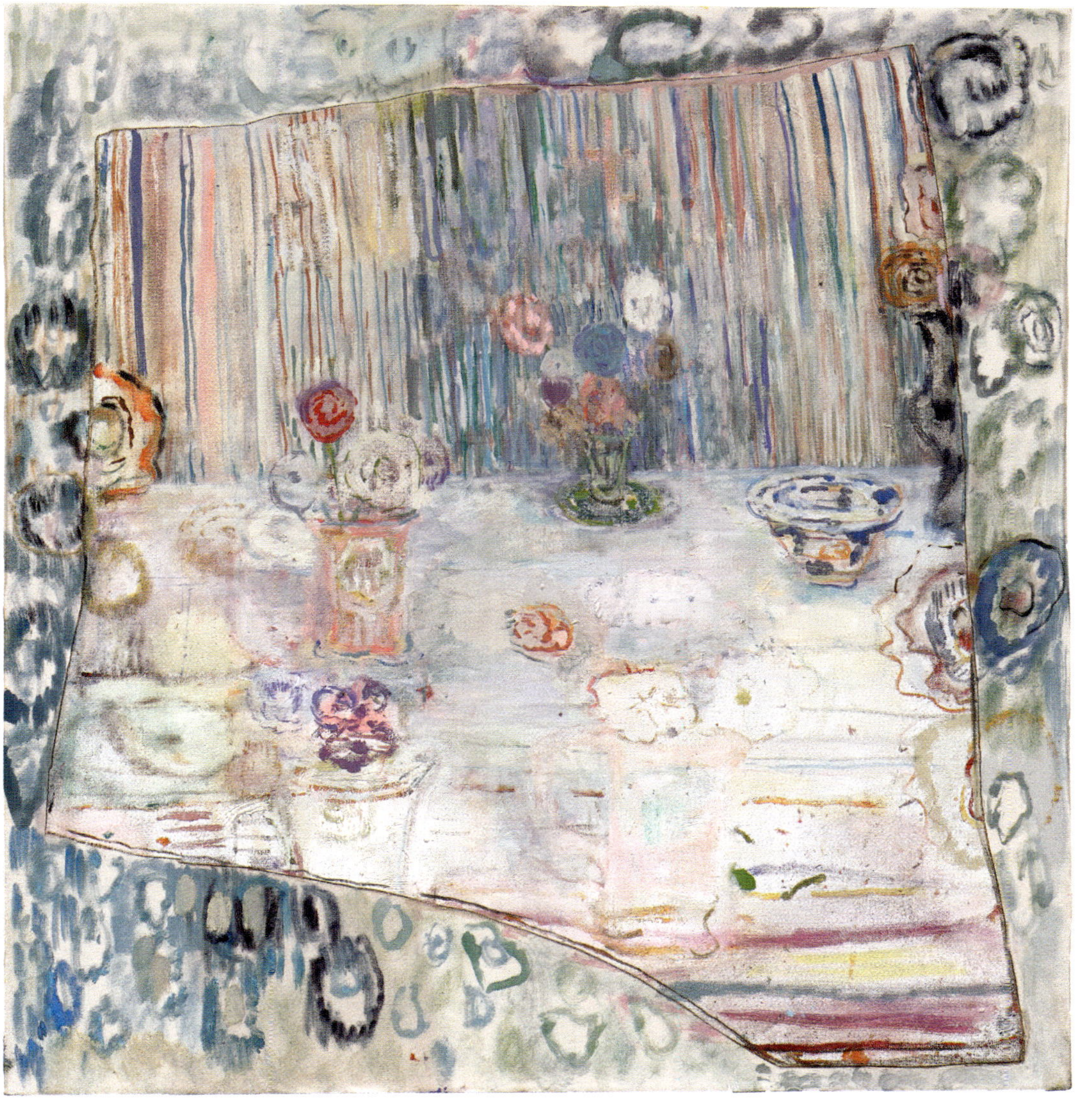

 *Benedictus*, 2022, oil on canvas, 82 x 95 cm

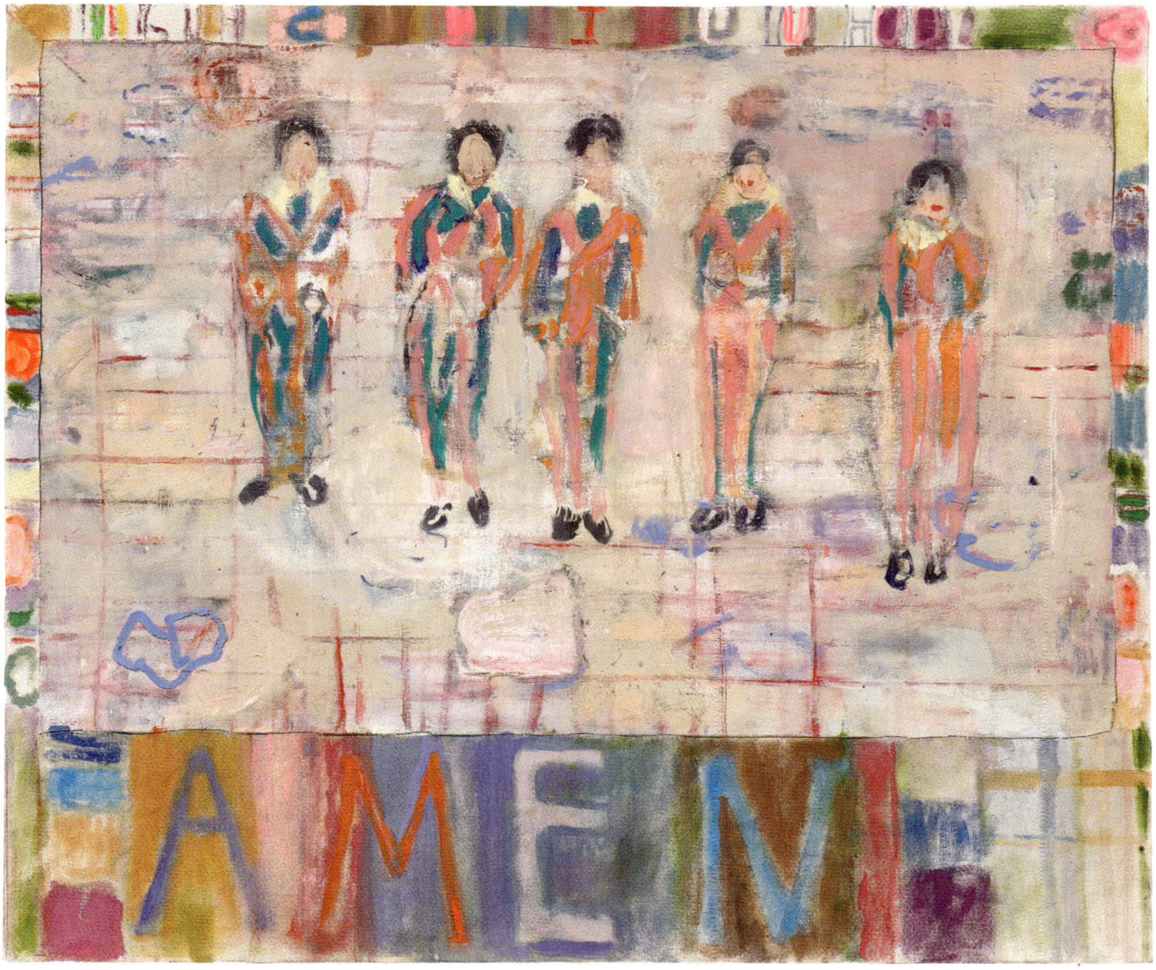
AMEN

 *We are, we are*, 2022, oil on canvas, 59.5 x 63 cm

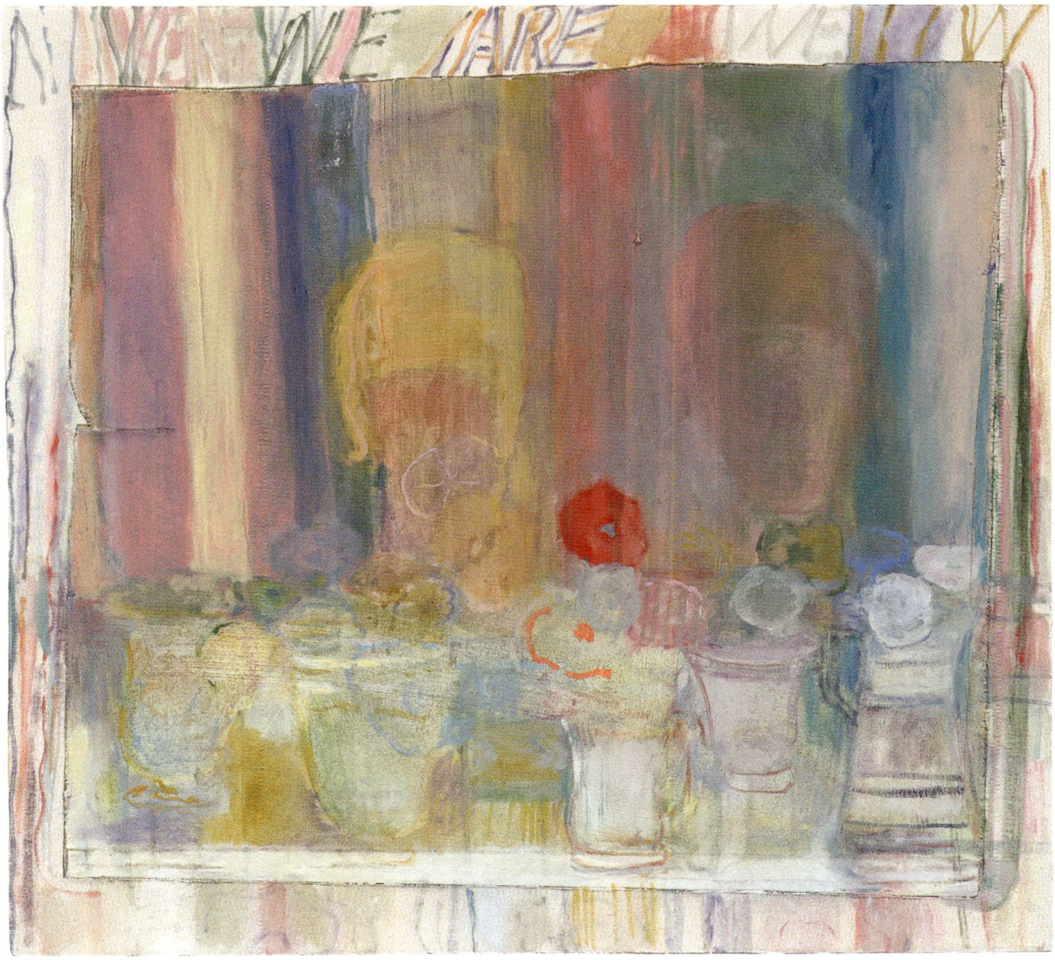
WE ARE

 *Morning rain*, 2022, oil on canvas, 115 x 109.5 cm

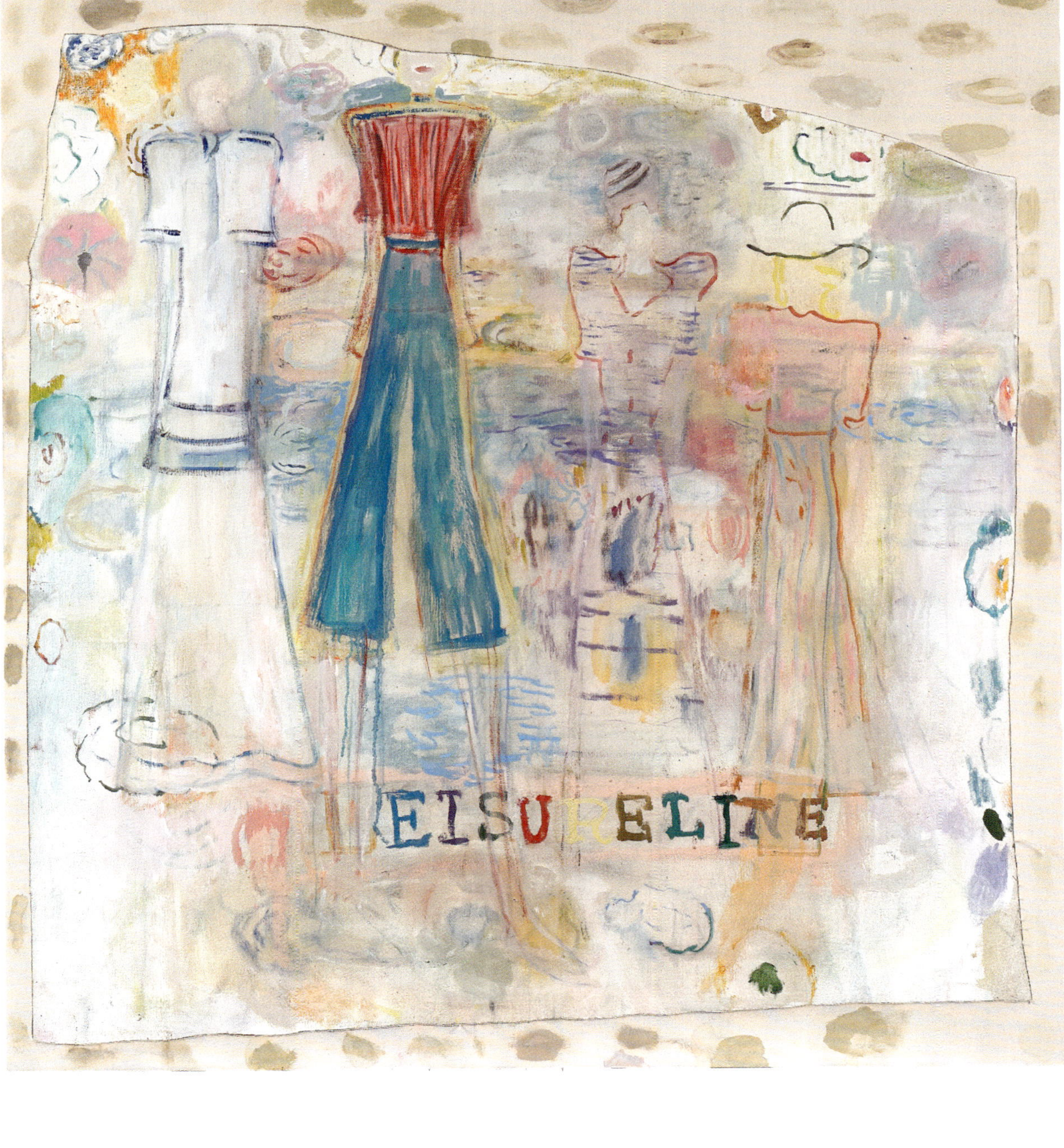
EISURELINE

 *Train song*, 2022, oil on canvas, 63 x 85.5 cm

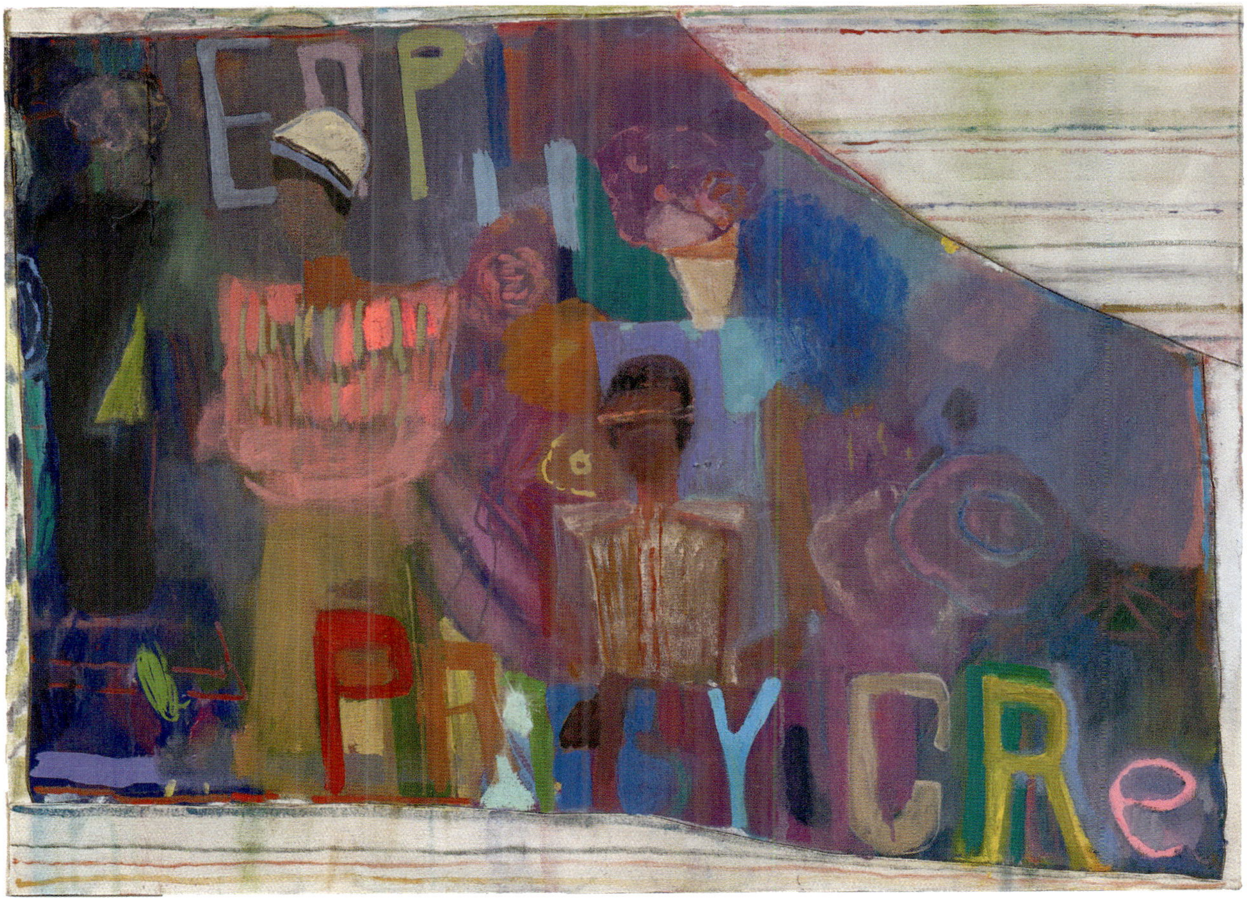

64 *A cure*, 2022, oil on canvas, 87 x 62 cm

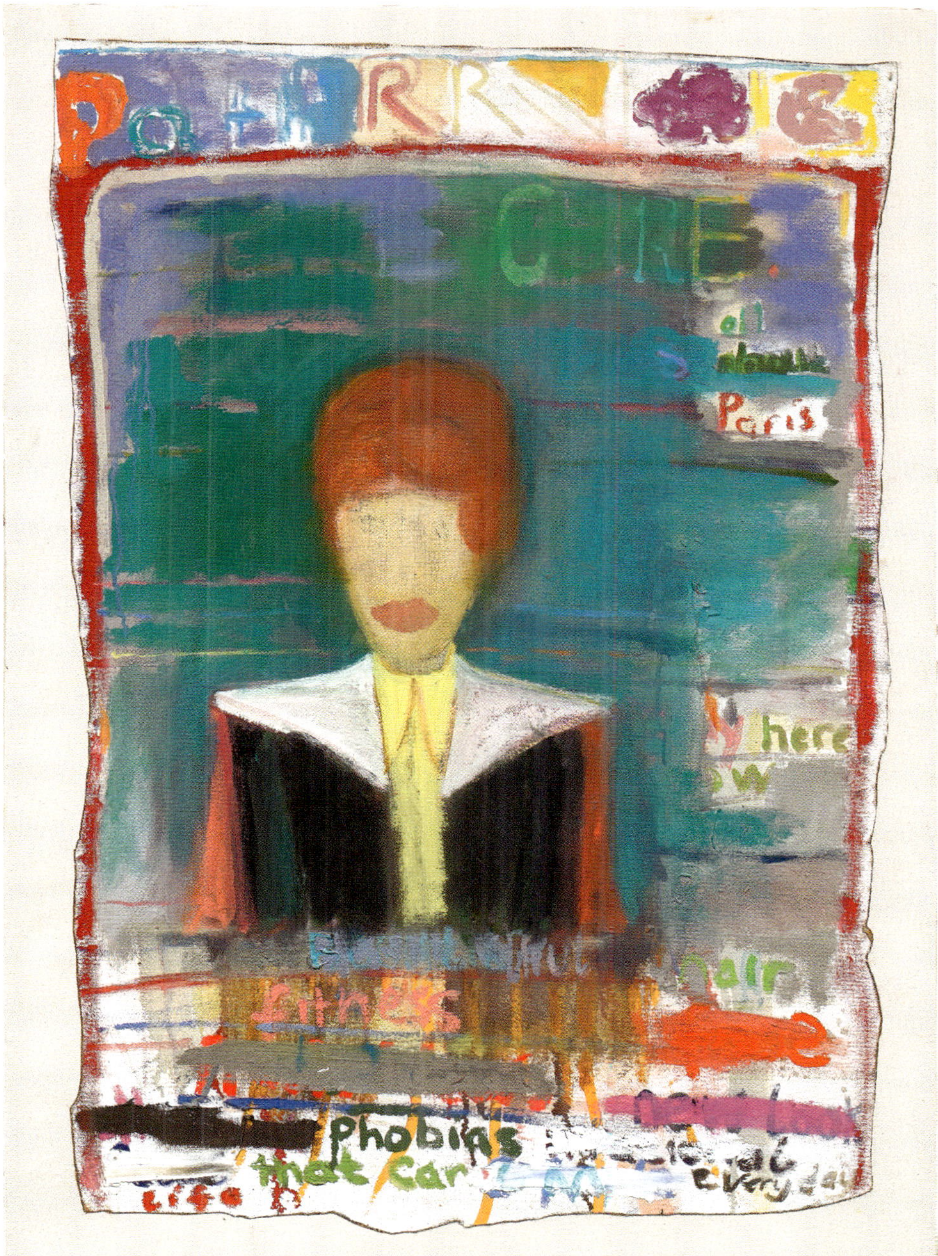
CURE
all
Paris
here
hair
Phobias
that car
every day

 *If they were not*, 2022, oil on canvas, 75 x 114 cm

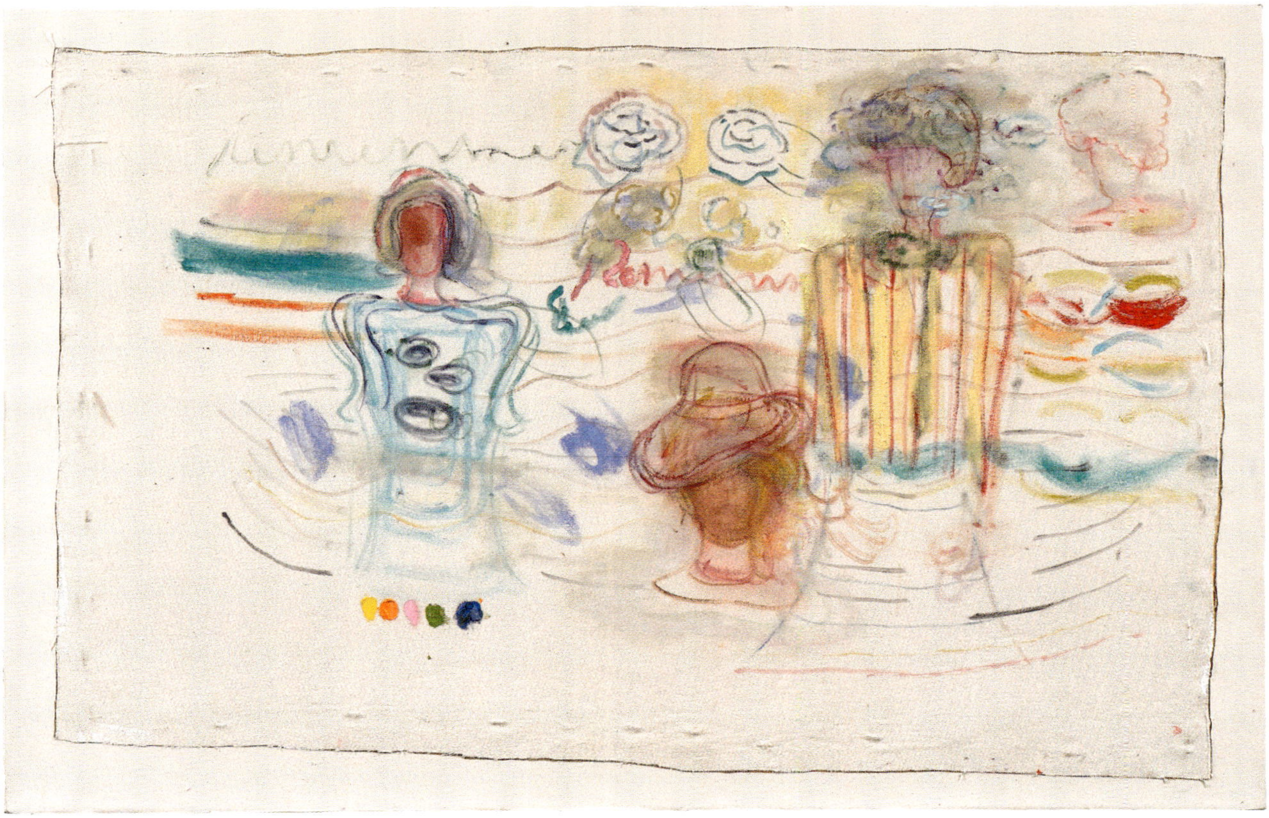

 *In snow white cottages*, 2022, oil on canvas, 101 x 76.5 cm

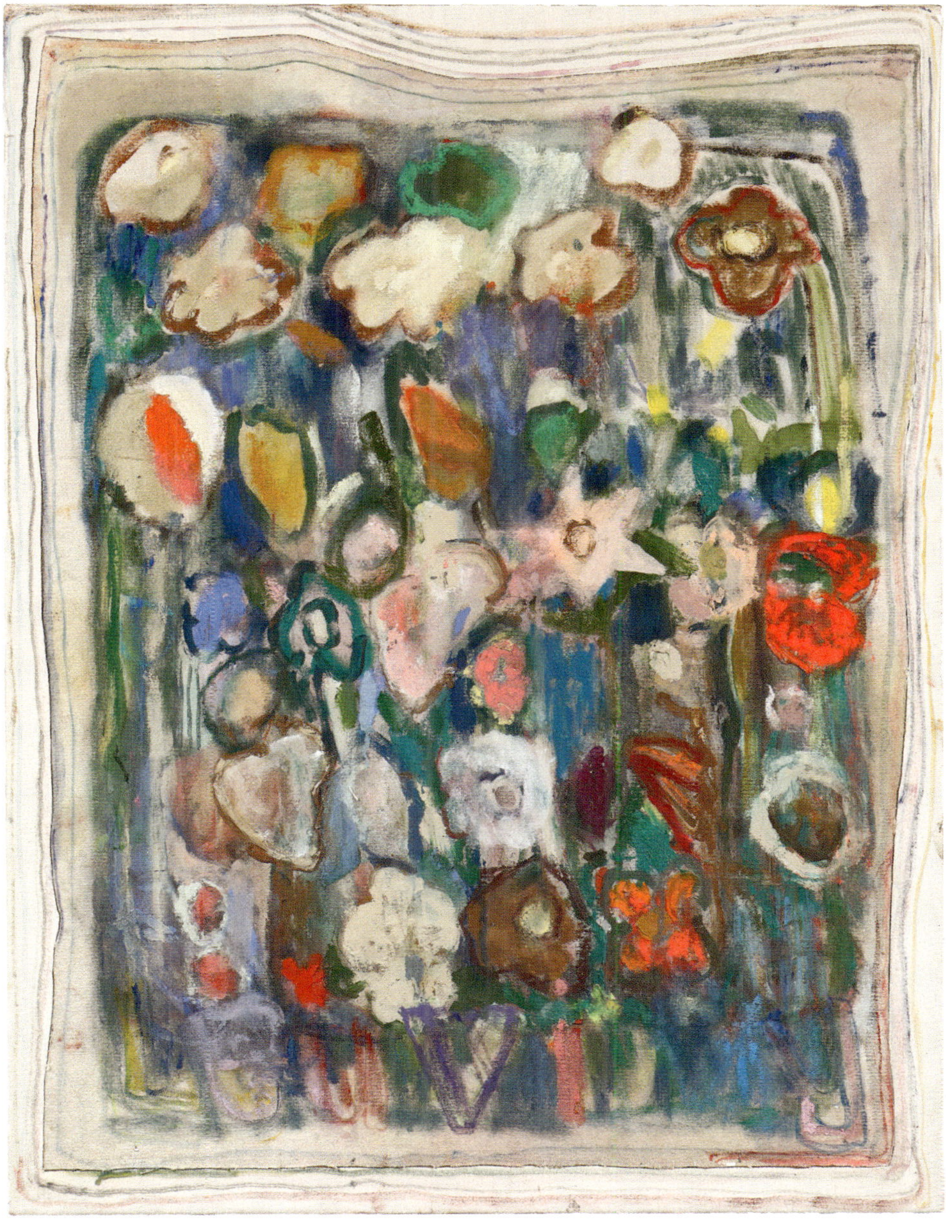

 *Dumb*, 2022, oil on canvas, 90 x 82 cm

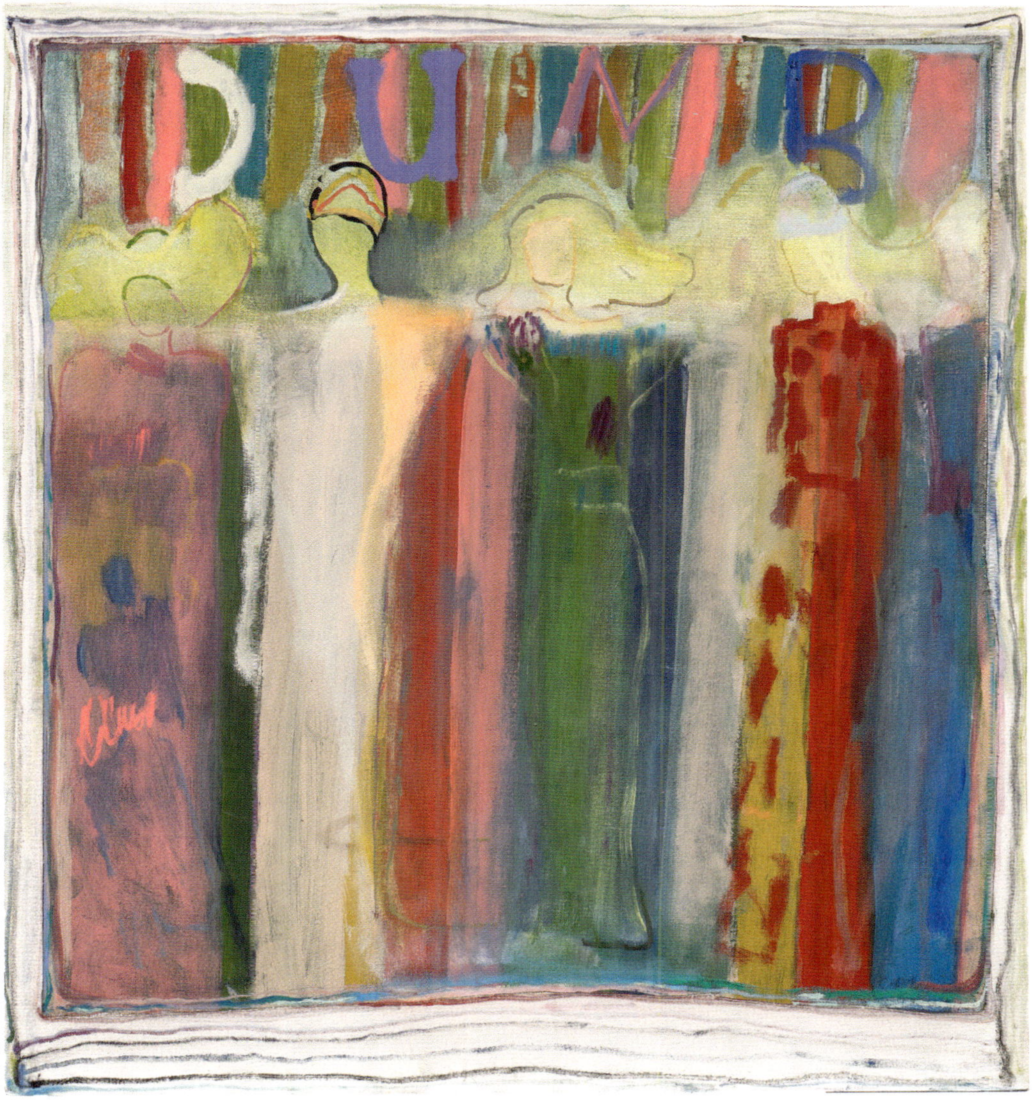
DUMB

LORNA ROBERTSON *in conversation with Mikey Cuddihy*

**MIKEY CUDDIHY**: *So, something I've been thinking about a lot, in terms of your work, is the sense of scale. How you make that jump from the smaller works on paper to these huge canvases. When I saw that painting with the yellow jug in it* [This is not a love song] *I was stunned by how huge it was. It looked so intimate when I'd first seen it as an image, and then to suddenly be confronted with this giant work was a real surprise. I wondered how you managed to navigate that.*

**LORNA ROBERTSON**: I suppose I'm not aware of how the paintings are seen by other people, or of the difference between how they see the big ones or the smaller ones, but in terms of making them, in some ways I find it almost easier doing the big ones, which surprises me. Although I always feel quite frightened of them before I start – I'll often have the canvas up on the wall for a wee while before I touch it.

**MC:** *And how do you usually start? With a white primed canvas?*

**LR**: No, I usually turn the canvas around and work on the other side of the prime.

**MC:** *So it's not so pure; does that feel less intimidating than working on white?*

**LR:** Yes, I think so. I don't really like the whiteness of the canvas, I like the slightly stained, weathered feel of the other side that's got some colour in it.

**MC:** *I've been reading a huge tome called* Ninth Street Women *(by Mary Gabriel), about the women abstract expressionists in the 50s, Lee Krasner, Helen Frankenthaler, Joan Mitchell. I keep thinking of this image of Helen Frankenthaler in her studio where she was in the work, you know, the work is on the floor, and the wall, she's surrounded by it, and I wonder if that sense of working at that scale, whether you feel like you are part of the work itself?*

**LR:** Oh, I know that photograph, yes. There's maybe something in that. I think so, it feels like it's so important, that physical relationship to the work, to movement.

**MC:** *Yes, that comes into it, the gesture…*

**LR:** It's a bit like dancing or something, you've got to feel relaxed and trust that you'll find the rhythm and that your coordination to do it is going to work. I find it really interesting, because on some of them I'm working on a ladder. So I'm focused on one area of the painting without being able to see the rest of it and I have to make a decision; I've got to hold the bigger image in my head, and it's quite daunting. You think you're not going to manage, but it turns out you can do it. Somehow it is there in your head, and you can work on different parts of the canvas and draw all the bits together.

**MC:** *Years ago, I made large works in the studio in London. I would paint them on the floor so I was, sort of, in them, and then I would staple them onto the wall and then have to go outside to look at them because I couldn't get far enough away from them. There's something of that with your big paintings – that sense of your having been inside your work, but at the same time trying to hold it away to see how it operates.*

**LR:** It's quite exciting because you're so close to it and yet you're allowing yourself this freedom. And I suppose there's an element of chance because you can't have the control that you have with the wee ones; you can't get back to see them, but it's exhilarating because you're really in them.

**MC:** *And you usually work with the canvas stapled onto the wall, don't you? You've got that hard surface, so in a way it's still referencing drawing in some way, with a harder surface to work against.*

**LR:** Yes, on the wall so it's flat, and with a canvas you can scrub into it, and I like that. Sometimes I will cut it up. It's not precious. I quite like finding ways in which I'm almost deliberately making it difficult for myself. I feel that, for me, I need that kind of difficulty. It's like with the shaped canvases, it's just a harder way to make them work somehow. And I sometimes struggle more with the smaller ones. I'll quite often start in the studio with smaller paper pieces and get quite annoyed with them and rework them and rework them. And then I'll go on to a big canvas, and it'll just be so much easier.

**MC:** *One of the things I love about painting, and especially painting large works, is that they are so physically present. It's like, 'Here I am. I've got this studio, and here are these big paintings I'm spending loads of time on.' There's no two ways about it, you know, it feels like a statement of intent; it's not quite masculine exactly, but it feels assertive.*

**LR:** I know what you mean. It does feel assertive somehow, and maybe there is sometimes an association between big paintings and a kind of masculinity, but at that scale you're creating something theatrical, and I like the idea that you can, sort of, be 'in' the big paintings. And the audience can be in them too.

**MC:** *They're fearless, or so they seem to me. And so full of colour. Can I ask you about that? How you use colour and whether you have a colour theme worked out before you start.*

**LR:** No, not really. I work quite intuitively but I do try and push myself from always using the same colours, or to do something unpredictable. Like I said before, to make it more of a challenge, or stop it from getting too easy.

**MC:** *When that happens, do you go back to drawing and something more basic?*

**LR:** I quite often draw into the paintings. Sometimes I find that a painting just needs drawing in after I've painted it for a while. It's as if the painting has to get worked out in the process of making. I've got lots of research material, drawers full of stuff, but I don't really look at it. It's kind of like I've absorbed a lot of it, so it's still with me. And I think it works better for me if I'm just working completely intuitively and I'm almost not aware that I'm thinking. Once I get into that nice state where I've been in the studio a few hours and I'm completely in the painting – it's not necessarily that I feel very relaxed, it can be quite tense, but I'm completely zoned in and...

**MC:** *Focused.*

**LR:** Yes. And I sort of lose track. I can be there for hours and hours without stopping and be really surprised that it's five hours later.

**MC:** *And sometimes there are bits of text in the paintings, or phrases. Is that something you bring in later or which is there from the start?*

**LR:** Sometimes I'll start with words. I'll maybe be thinking about a word in my head, and I'll just paint it in, although quite often you can't really see the text, but I like the idea that it can be whatever the person looking at it wants it to be.

**MC:** *I'm just staring across the room and there's one of the fragment canvases that have been stretched, and I've just realised it says 'amen'.*

**LR:** Well, this fragment of canvas that I'd been working on was taken from an image I had of Vatican guards. So, I mounted it onto canvas, and then I added more canvas round it, and it brought up a bit of a pun, the 'ah men'. I was raised Catholic, though I am very much not one now, so there may be an element of owning the image for myself, and in altering the image it was almost like a kind of personal iconoclasm.

**MC:** *What I like about the words is that they're still very much part of the actual painting, you know, they're coloured and painted, integral to the fabric of the painting itself.*

**LR:** Yes, the look and sound of the text is important. I really enjoy painting the writing as well because I've actually got terrible handwriting.

**MC:** *That's really funny. And there's the big painting that says, 'leisureline'. Does that come from a magazine?*

**LR:** Yes, it was in a magazine, and I'd cut it out because I was attracted to the colour and I liked the graphic, the way it was written. And I thought it was such a funny word, 'leisureline', and the idea we might dress for leisure. I'm interested in how clothes reflect us or allow us to project an idea of ourselves. I often cut things out from fashion magazines, scraps and fragments, and make these arrangements on walls in the studio with bits of things – watercolours and drawings and bits of patterns and figures.

**MC:** *And the wall is your backdrop, and you work to those limits; that sense that it's not separate from the room, but part of it.*

**LR:** Making a space where everything is playing off everything else. Shapes and colours playing off one another, and you can allow these relationships between things.

**MC:** *I do something similar, but I find it frustrating when I'm making an installation on the wall with fragments of drawings, colours and shapes, when I take it down it's no longer a work – it's gone. But when you're making an actual painting, you can make those relationships permanent – they won't be lost.*

**LR:** Like you, I enjoy the paperiness of paper. The paper is fundamental. It breathes.

**MC:** *The thing I like about paper is that it's a given – you don't have to construct anything. If you're making a painting on canvas, there's a whole construct that you have to create before you've even started. With paper, you respond immediately to a page or a sheet.*

**LR:** And it's quite fragile. In your work with your paper skirts, they're stained and torn…

**MC:** *Yes, and the cheaper the paper, the better: newspaper, flipchart paper…*

**LR:** I like newspaper too.

**MC:** *But years later it's all falling apart! For me, canvas always feels like fabric.*

**LR:** I like the sense of canvas as fabric, but I don't like the limits sometimes of the stretcher, so that's why I've been working on those shaped canvases.

**MC:** *They're great.*

**LR:** I like their openness. I can add things. They can grow or I can cut them up. Sometimes I feel if I have too much of a fixed idea about a painting when I'm going into the studio, it can get in the way of the painting – it gets overtaken by the idea, and it doesn't work. It's like I'm illustrating an idea. I need to hold on to a sense of a feeling about the thing, rather than an idea or an idea of an image. It's taken me so long to learn that, to believe in that, which might not feel like a solid thing, but it is.

**MC:** *Can I ask you about titling the paintings? Which is something that I know you do at the end – kind of the last thing – and which, inevitably, sometimes suggests a narrative. It seems like quite an important part of the process. You have paintings called* Where left is always right, Big dark dying, Fleeing and fleeing and being, Softly, so softly. *And then there was one that mentioned the composer Arvo Pärt; what was that about?*

**LR:** Yes, *The part Arvo played*. This was a bit unusual for me in that I'll often listen to music, but I've never really painted to just one piece of music, in this case Pärt's 'Spiegel im Spiegel' played over and over on repeat as I painted it, mainly in one session, for probably four or five hours. I then put it aside for a year before revisiting it and finishing it.

**MC:** *Do you choose the music beforehand to suit how you want to approach the painting, or does it happen the other way round?*

**LR:** I'll spend time finding the right piece of music but then to be honest even though it might be still playing I sort of forget about the music once I'm painting. It's on in my earphones, and it just plays and plays, but I'm not really listening.

**MC:** *All kinds of music?*

**LR:** Yes, a real mix. At the moment it's certain modern classical music, that edges towards the ambient like Max Richter, Pēteris Vasks, Nils Frahm, and lots of singer-songwriters like Karen Dalton, Judee Sill, Linda Perhacs, M. Ward.

**MC:** *I was watching a short film, with you talking about your work, and you were describing the joy of putting a thick, fleshy lump of paint next to a clear graphic line, and that you revel in this wide range of notes that you can use. And I was wondering, when you said that, were you thinking about notes in terms of music?*

**LR:** Yes, I find it really useful to think in terms of music. You know, thick and thin, pitches of colour, and the spaces between things, pacing and rhythm.

**MC:** *What about other routines? I know that you like to swim before you come to the studio. Is that an important part of your whole working process?*

**LR:** Yes, definitely. It's something that's taken years to learn – the whole way to feel and to come into the studio. It's a kind of preparation, to swim and breathe and then walk into the studio, and have the earphones in, music chosen. Getting to a place where I'm physically comfortable and relaxed and ready to paint.

**MC:** *And I guess with swimming there are rules and parameters, you've got that rectangle and that grid of the lanes.*

**LR:** It is a bit like that. I sometimes need to put grids into the paintings to offer structure to them, to pull them together, and when I'm swimming up and down, I quite often think it is like the structure that I need in the paintings to hold them together. I try not to think about painting until I enter the studio. I mean, sometimes when I go home at the end of the day it takes a wee while to stop thinking about it, but it's not useful for me to think about it until I'm in the space. It's almost like I need to do it – to be in the act of doing it – rather than to think too much.

**MC:** *Do you always work in the studio, or can you work at home as well?*

**LR:** Mostly the studio. I sometimes draw at home. I often draw in bed if I can't sleep, and I sometimes do watercolours if for any reason I can't get into the studio, or if we go away. But I really like having a space of my own that nobody else really comes to.

**MC:** *And that separation is quite crucial with a family and all the domestic stuff. I've always worked at home, but I didn't have my family until I'd already established that I worked from home. And even then, it was always as if the rules of my workspace were different from those of the rest of the house. There was one not very comfortable chair, bare floorboards, cobwebs everywhere…*

**LR:** I know, it's strange. It's not about comfort, but I do really like the feeling of shutting the door and being alone in the studio.

**MC:** *So, have you always had a studio as a separate place to work?*

**LR:** Yes, mostly. Except from when I had my first baby and I didn't have a space for eighteen months, but apart from that it's always been a priority to have a space to work. Even when we were really skint, I had somewhere to paint. And I think just keeping at it, even if it was just stolen hours. I remember when my kids went to nursery, it would be two hours, and I'd go in and think, 'What can I do in two hours?' But that was a dead useful discipline, I think, because you're using your time well. You have to.

**MC:** *When I had my child, and I only had one, when he was a baby, I suddenly decided I wanted to use oil paint, and I don't paint with oils usually, but I wanted to paint this huge painting. And I had him in a play-pen in the studio, and I thought, 'This is so stupid…'*

**LR:** Yes, the turps and everything, it's so messy.

**MC:** *It didn't work. He'd wake up crying, be picked up and get covered in paint.*

**LR:** I did once have a studio in our living space. It was in Dusseldorf where Andy and I did a residency. We both used the studio at the same time. It was an amazing, big studio with a small living space, and we had our boys who were quite young. It was good, actually, it was fine, especially at that age. They'd go to bed, and somehow we had the energy to paint until three in the morning and still get up early.

**MC:** *So, in terms of having your show, you'll suddenly have that transition from your crowded studio space to this lovely gallery space. How do you feel about that?*

**LR:** It'll be interesting to see the work. It always looks so different from how you think it's going to look in your head. Some of it I've been working on for maybe over six years off and on, so it's nice to finish things. And it's such a different thing to see it up on a wall and out in the world. I am looking forward to that part of it, yes.

**MC:** *Can I ask you how things have changed in your work as your life has changed?*

**LR:** I left art college when I was twenty-two. I'm fifty-four, and I've always painted. I've probably always made quite a lot of work and I feel like it's been through lots of different stages, but it's taken a long, long time to find the right way for me to make work. I painted and drew from life to begin with, trying to understand or believe in a language of painting that was authentic. I worked outside a lot. The work was always quite rough, it still is quite rough; I enjoyed the canvases getting really weathered.

**MC:** *So you worked from landscape?*

**LR:** Yes.

**MC:** *Like that wonderful Scottish painter?*

**LR:** Joan Eardley. She was a big hero of mine. I went out and drew in cafes and in the landscape, and I also did a lot of still life. I remember throwing pigment onto paintings, and I was always covered in paint; I'd go outside and just make such a big mess. And then I got a scholarship to Florence just when I finished art school and that was really great, because I kind of felt, 'I don't know if I'm really interested in old paintings,' but actually it was so good. Because I could see that the paintings were about belief. The subjects may have been religious, but the belief was in the language of painting as a way to communicate something. Particularly the Fra Angelicos, I just was really touched by them.

**MC:** *Another artist who I sometimes think of when I'm looking at your work is Rose Wylie. Is she someone that you think about?*

**LR:** Yes, I think I first saw Rose Wylie's work in Norwich at EAST International in 2007. She'd done these big Posh and Becks paintings, they were huge. And I was so excited by them, and maybe as well by the idea of her. I think she was maybe seventy-two at the time, and I just thought, 'This is so good, because you can just keep on going.'

**MC:** *She went to the Royal College to do her MA when she was in her fifties, I think, so after her children were grown up.*

**LR:** I found the ambition of her work really inspiring. And her freedom, you know?

**MC:** *Yes – those bright colours and thick lines on raw canvas, the way she physically builds the paintings; they're almost sculptural.*

**LR:** There's a very graphic element to them. I think there are lots of differences about how she and I approach painting, but yes, it was a kind of a relief to see them. So bold and big. They're so enjoyable, her paintings. And that rings true. I hope that I make paintings that are something to be enjoyed.

# WORKS ON PAPER

All dimensions refer to paper size

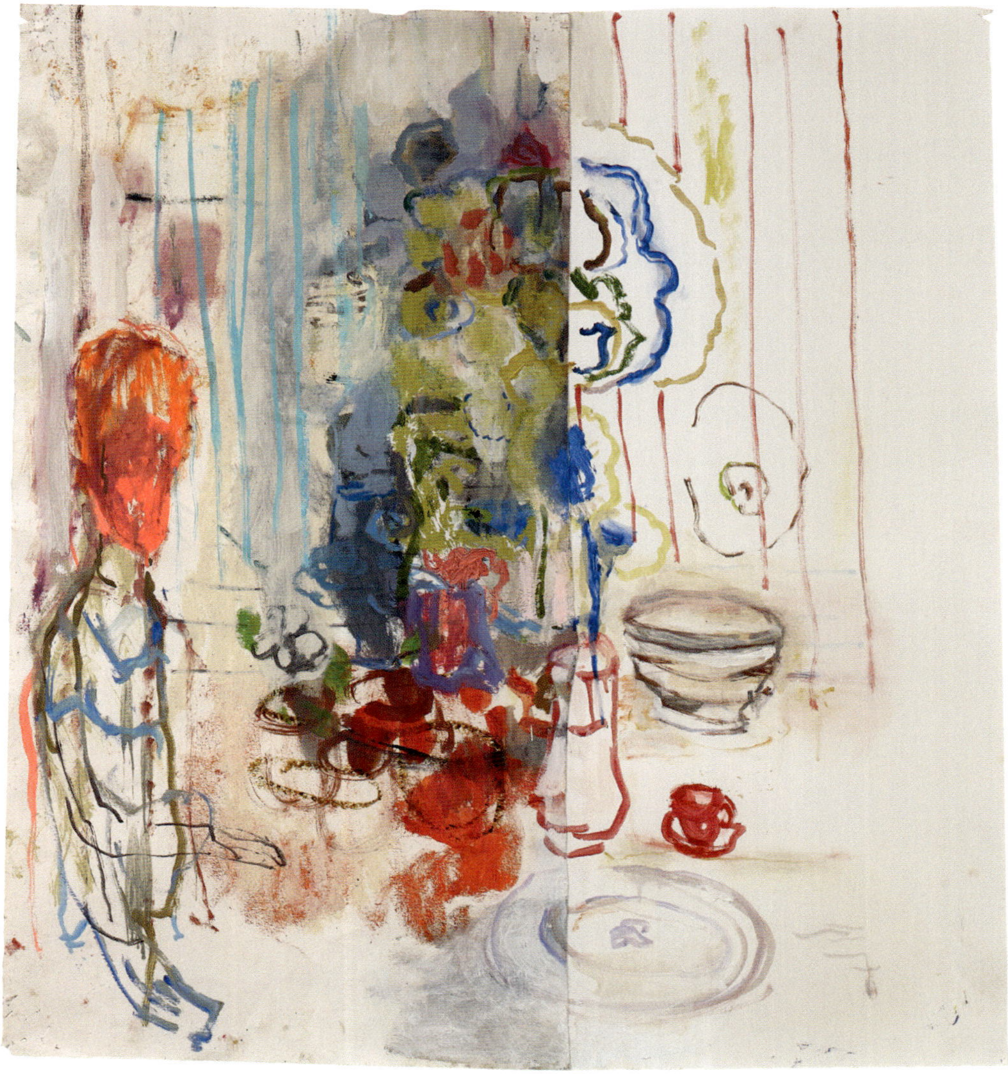

 *Yes and no*, 2021, oil on paper, 86 x 78 cm

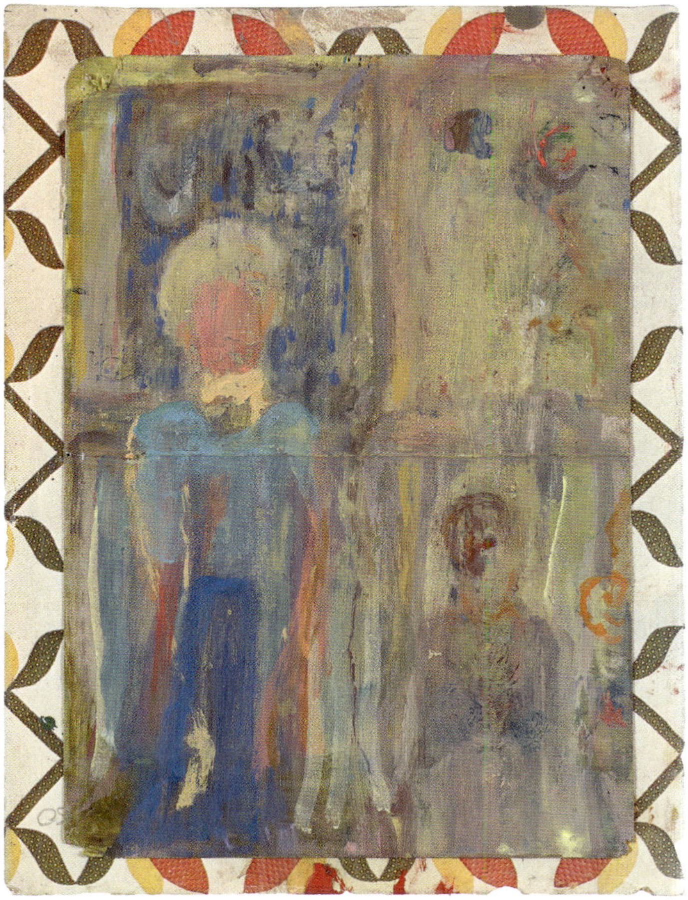

*Once I was*, 2020, oil on paper, 23 x 20.8 cm

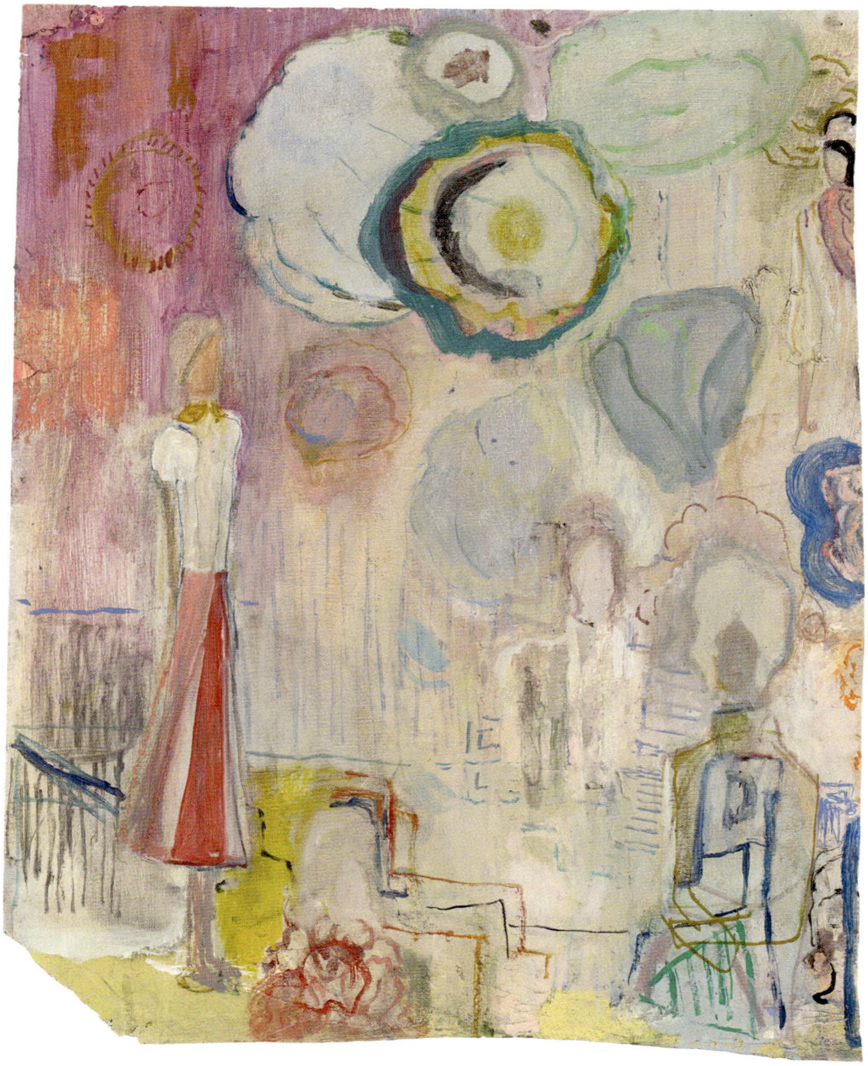

 *Sun spangled*, 2020, oil on paper, 74.5 x 61 cm

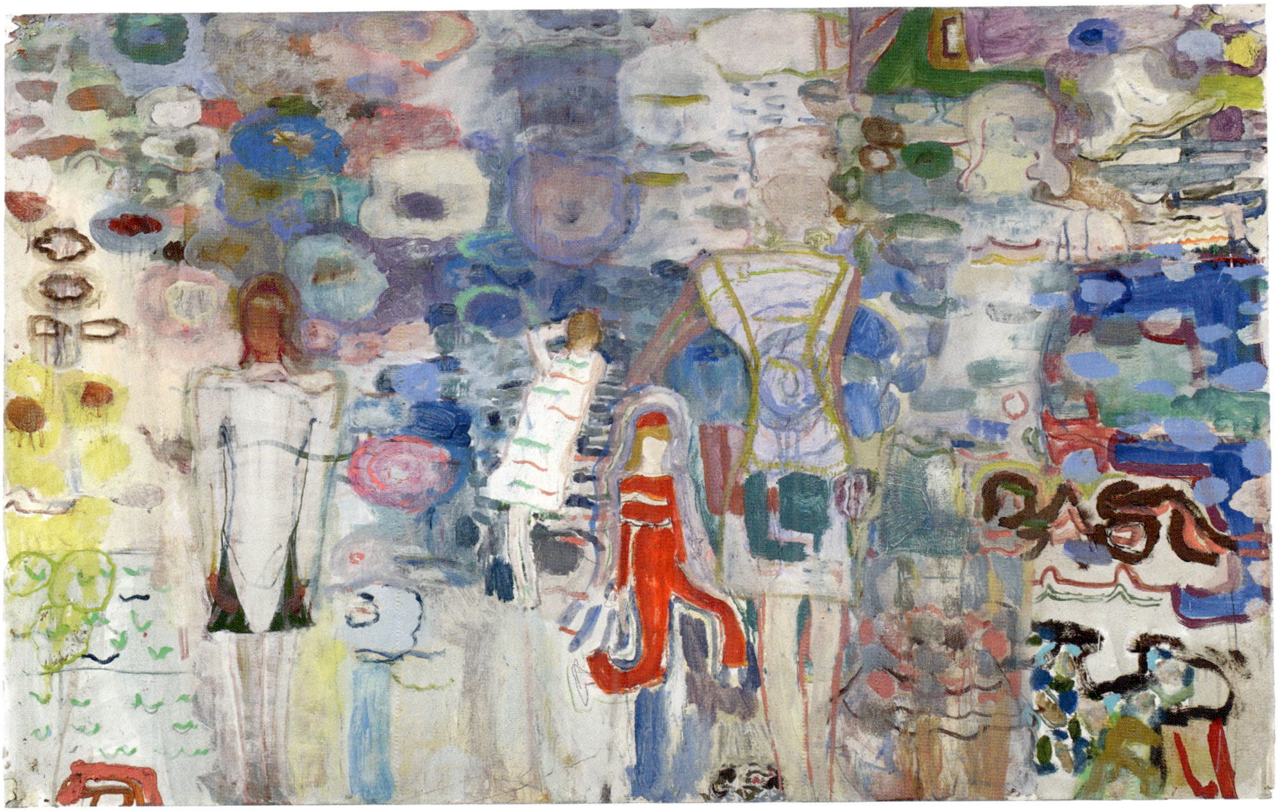

*Mountains and electricity*, 2021, oil on paper, 81.8 x 126.5 cm 

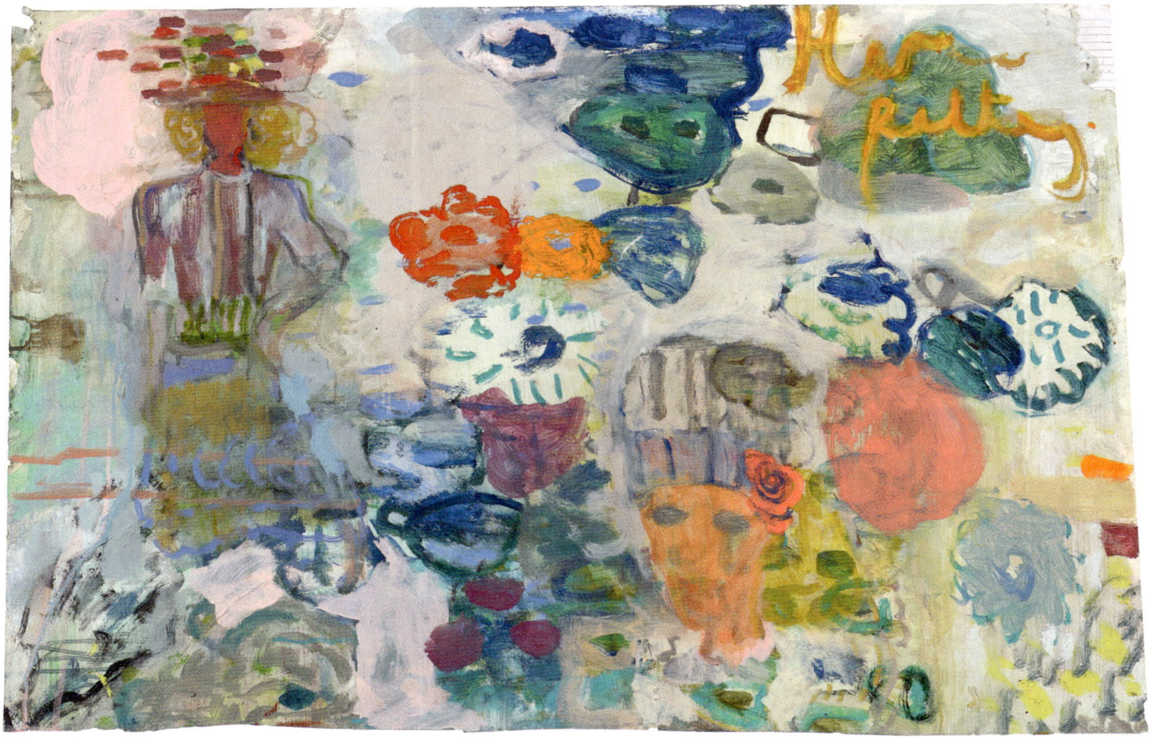

 *Damp fragrance from roses*, 2021, oil on paper, 56 x 82 cm

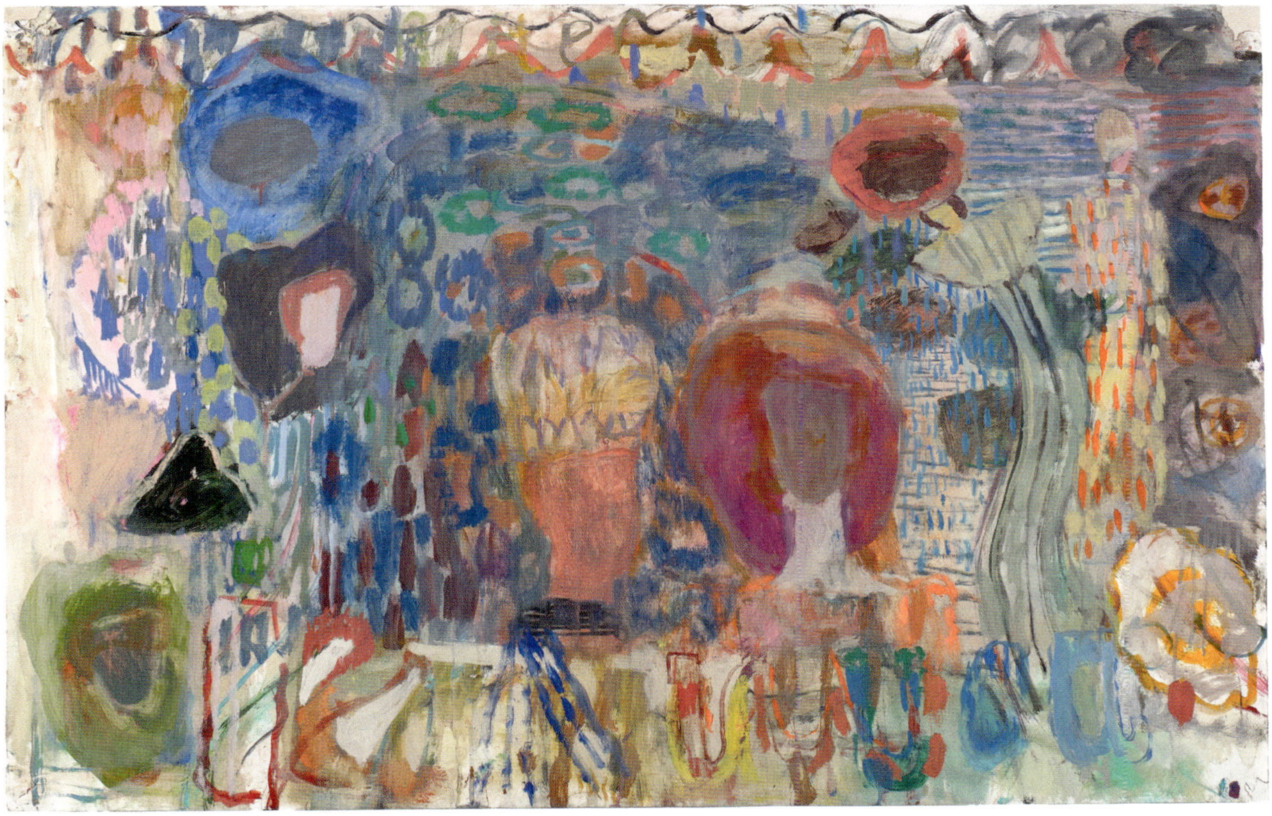

*Weed, nettles and thorns*, 2022, oil on paper, 82 x 126.8 cm

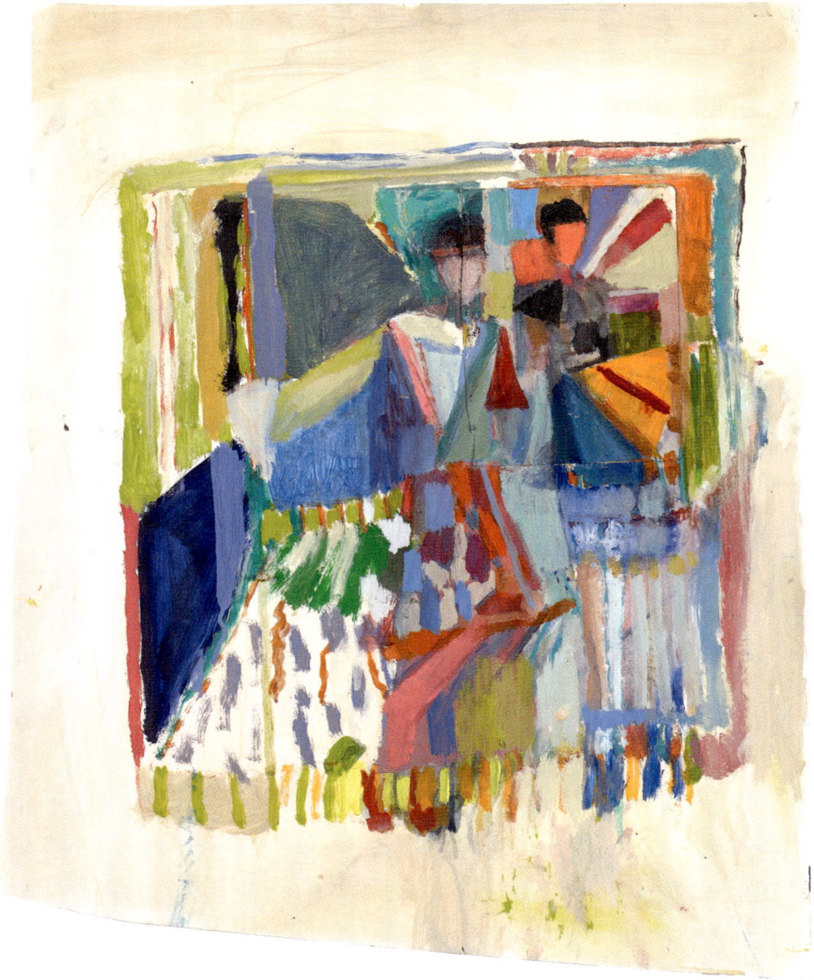

 *Salt, soil, stone*, 2022, oil and watercolour on paper, 60.3 x 48.7 cm

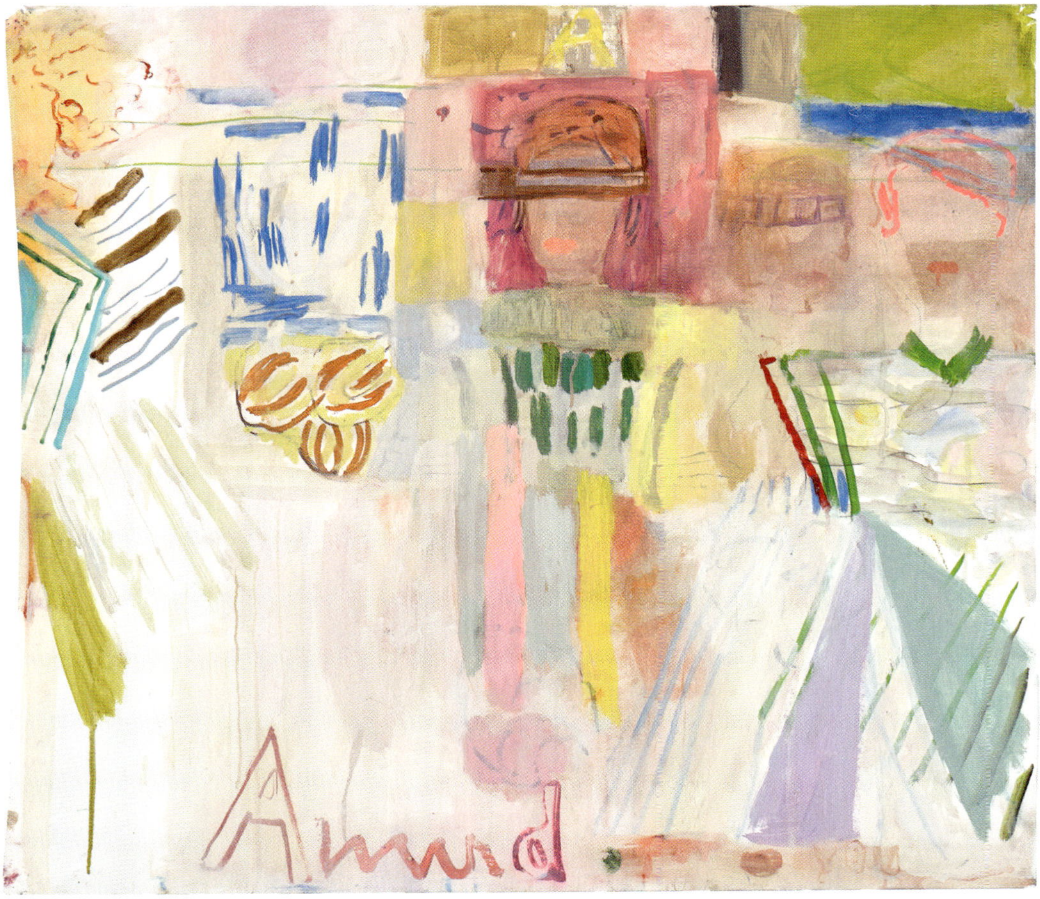

*Where the light comes to rest*, 2022, oil on paper, 81.8 x 90 cm 

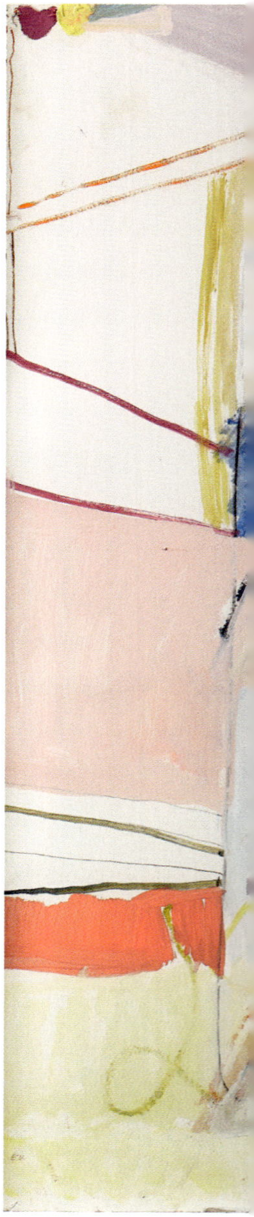

 *Courtyard*, 2022, oil on paper, 101 x 140 cm

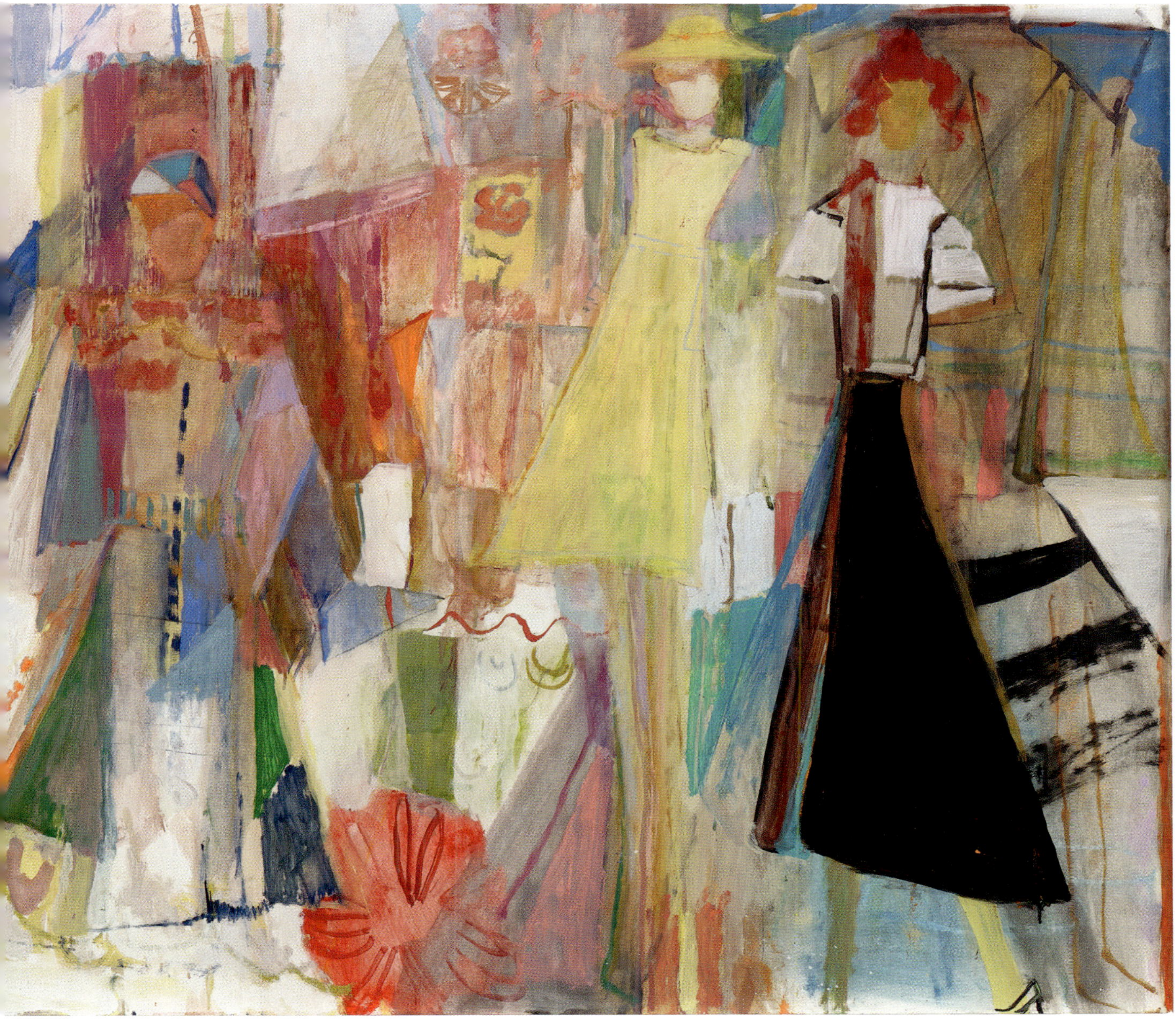

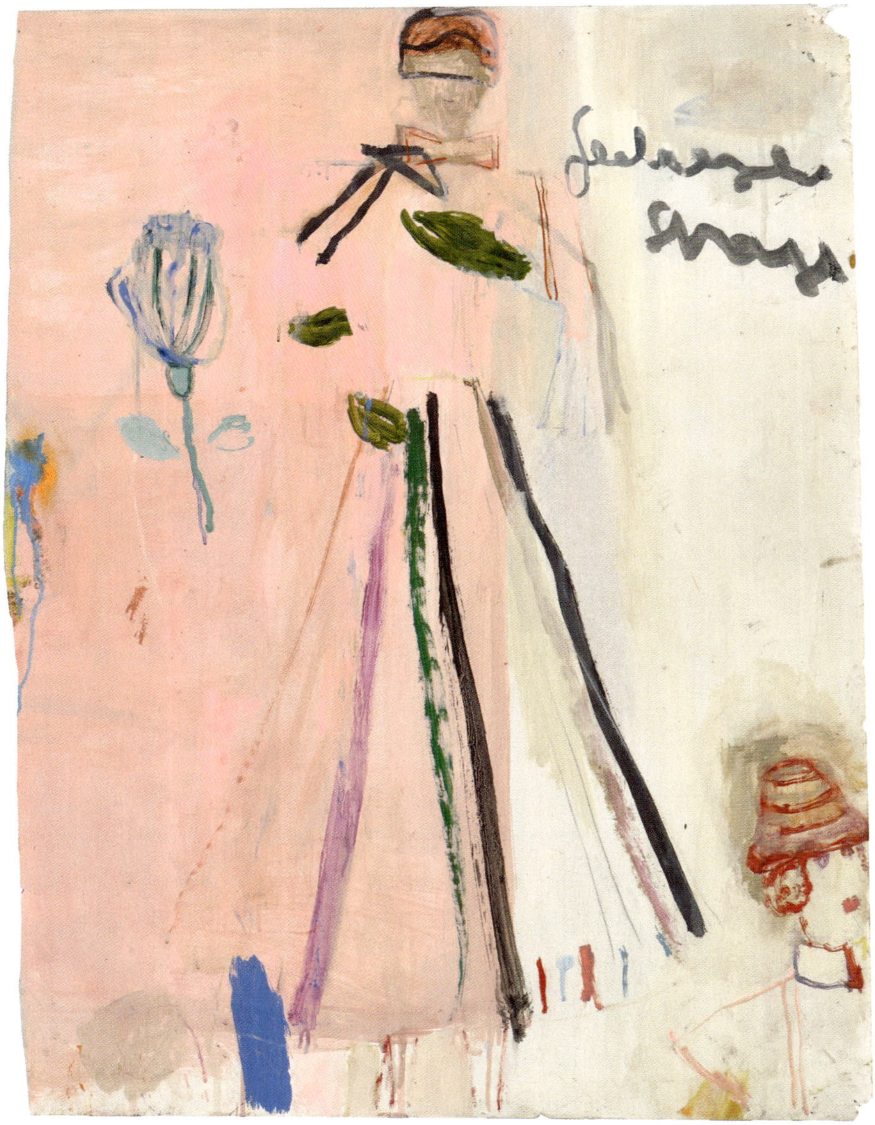

 *Where left is always right*, 2021, oil on paper, 81.8 x 62 cm

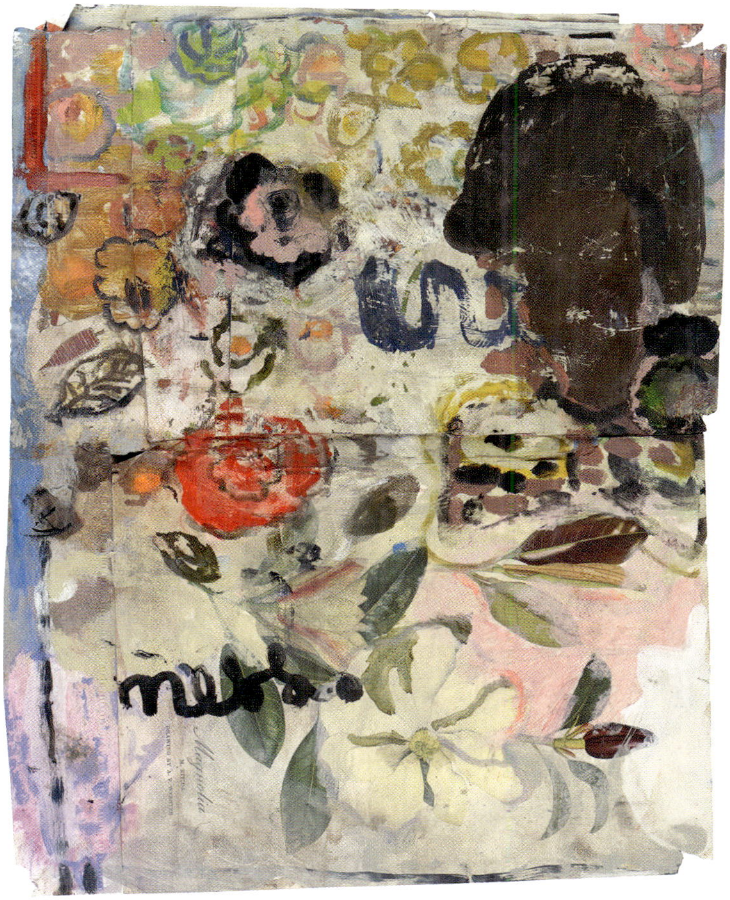

*Bistro Zicke*, 2020, oil and collage on paper, 44.8 x 34.5 cm 

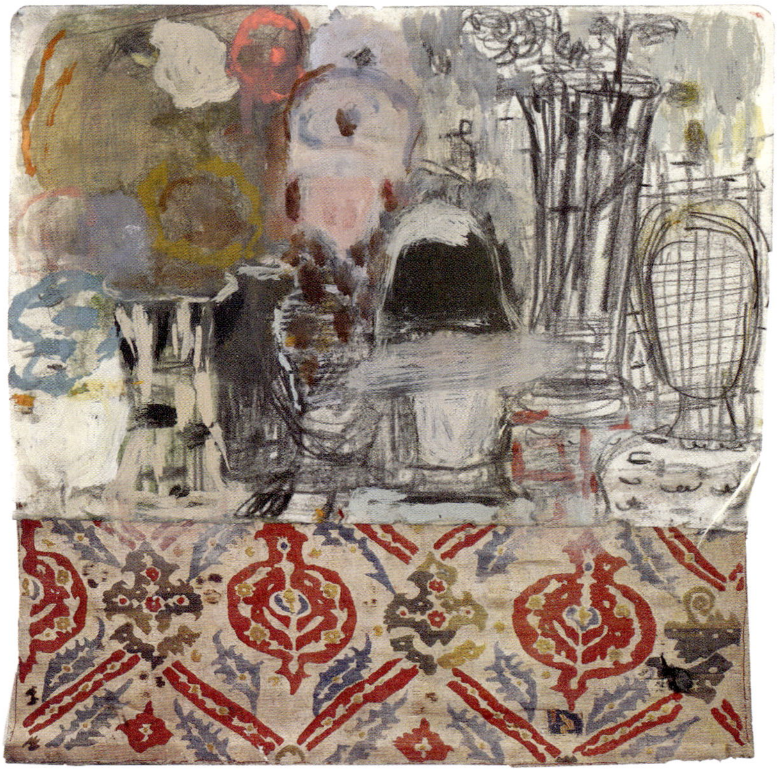

 *The tree in the room*, 2022, oil on paper, 21.4 x 20.2 cm

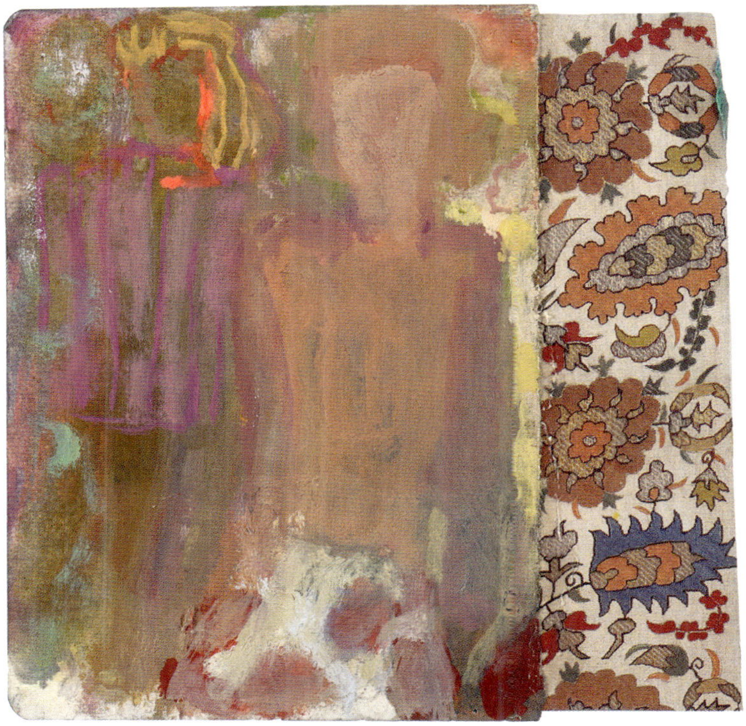

*The words in a poem*, 2022, oil on paper, 17.4 x 17.4 cm 

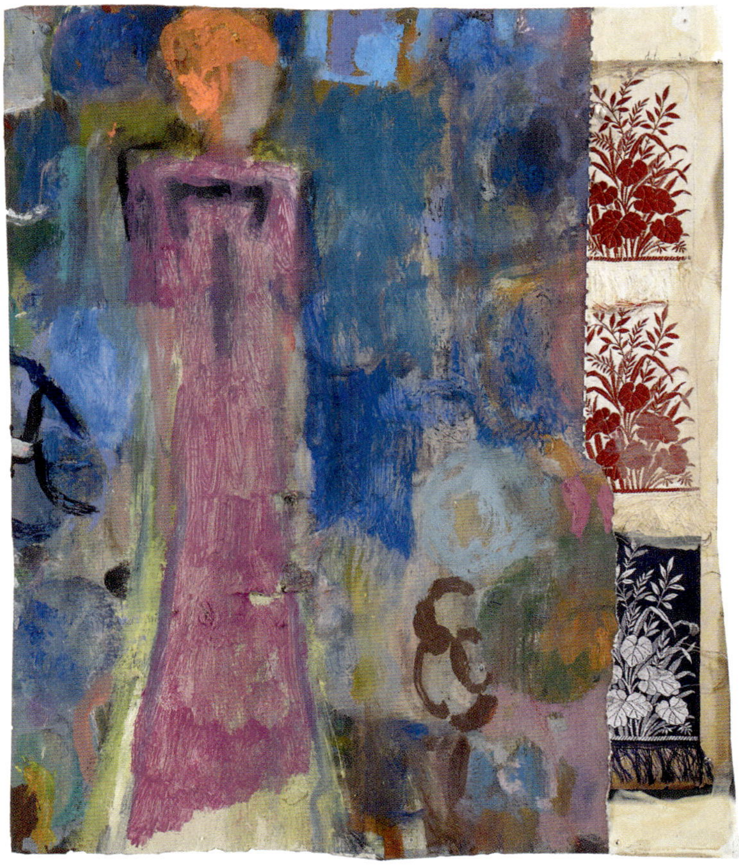

 *Side by side*, 2022, oil on paper, 27.2 x 22.4 cm

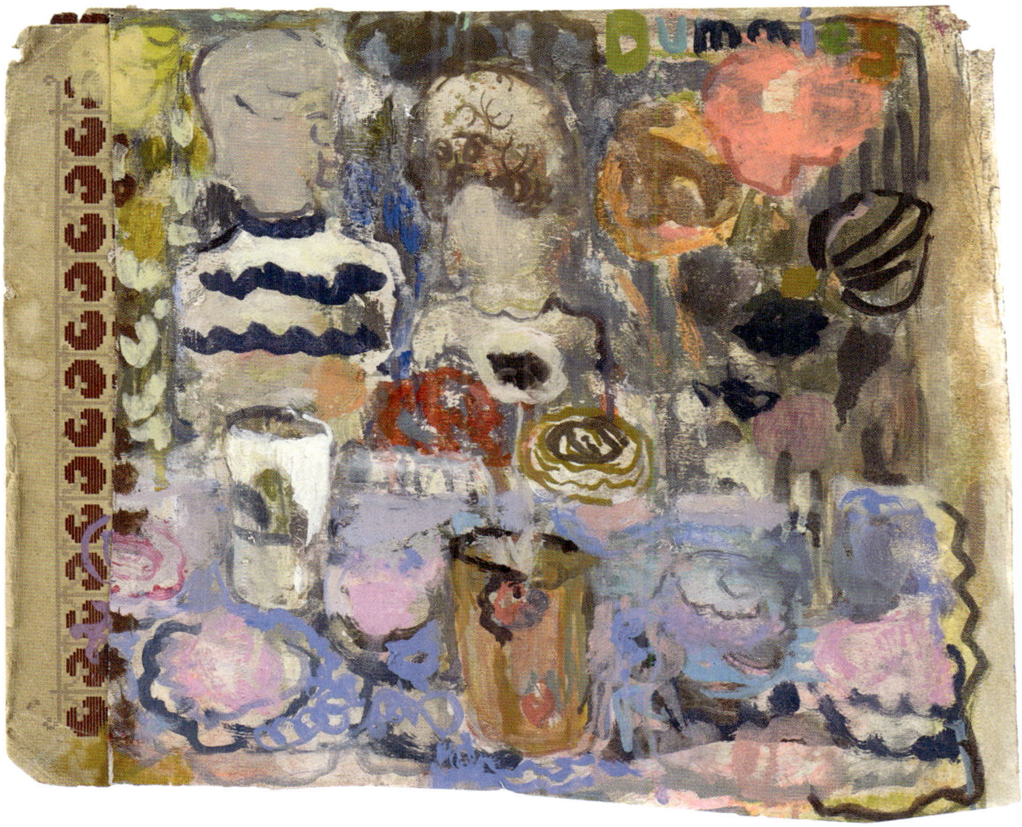


*Two of us*, 2020, oil and collage on paper, 30 x 37 cm

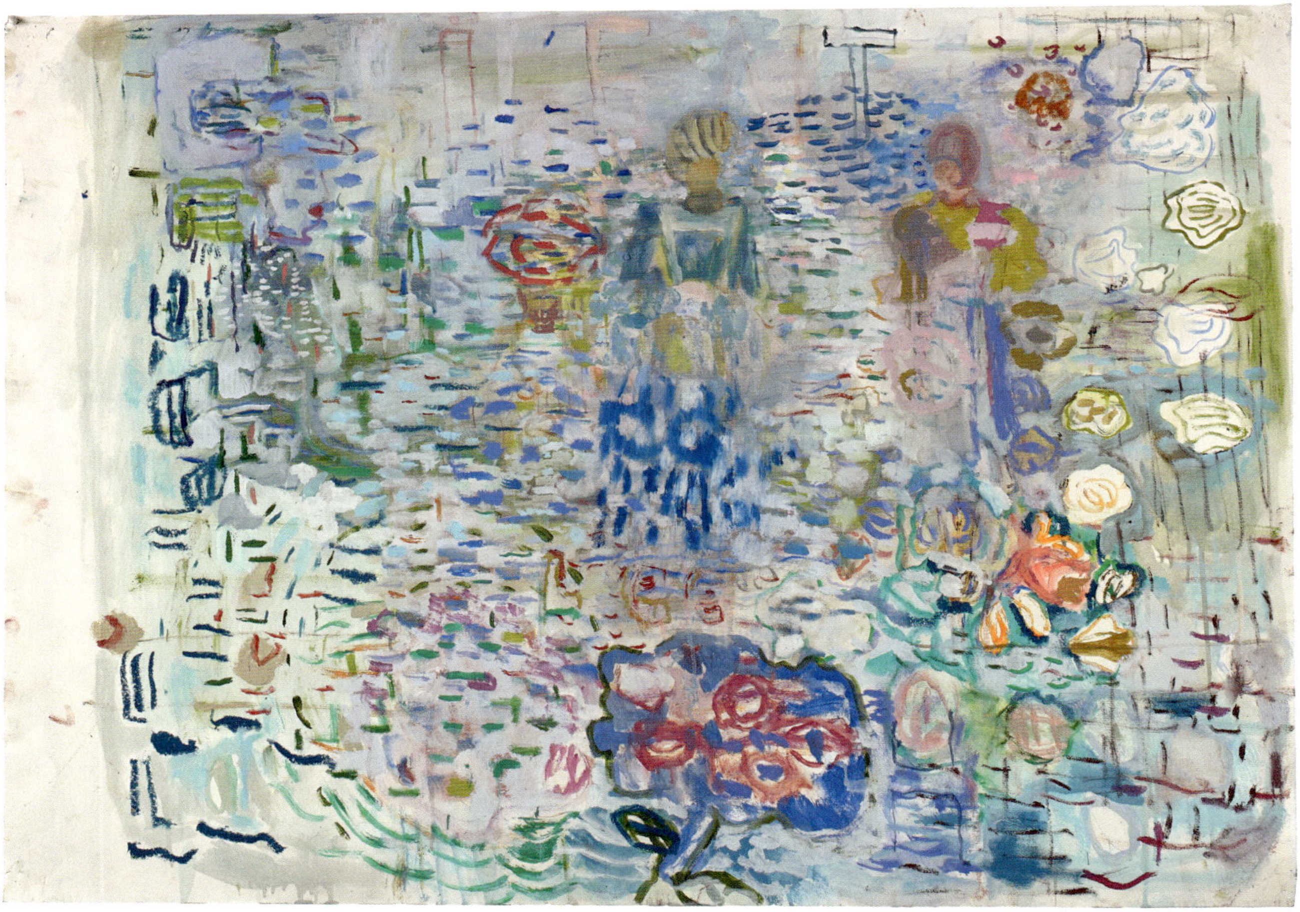

 *The part Arvo played*, 2022, oil on paper, 85.8 x 121.8 cm

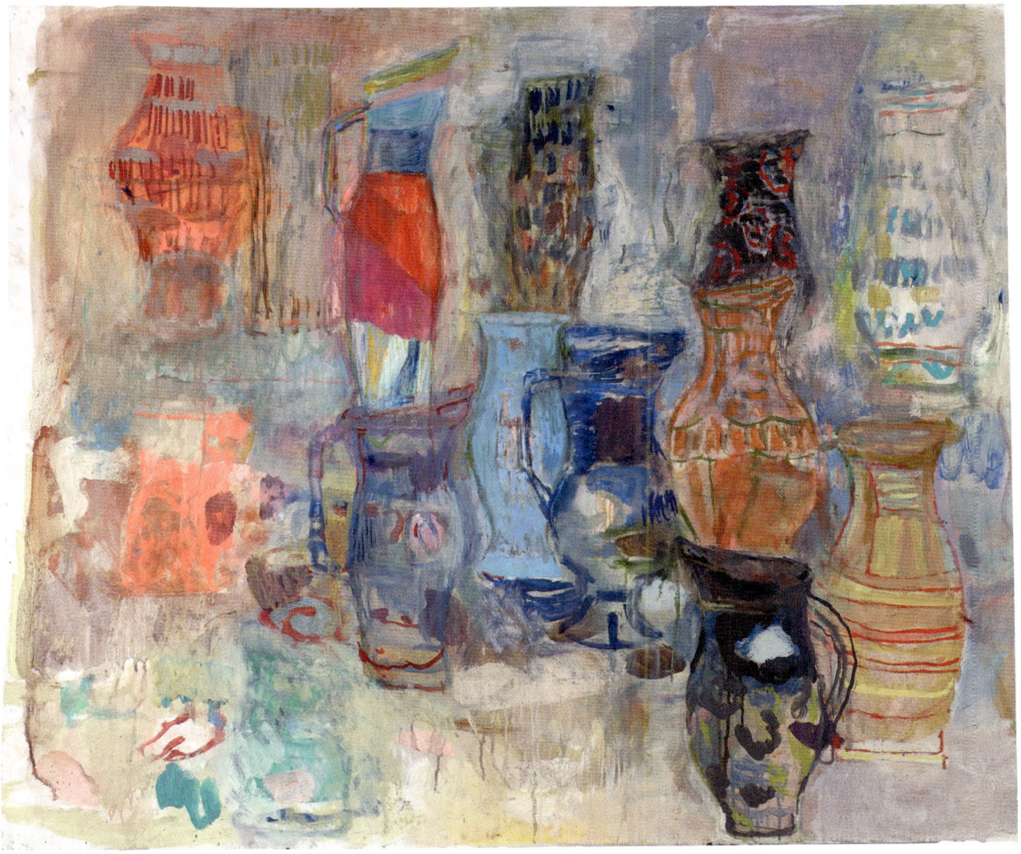

*Rhythm of rhythm*, 2022, oil on paper, 100.6 x 116.2 cm 

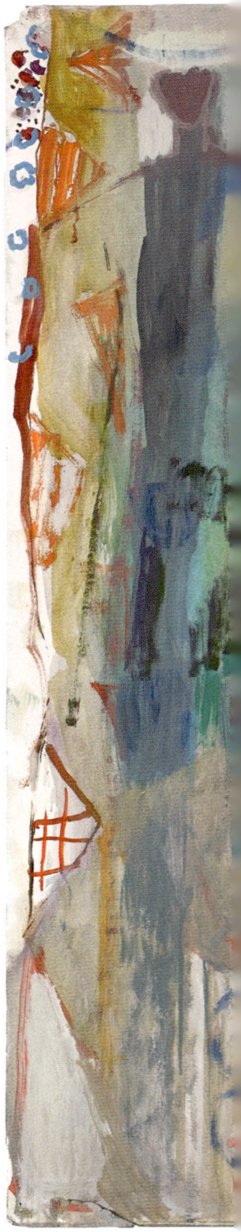

 *Big bright*, 2022, oil on paper, 99.8 x 140 cm

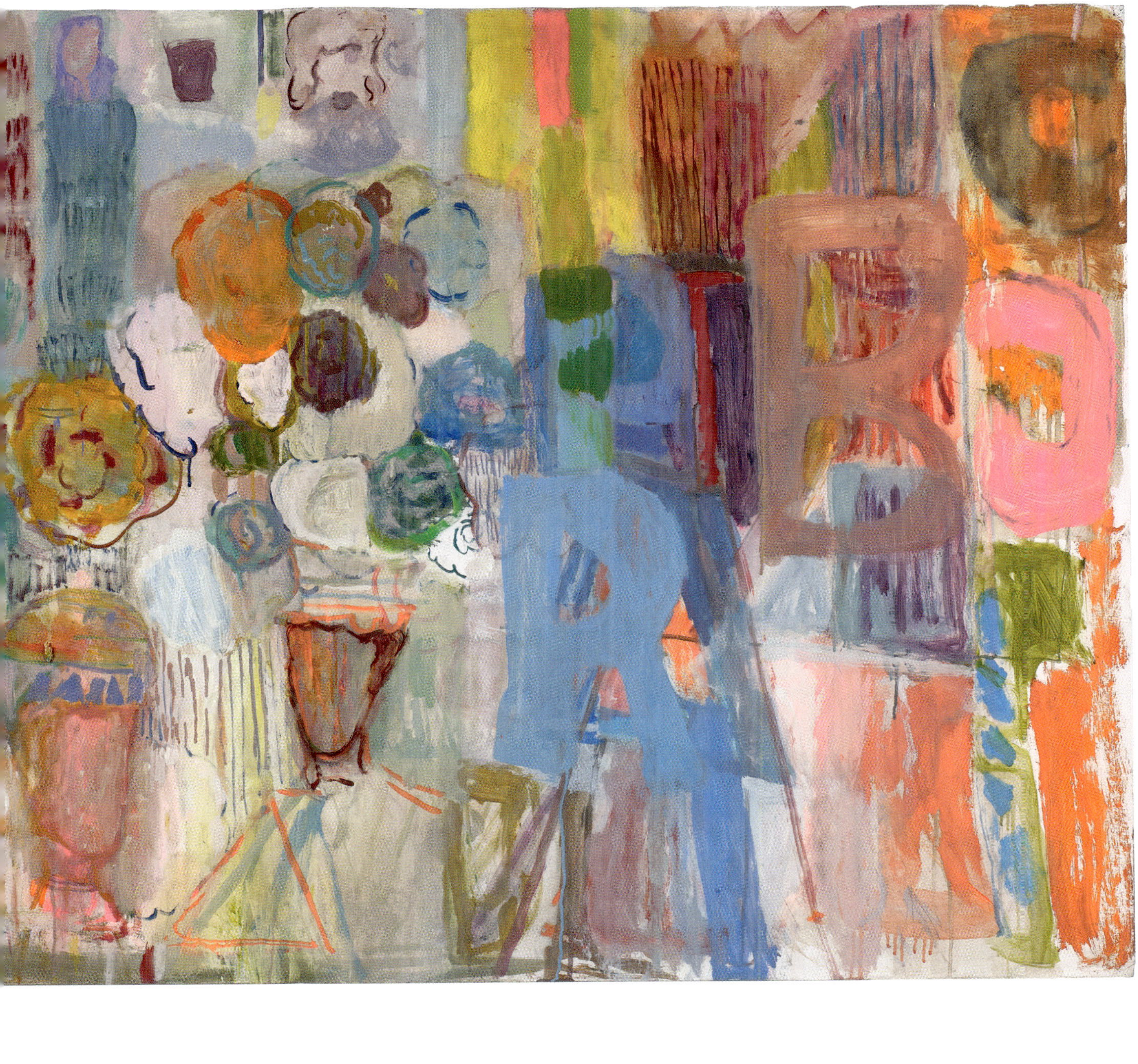

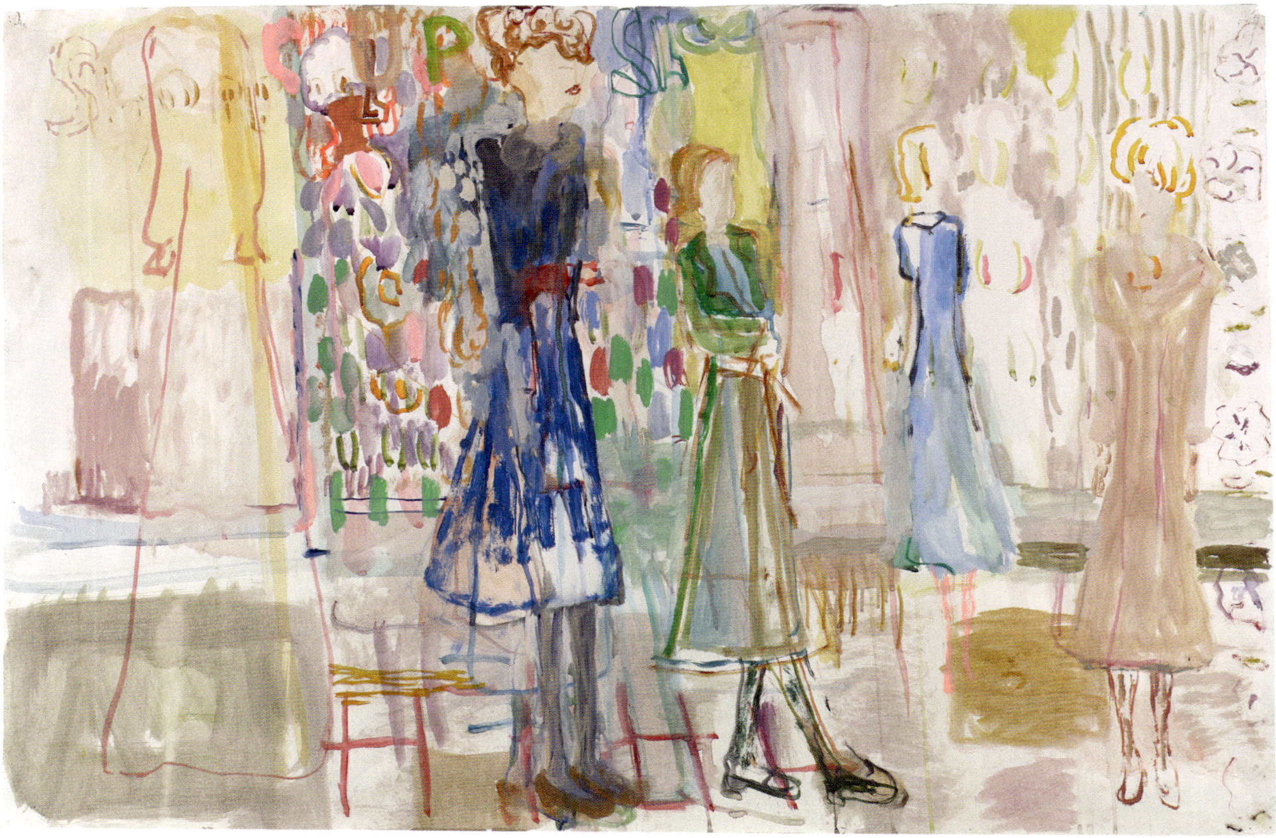

 *Washed, dressed, cleaned and tidied*, 2022, oil on paper, 81.8 x 126.8 cm

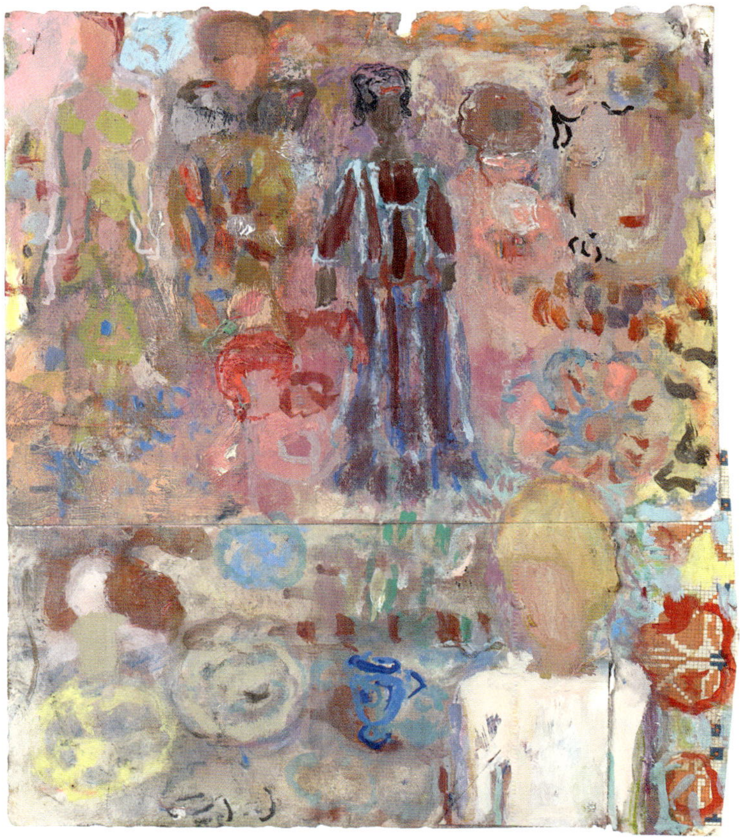

*A foreign journey*, 1990-2020, oil and collage on paper, 29.6 x 25.7 cm 

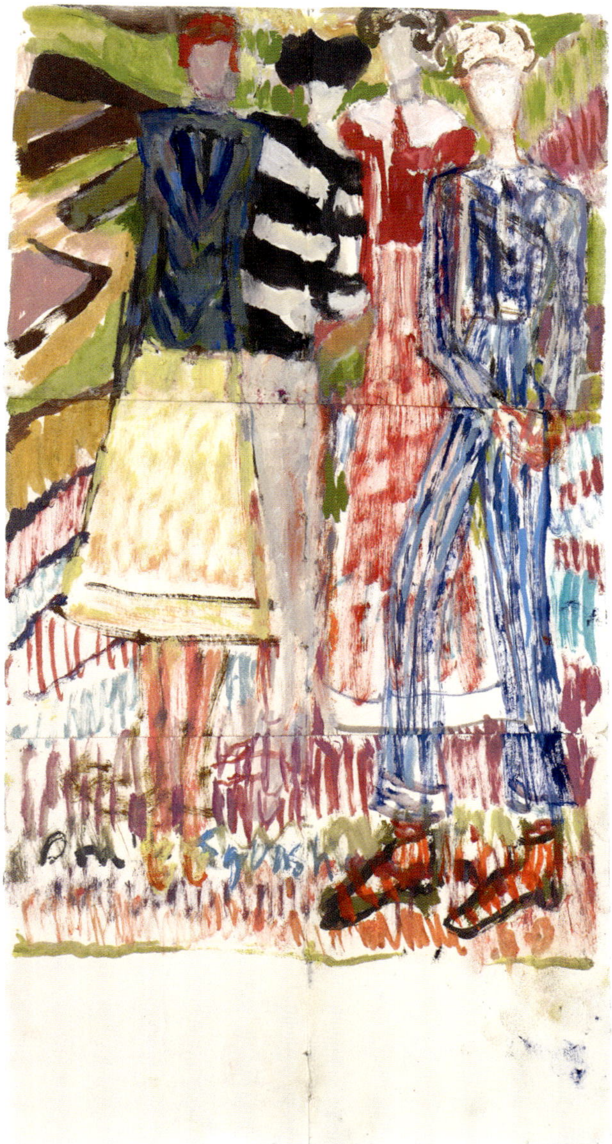

 *Patterns*, 2022, oil and watercolour on paper, 49 x 24.8 cm

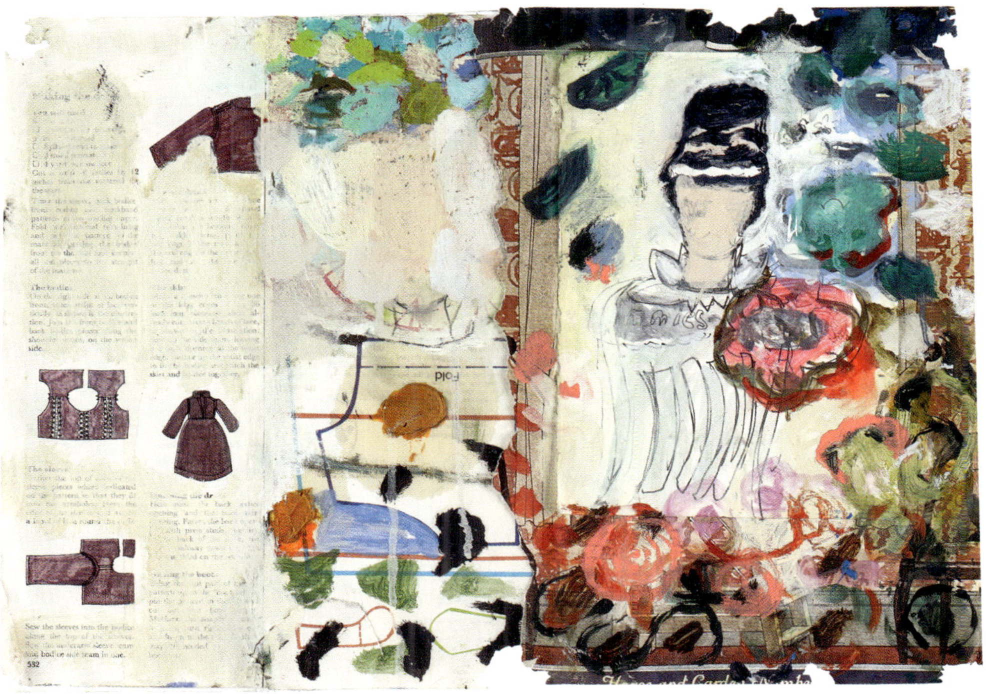

*Charlie perfume*, 2018, oil, collage, pen on paper, 29.8 x 41.6 cm 

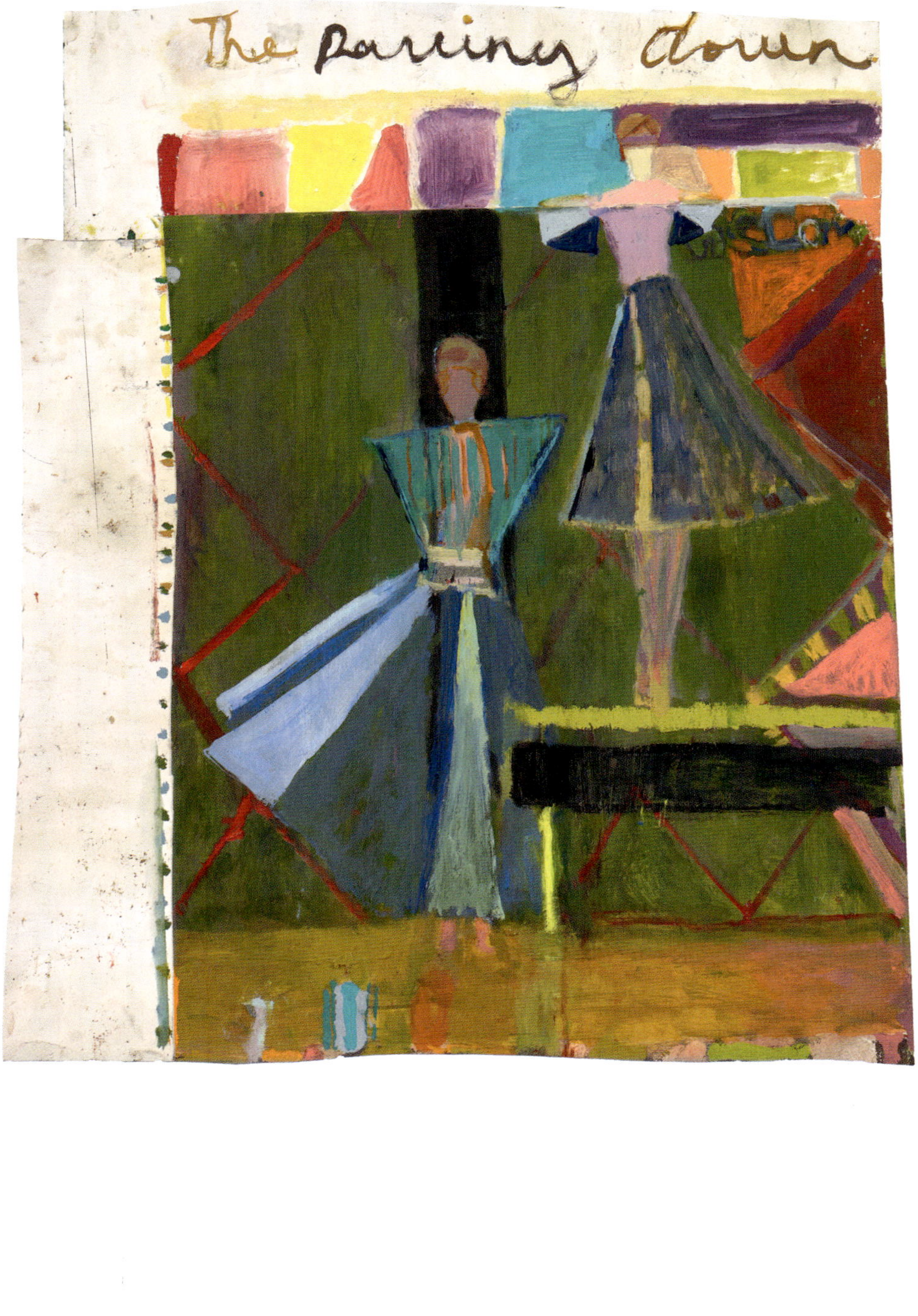

 *Jane Jane*, 2022, oil on paper, 88.5 x 72.3 cm

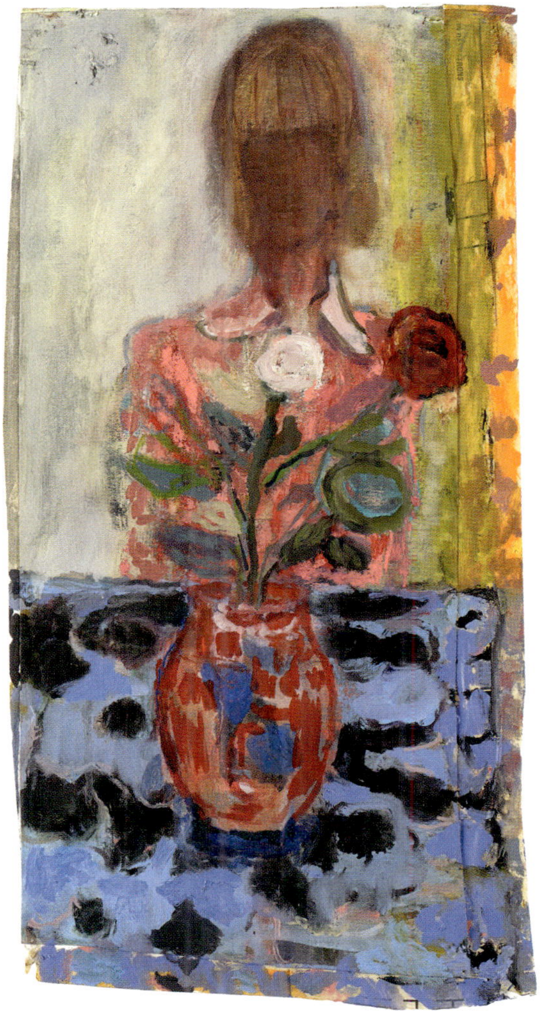

*The violinist*, 2020, oil on paper, 44.7 x 22 cm 

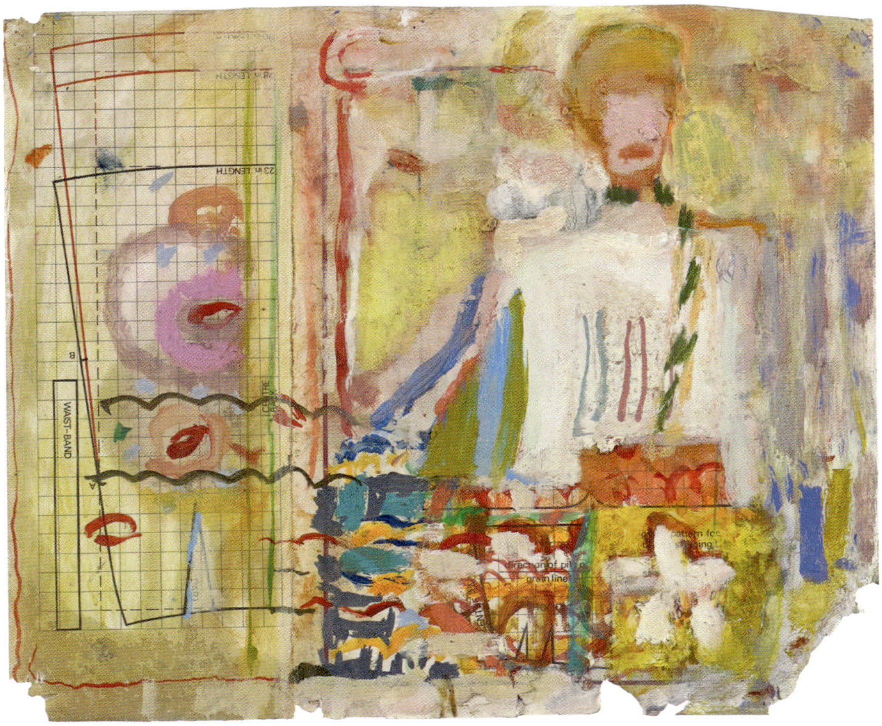

 *Woven and tightened*, 2022, oil on paper, 28.6 x 34 cm

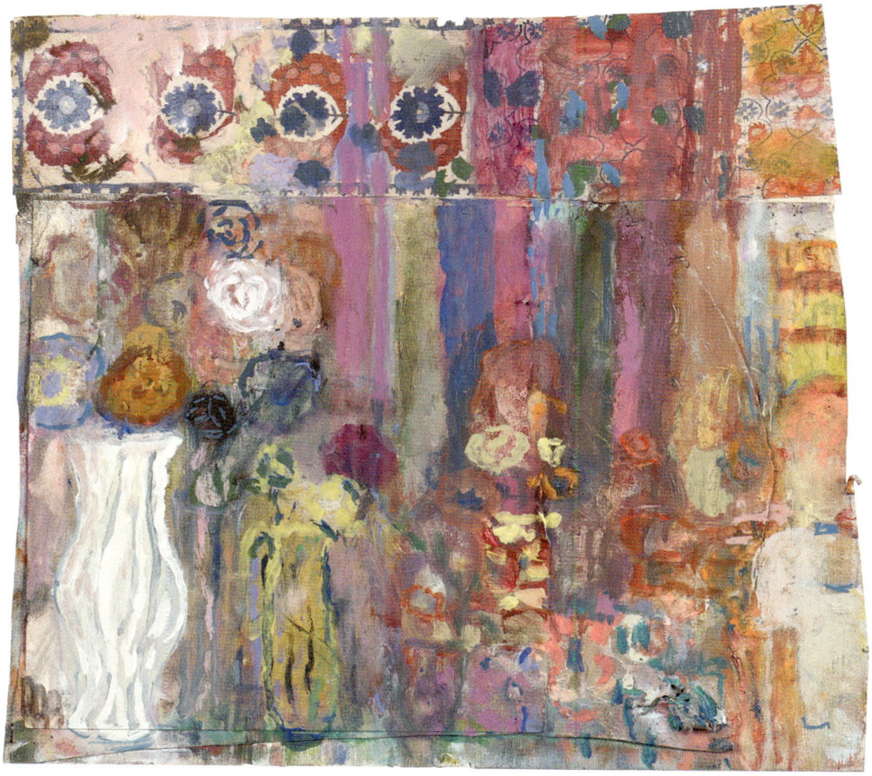

*Times told lovelier*, 2020, oil and collage on paper, 30.7 x 33.4 cm 

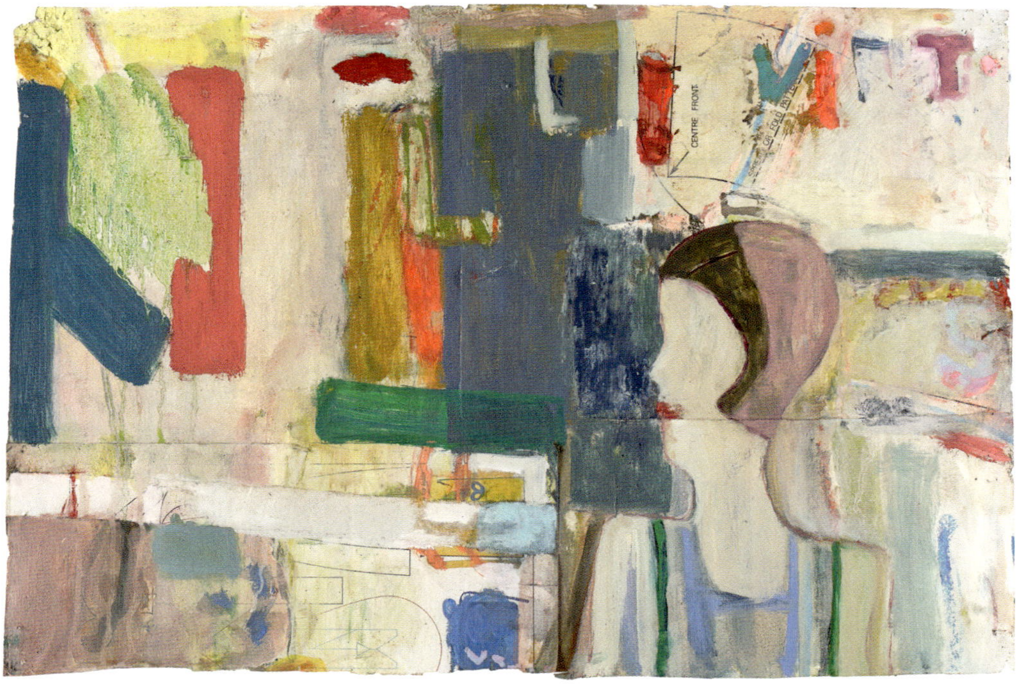


 *The swimmer*, 2020, oil and collage on paper, 37.2 x 54.4 cm

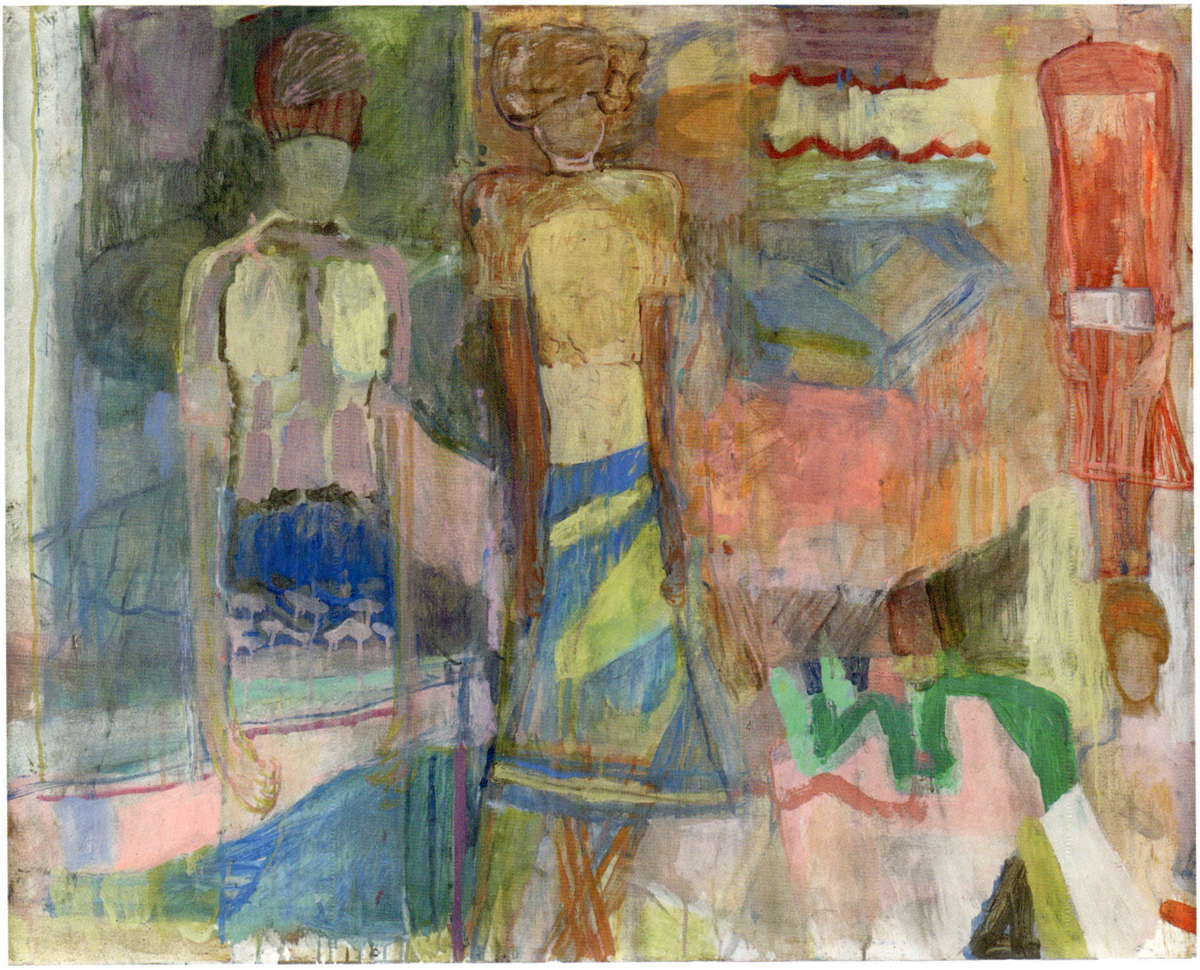

*Bellringers*, 2021, oil on paper, 82 x 101.6 cm 

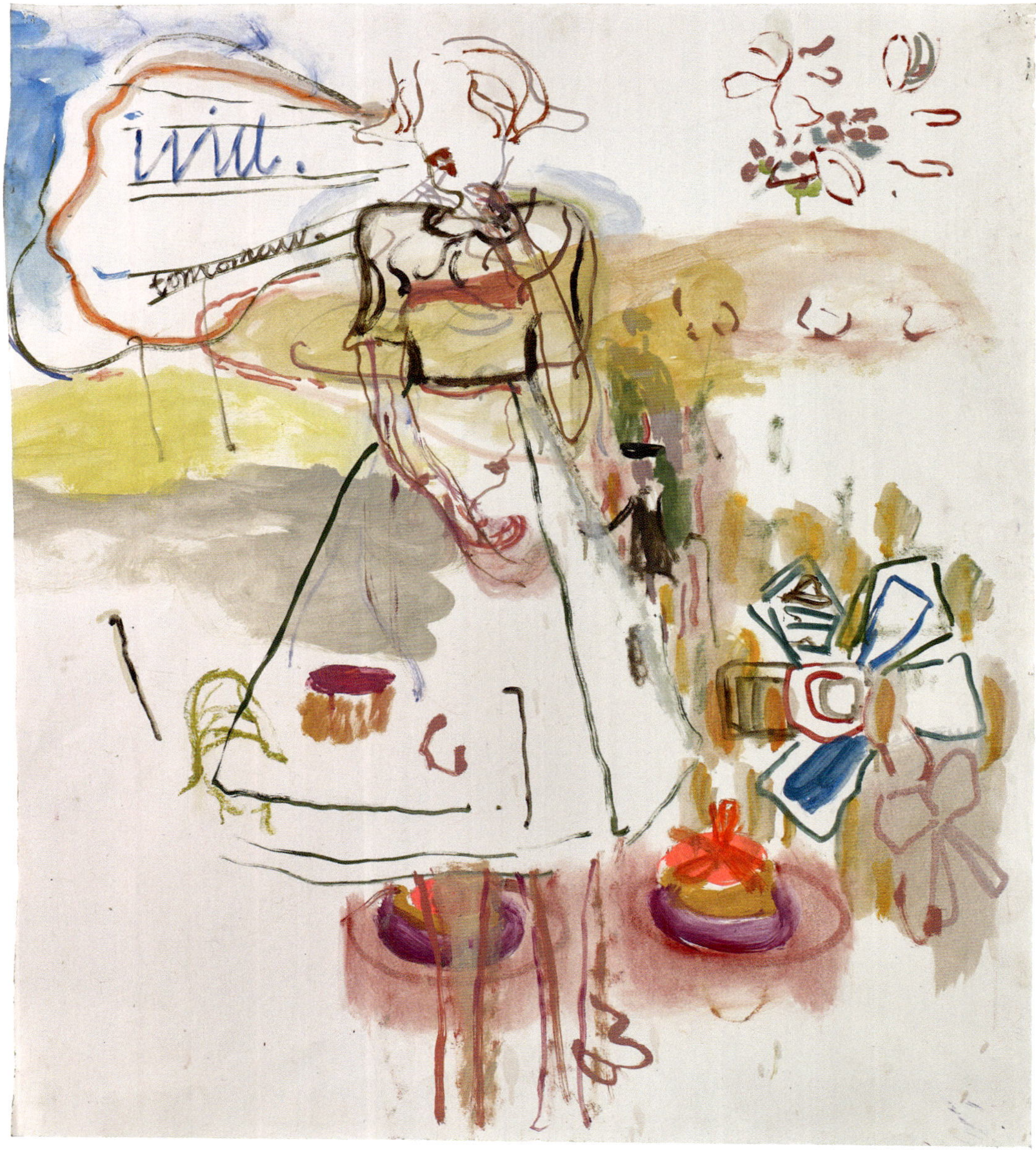

 *Cracked*, 2021, oil on paper, 81.6 x 69.2 cm

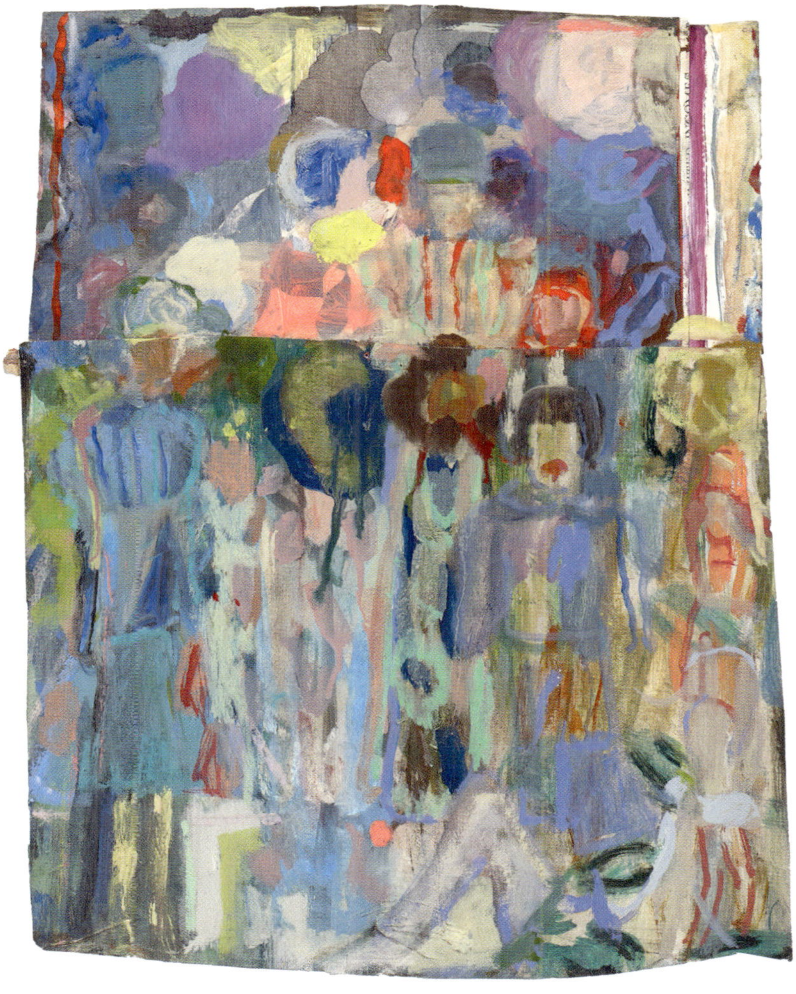

*A curtain behind a window pane*, 2022, oil on paper, 42.2 x 32 cm 

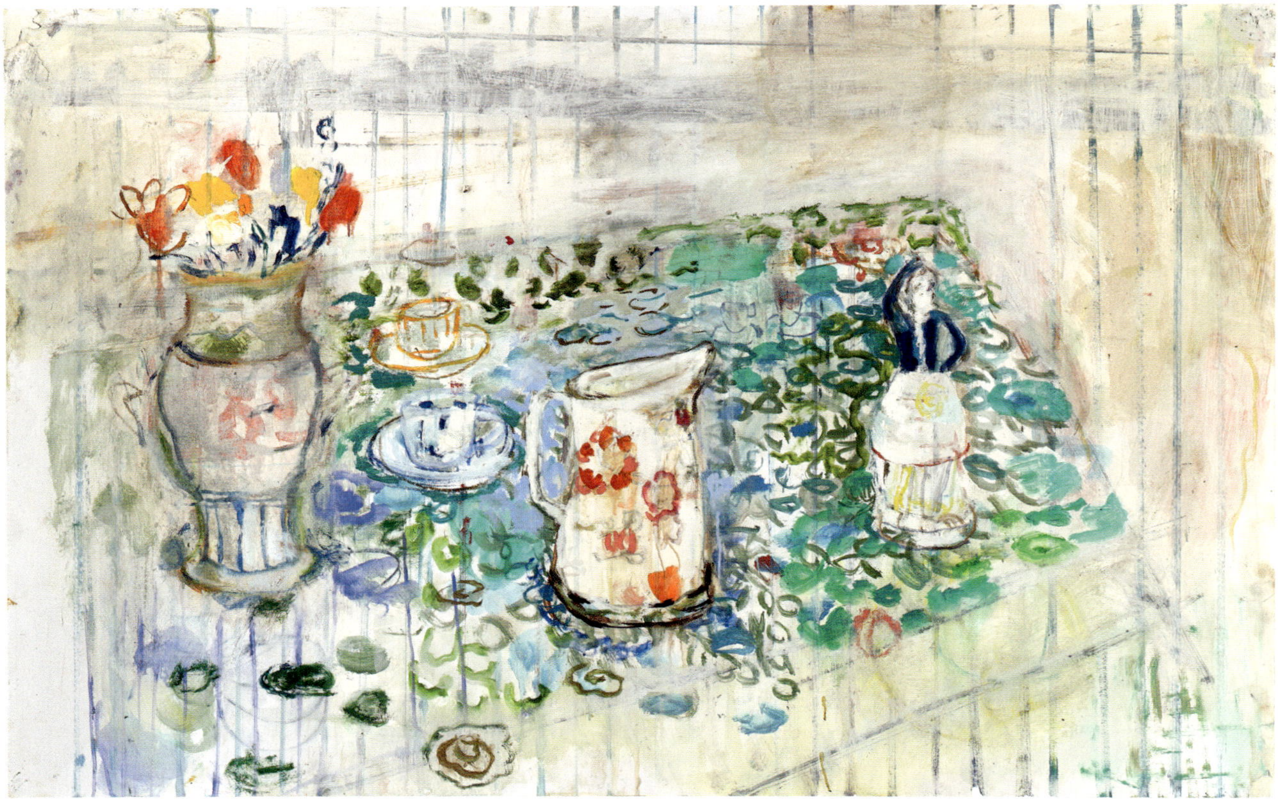

 *Still life at North Berwick*, 2016, oil on paper, 82 x 127 cm

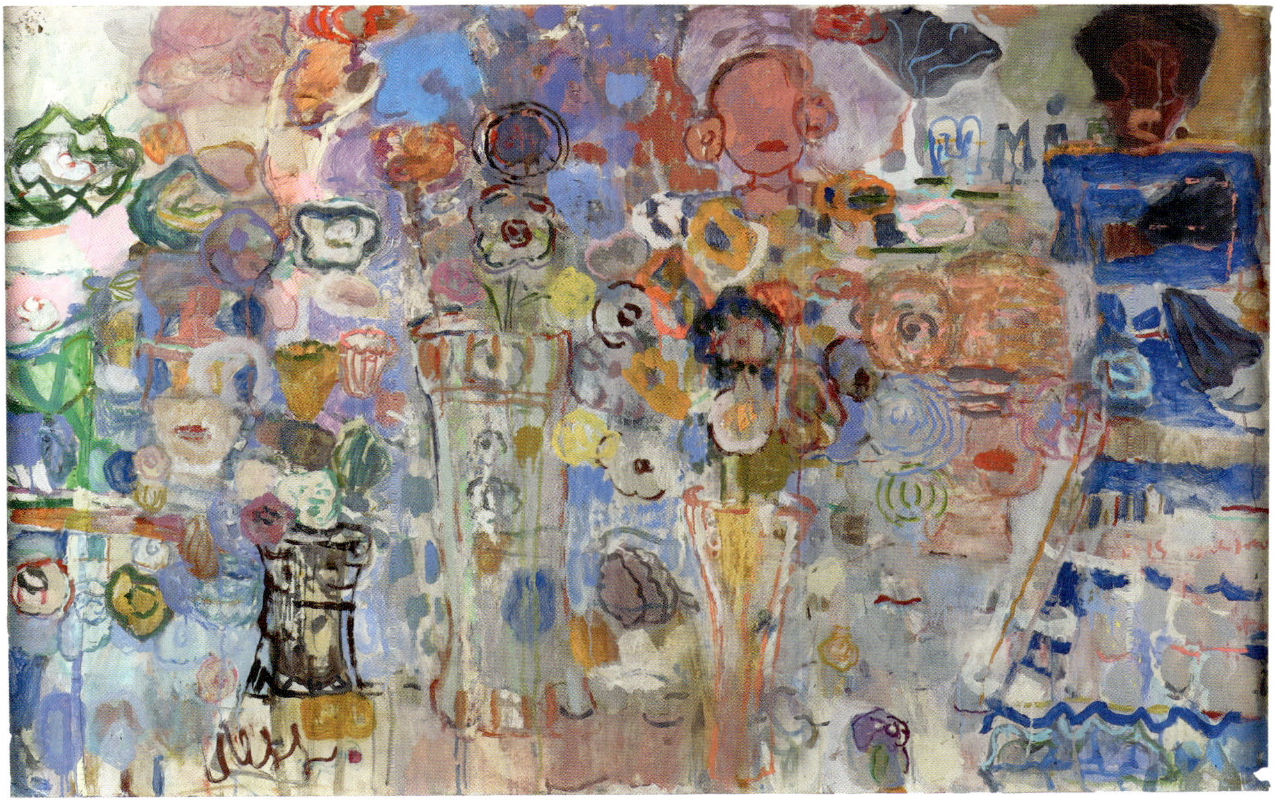

*The train*, 2022, oil on paper, 82 x 126.7 cm

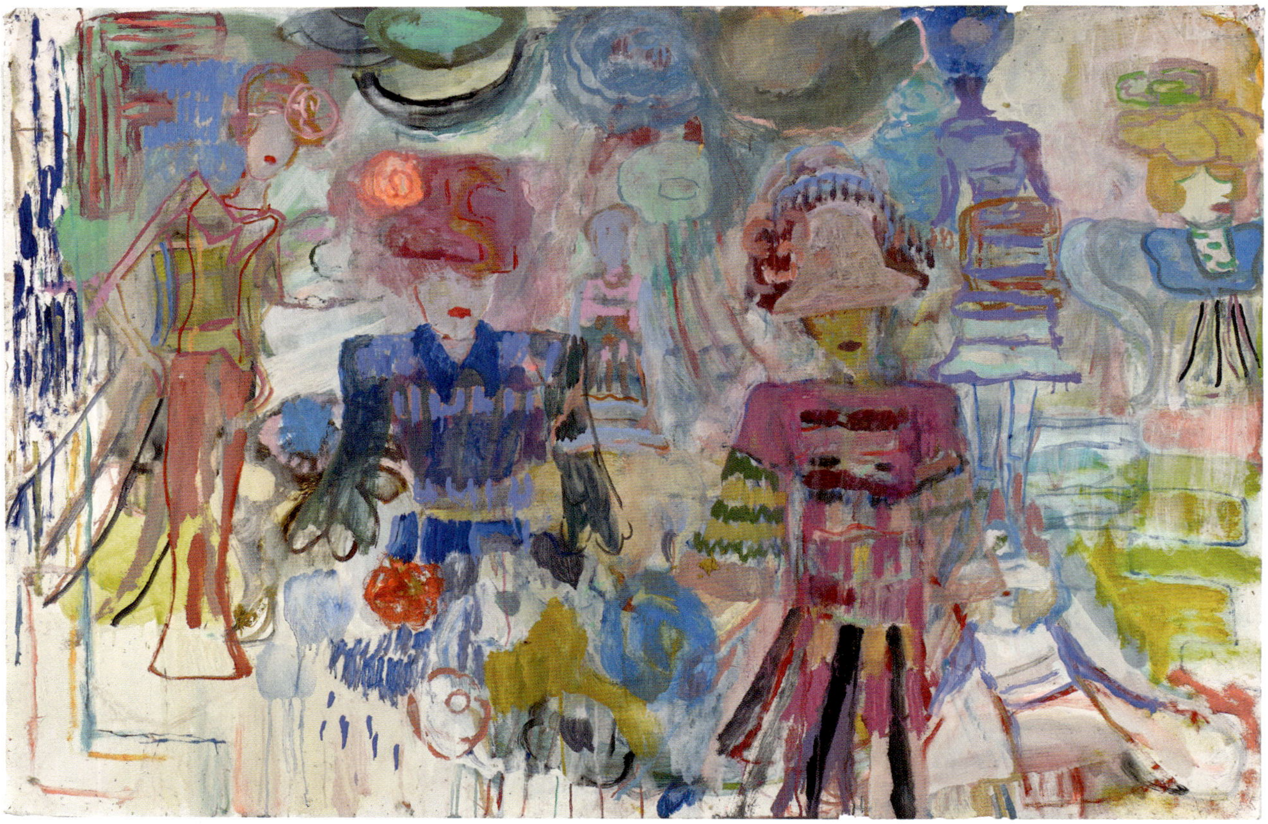

 *Softly so softly*, 2021, oil on paper, 81.8 x 126.5 cm

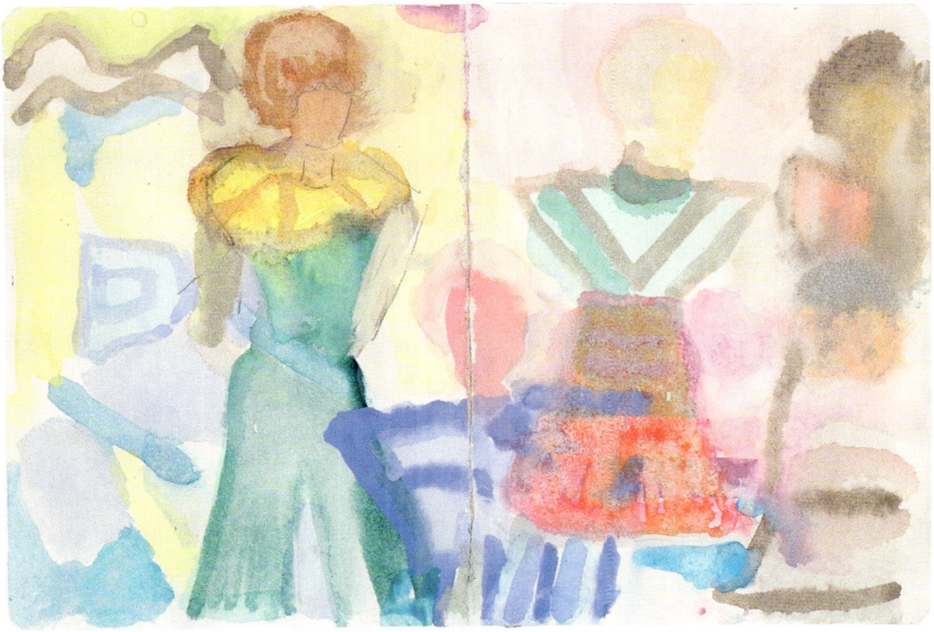

*We are glass*, 2022, watercolour on paper, 17.4 x 24.7 cm 

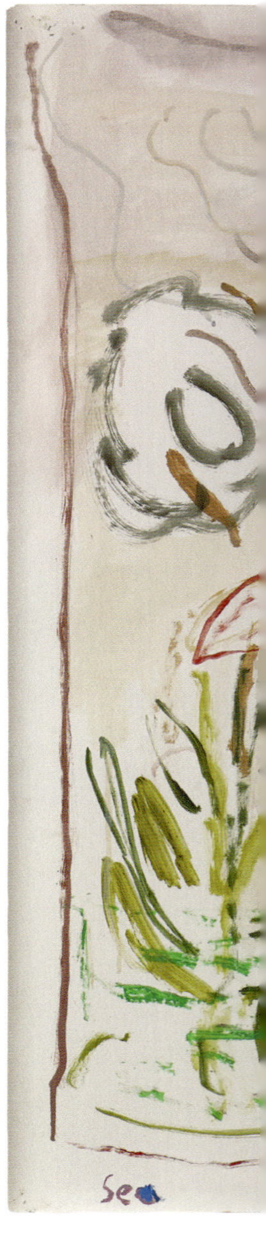

118 *Annie's garden*, 2021, oil on paper, 100 x 143 cm

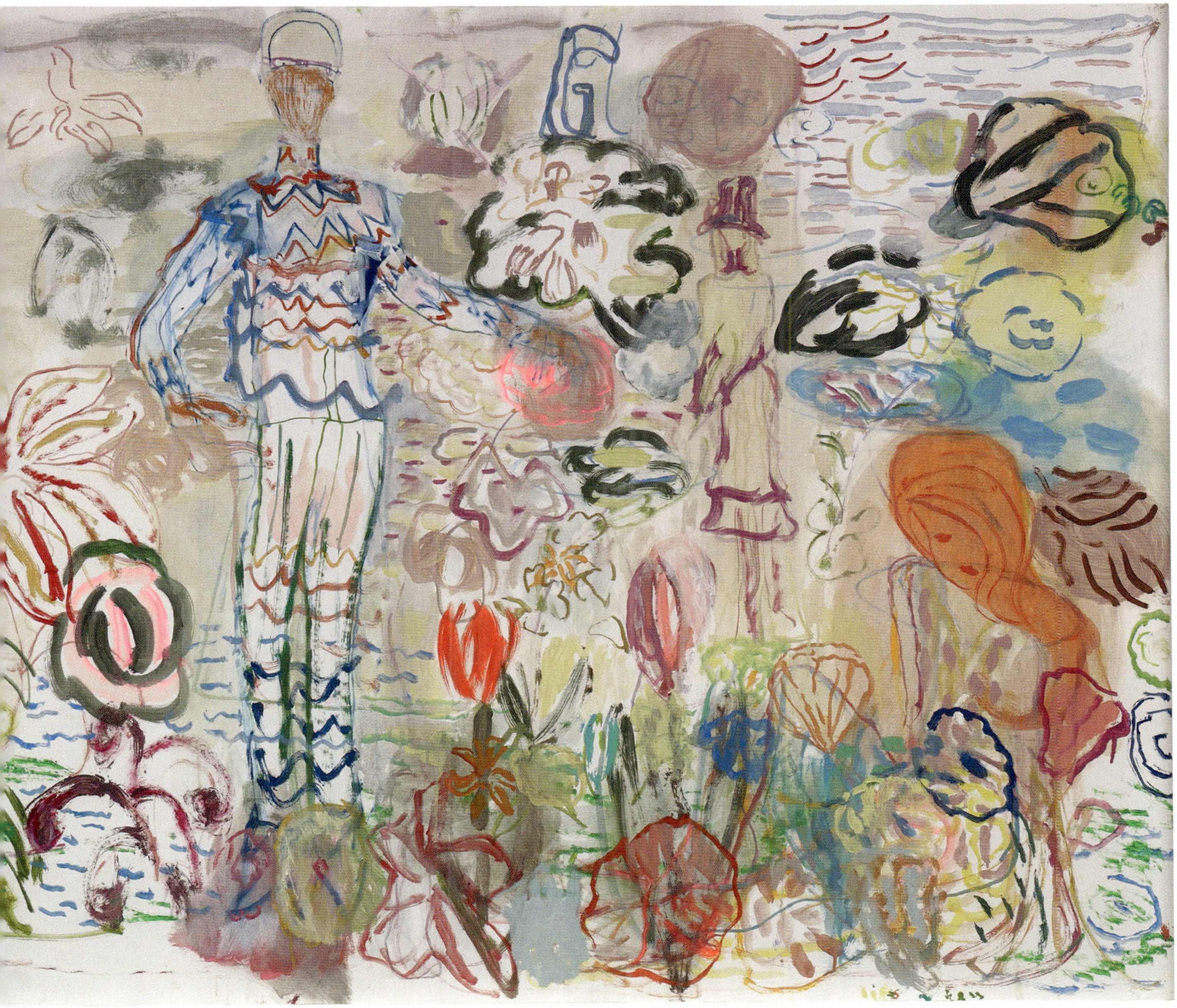

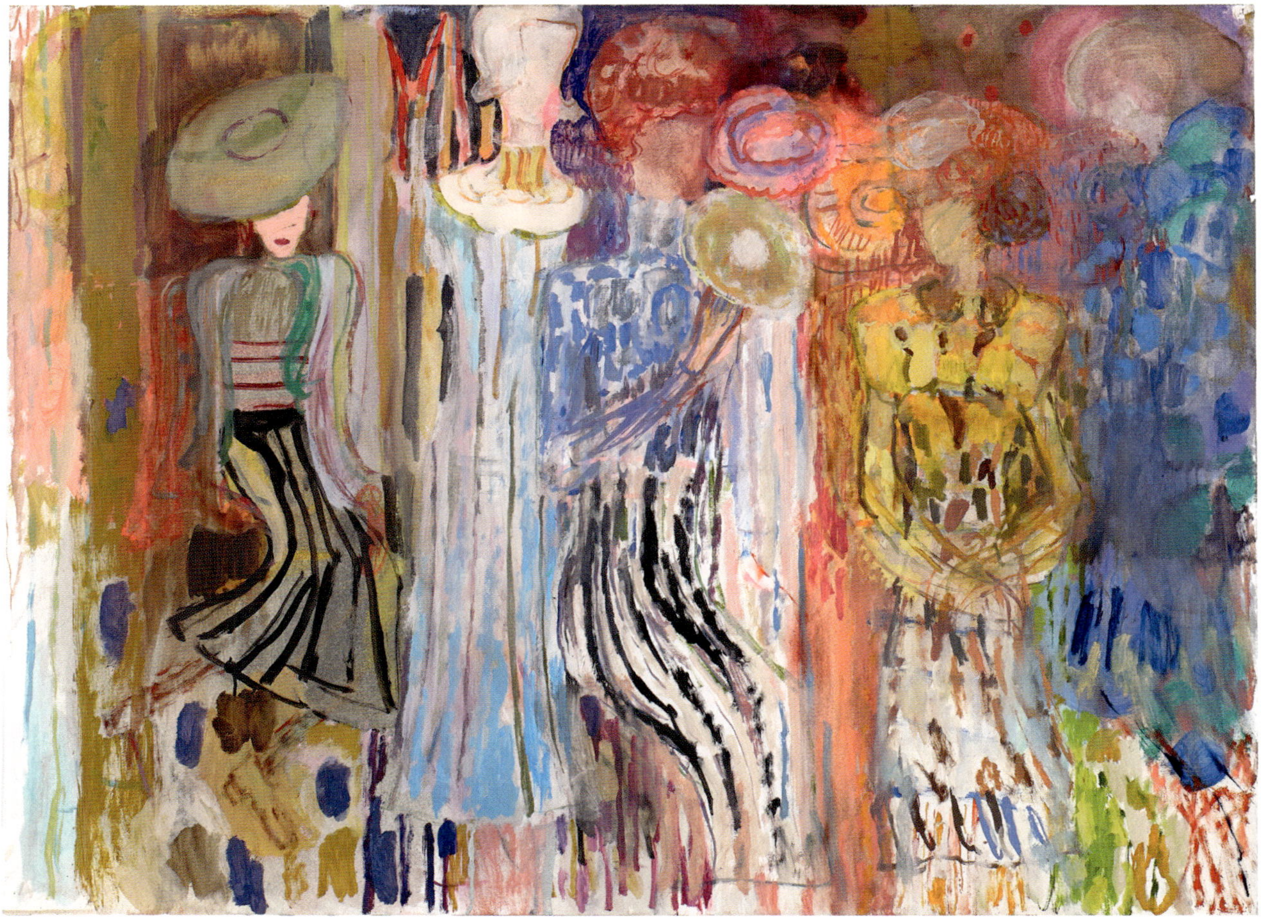

 *Fleeing and fleeing and being*, 2021, oil on paper, 81.8 x 109.8 cm

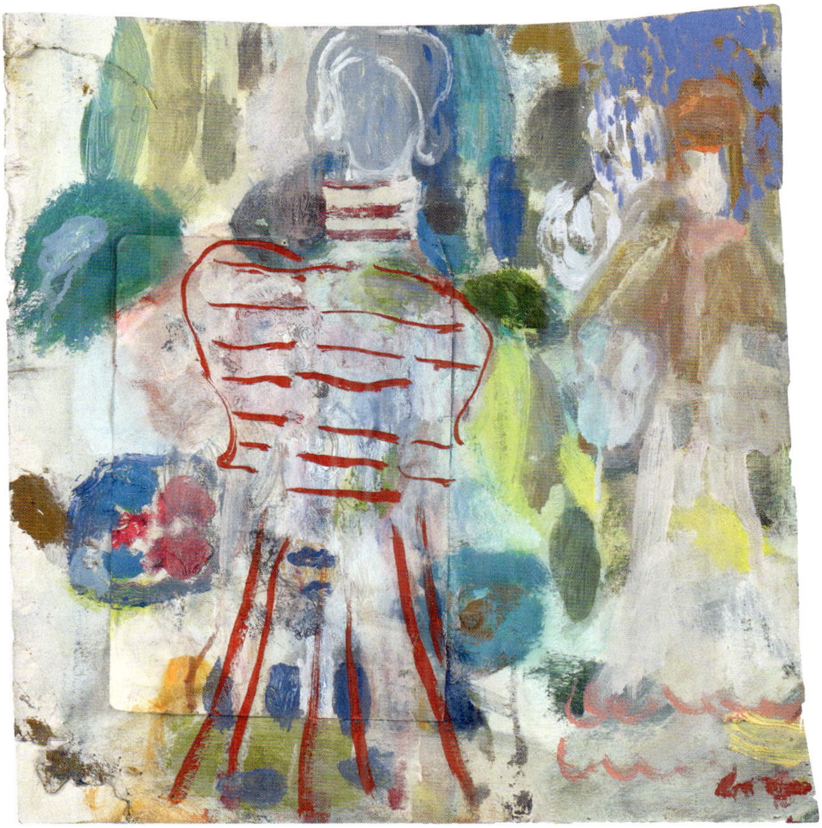

*Fields of stone*, 2022, oil on paper, 34.7 x 33.9 cm 

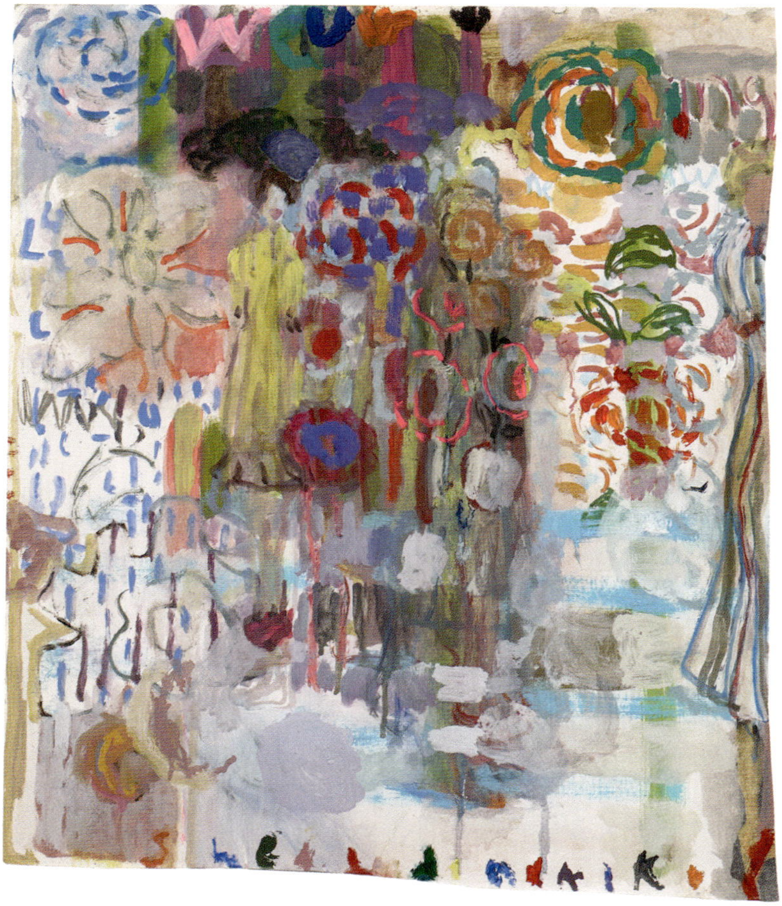

 *Rumours*, 2021, oil on paper, 46 x 39 cm

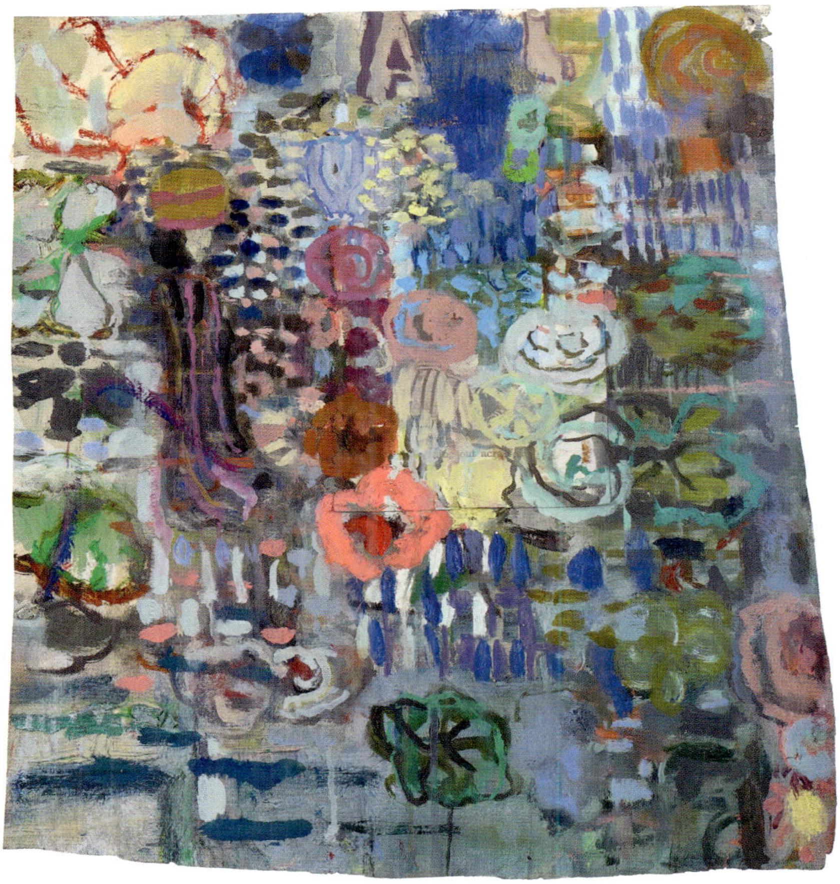

*Tears run rings*, 2021, oil on paper, 42.4 x 38.9 cm 

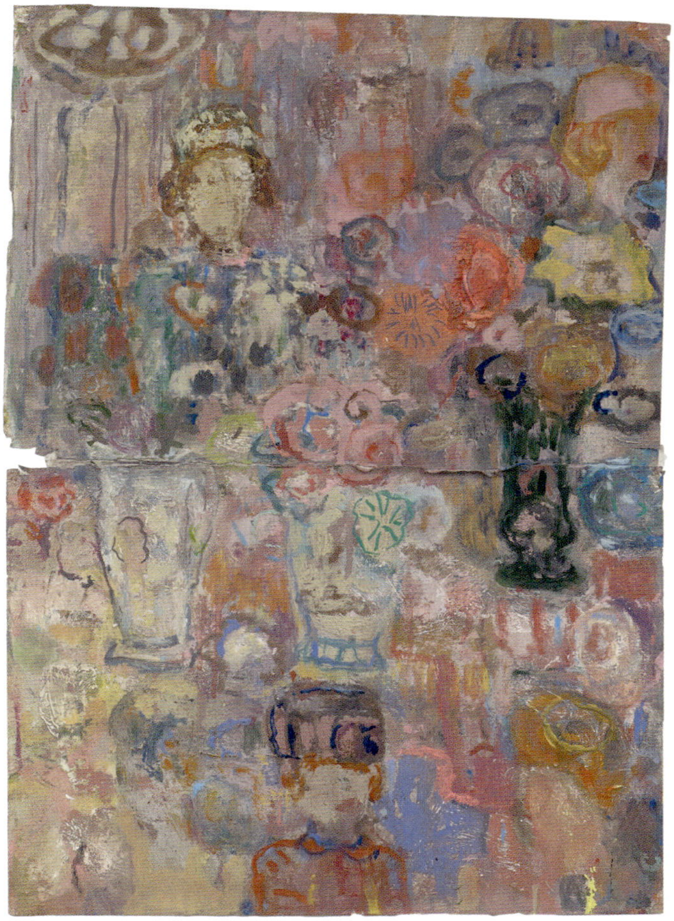

 *Blue China*, 2021, oil on paper, 42 x 29.5 cm

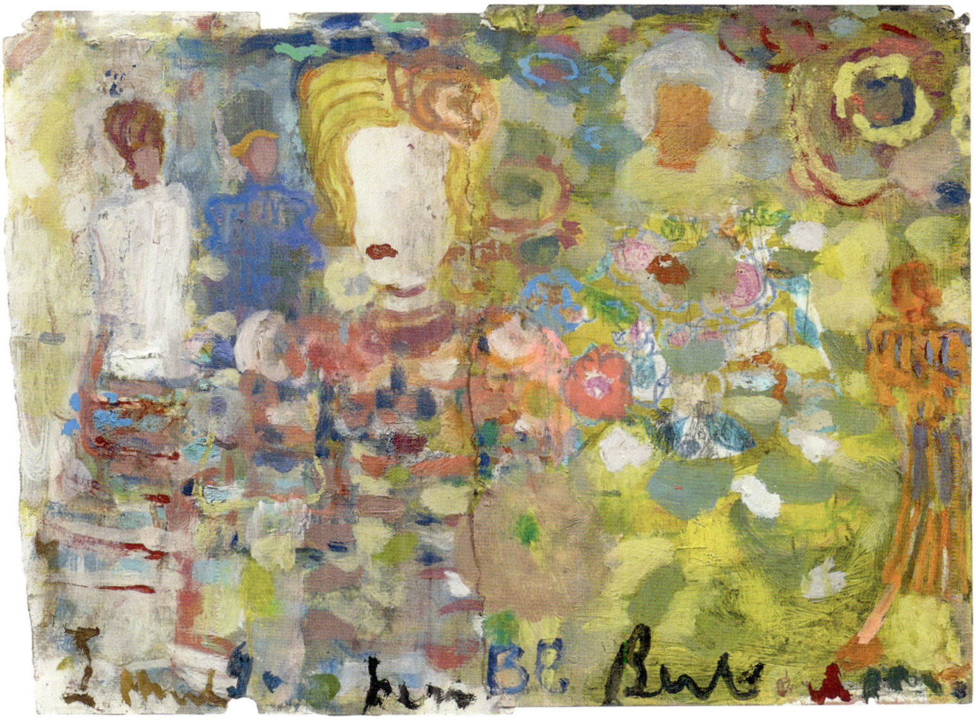

*Here before*, 2021, oil on paper, 29 6 x 39.5 cm 

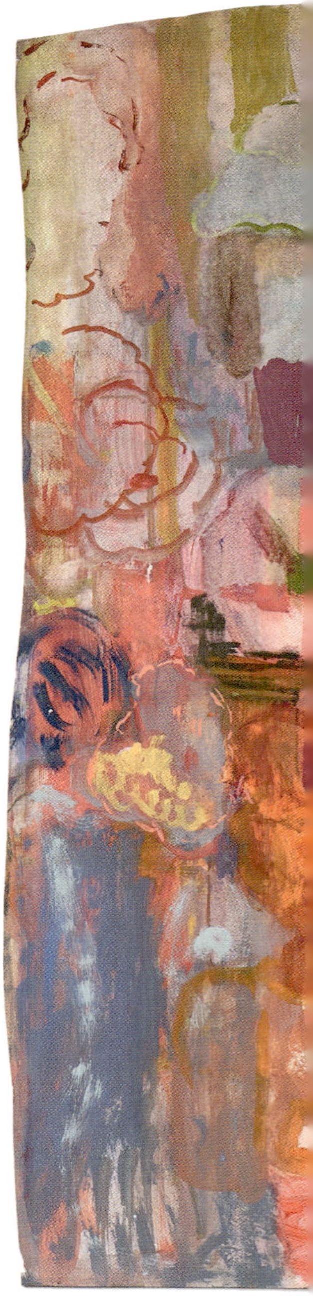

126 *Baubles, bangles, beads*, 2021, oil on paper, 93.5 x 124 cm

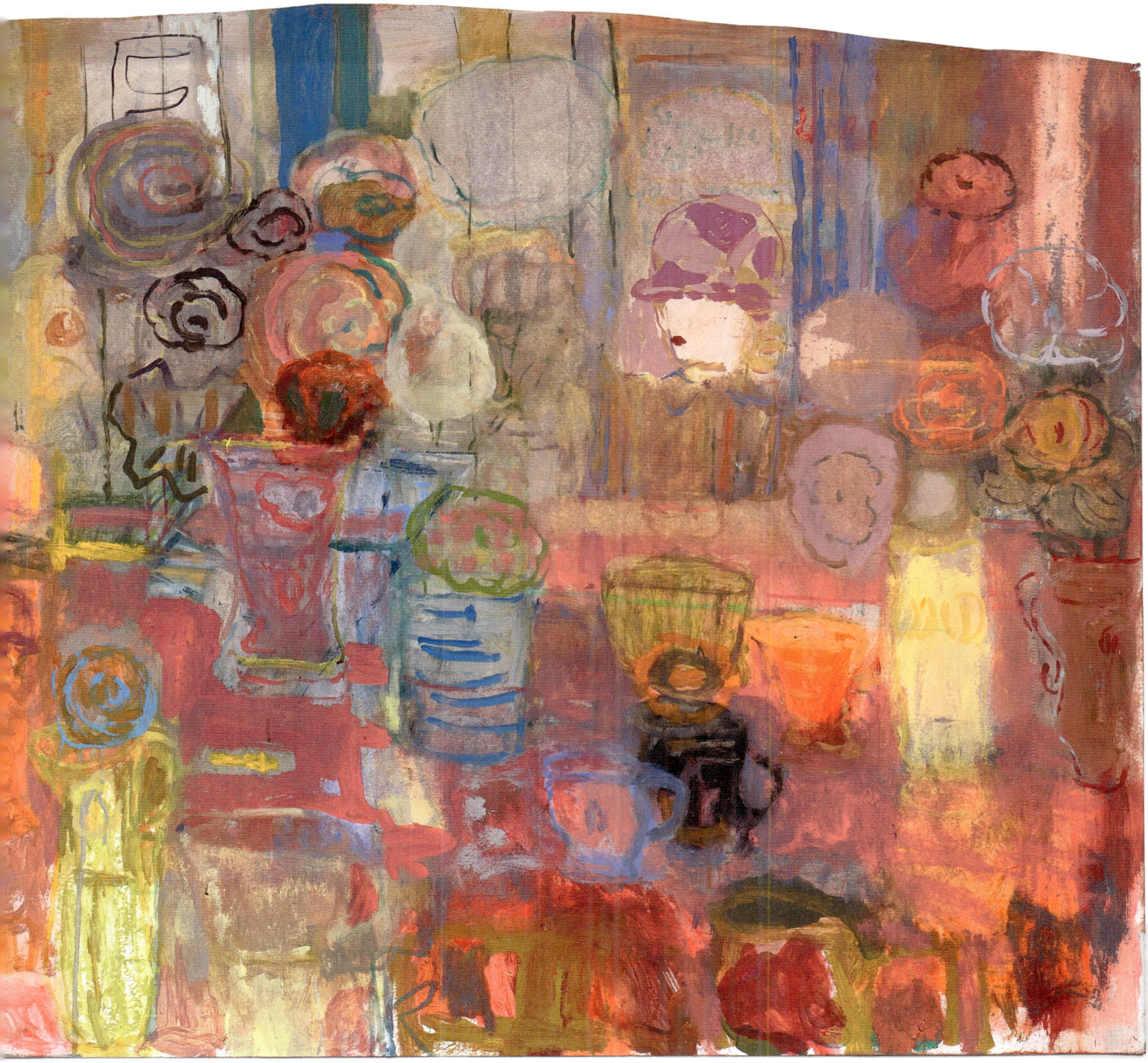

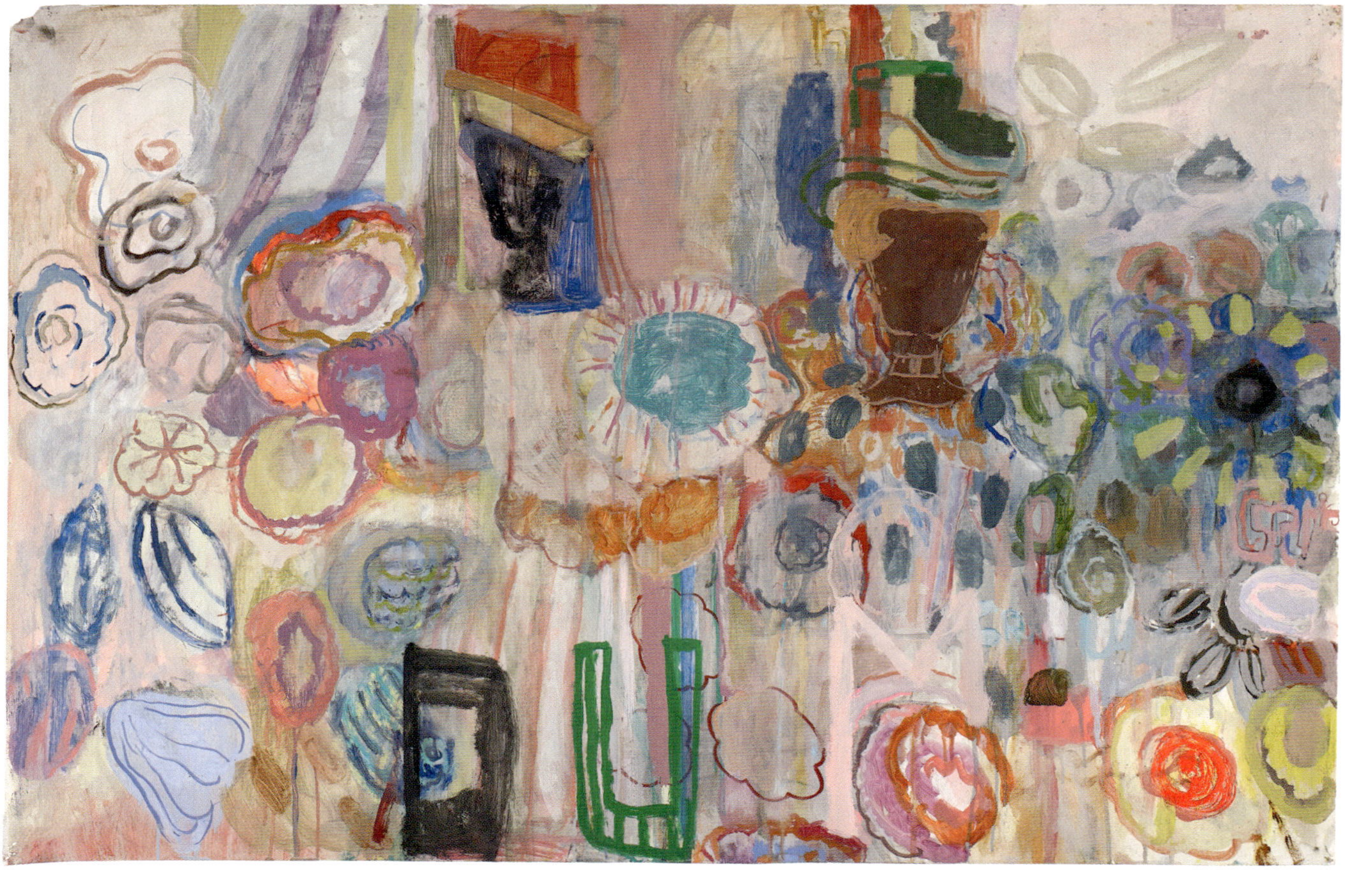

 *Dancers hidden*, 2022, oil on paper, 81.8 x 127.8 cm

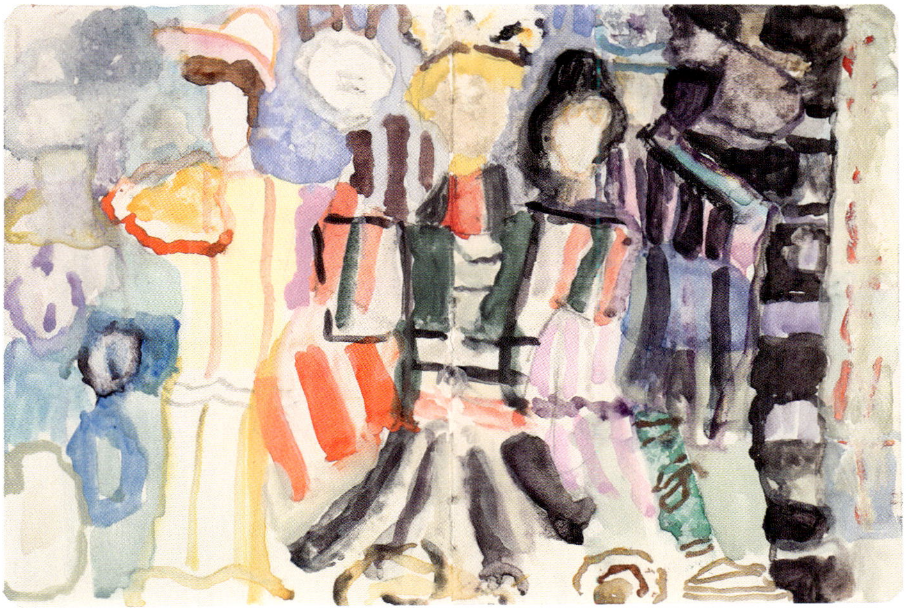

*Hats and coats II*, 2022, watercolour on paper, 17.2 x 24.7 cm 

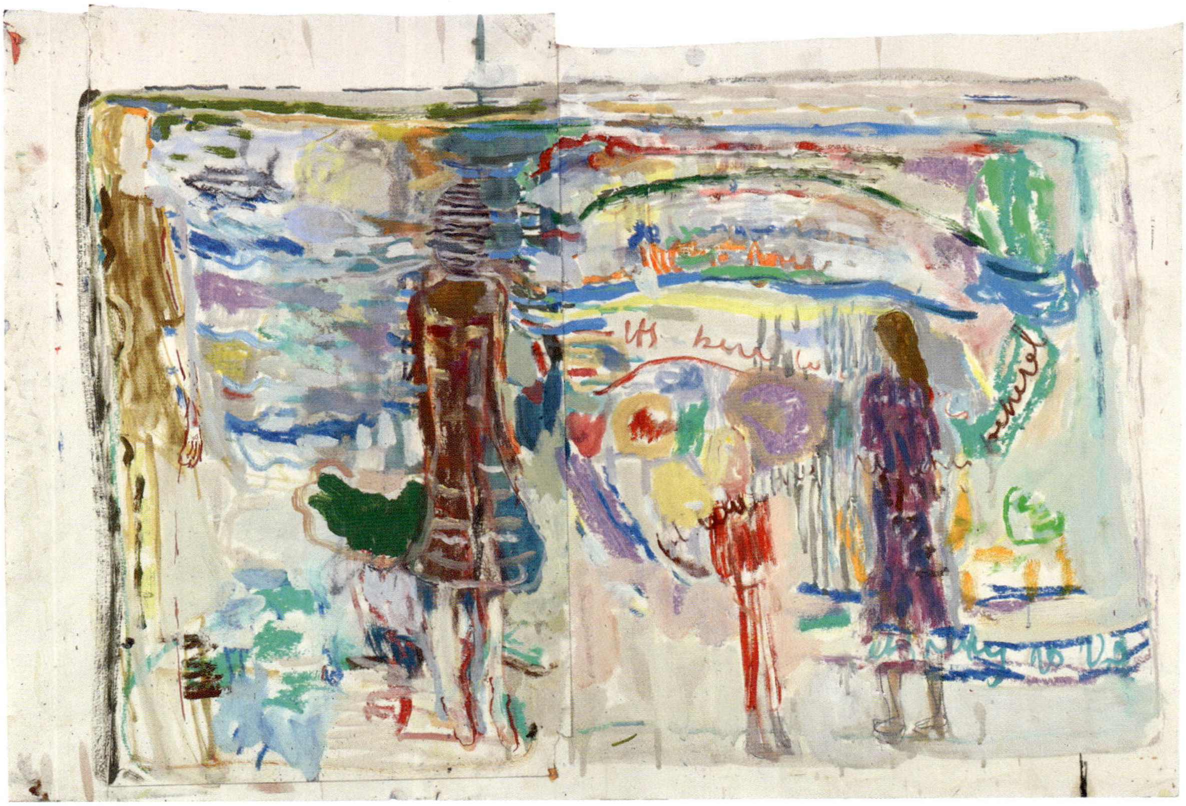

 *Big dark dying*, 2019, oil on paper, 57.5 x 84.2 cm

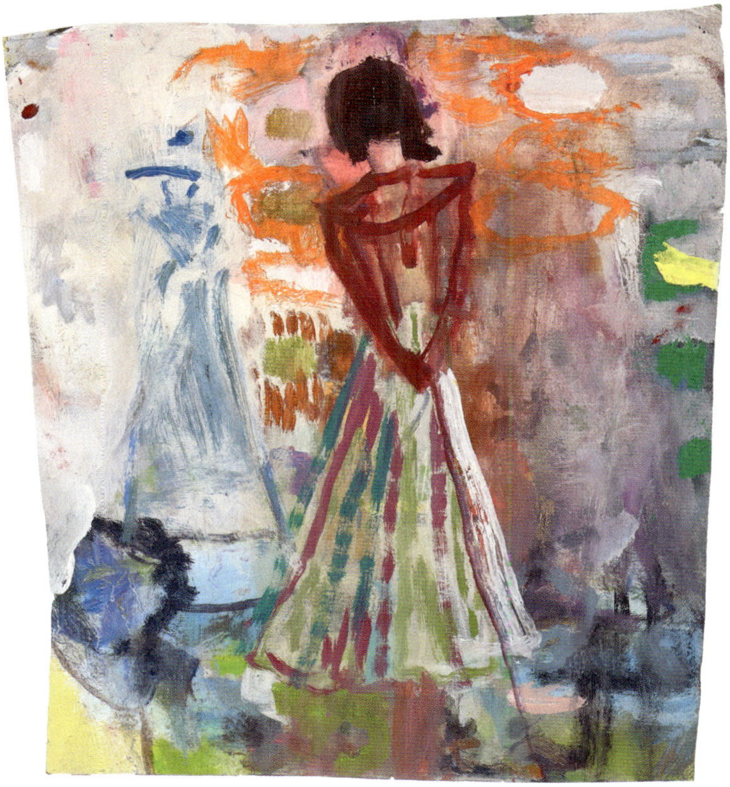

*Morning rain II*, 2021, oil on paper, 29.5 x 27.5 cm 

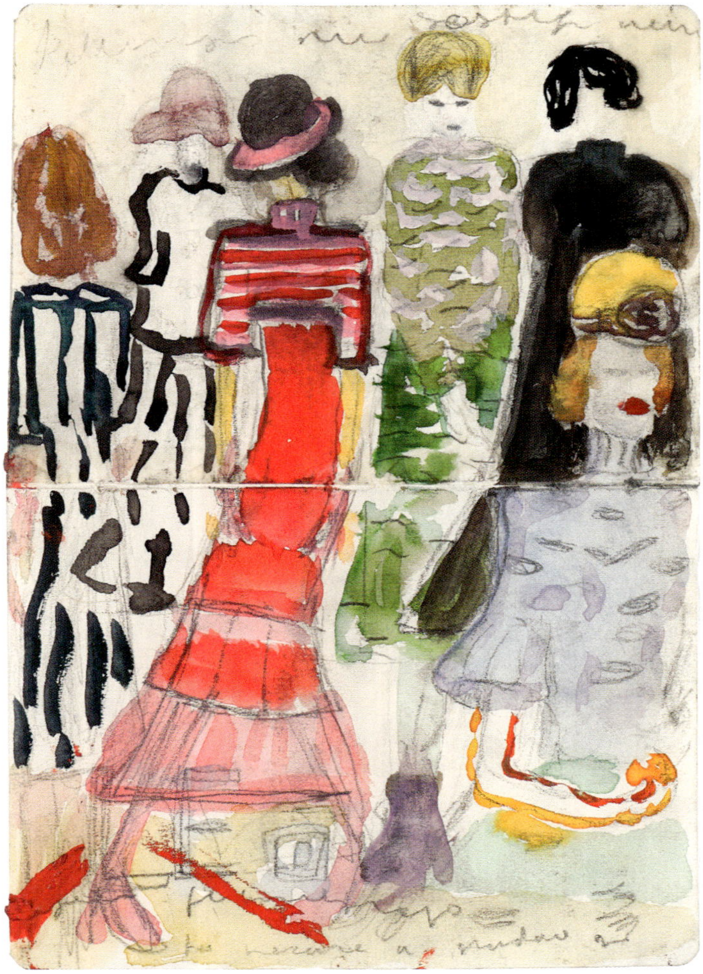

 *Tranquilisers*, 2021, watercolour and pencil on paper, 25 x 17.4 cm

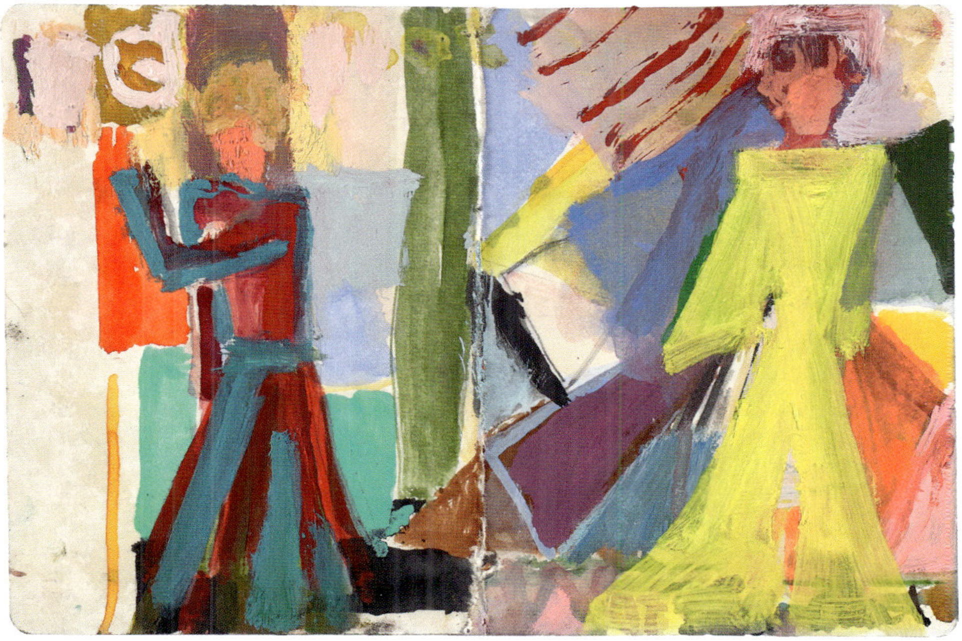

*Mirror on mirror*, 2022, oil on paper, 17.2 x 25.2 cm 

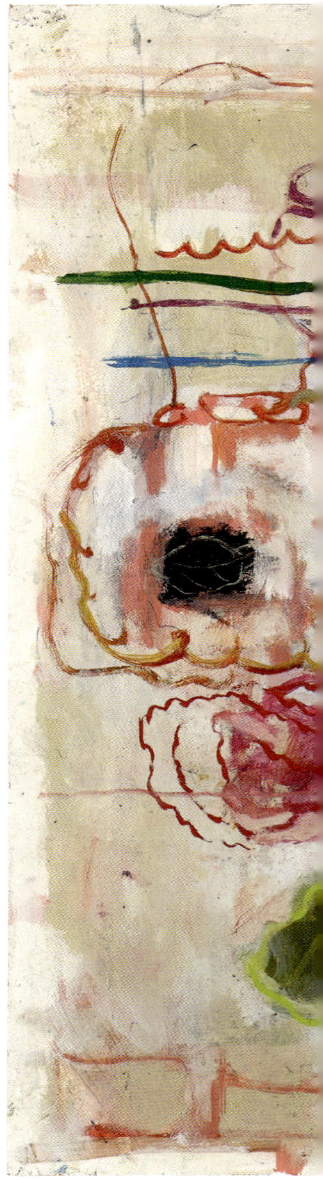

134 *Thoughts, meals, days*, 2019, oil on paper, 80 x 123 cm

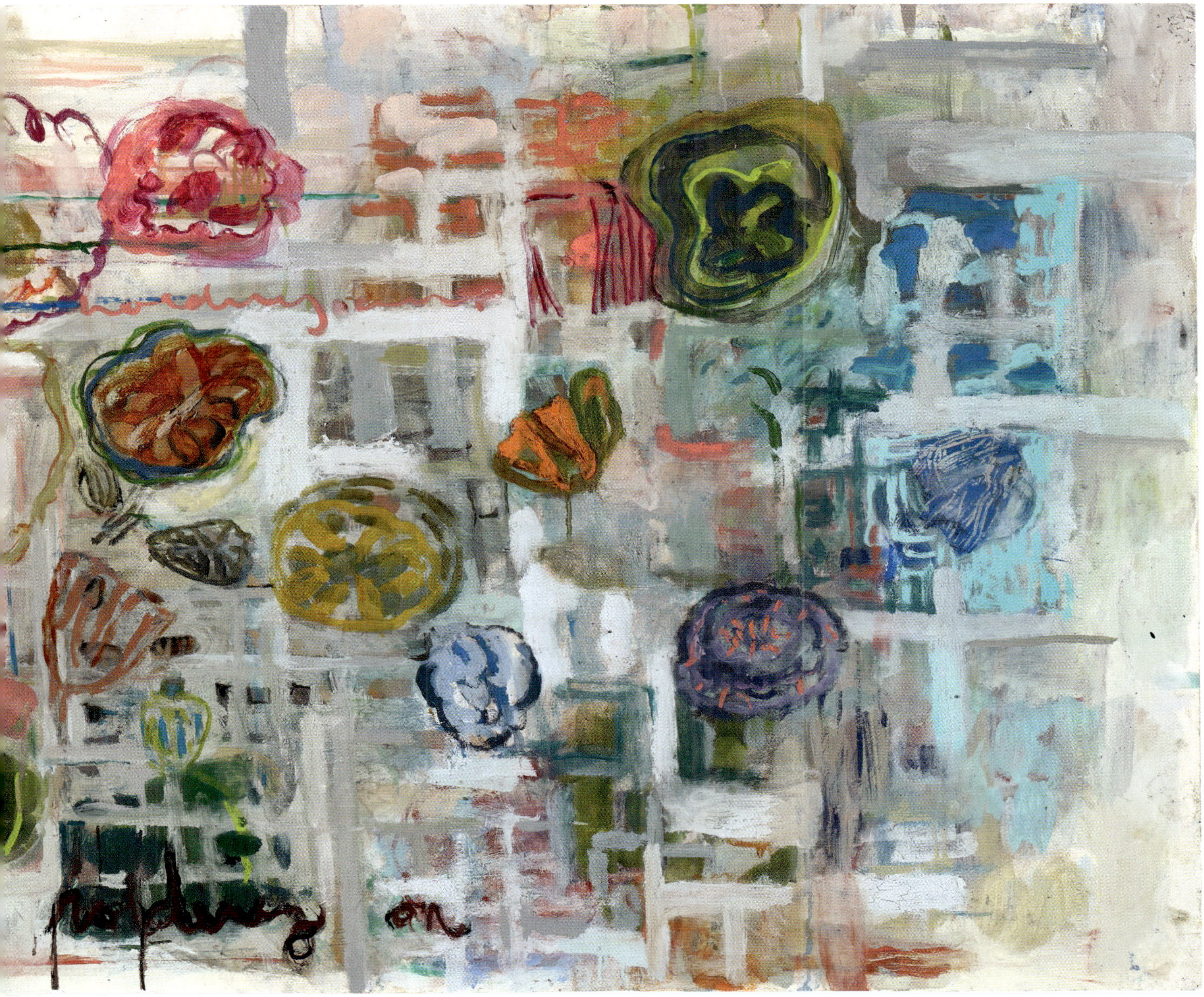
holding
on

# DRAWINGS

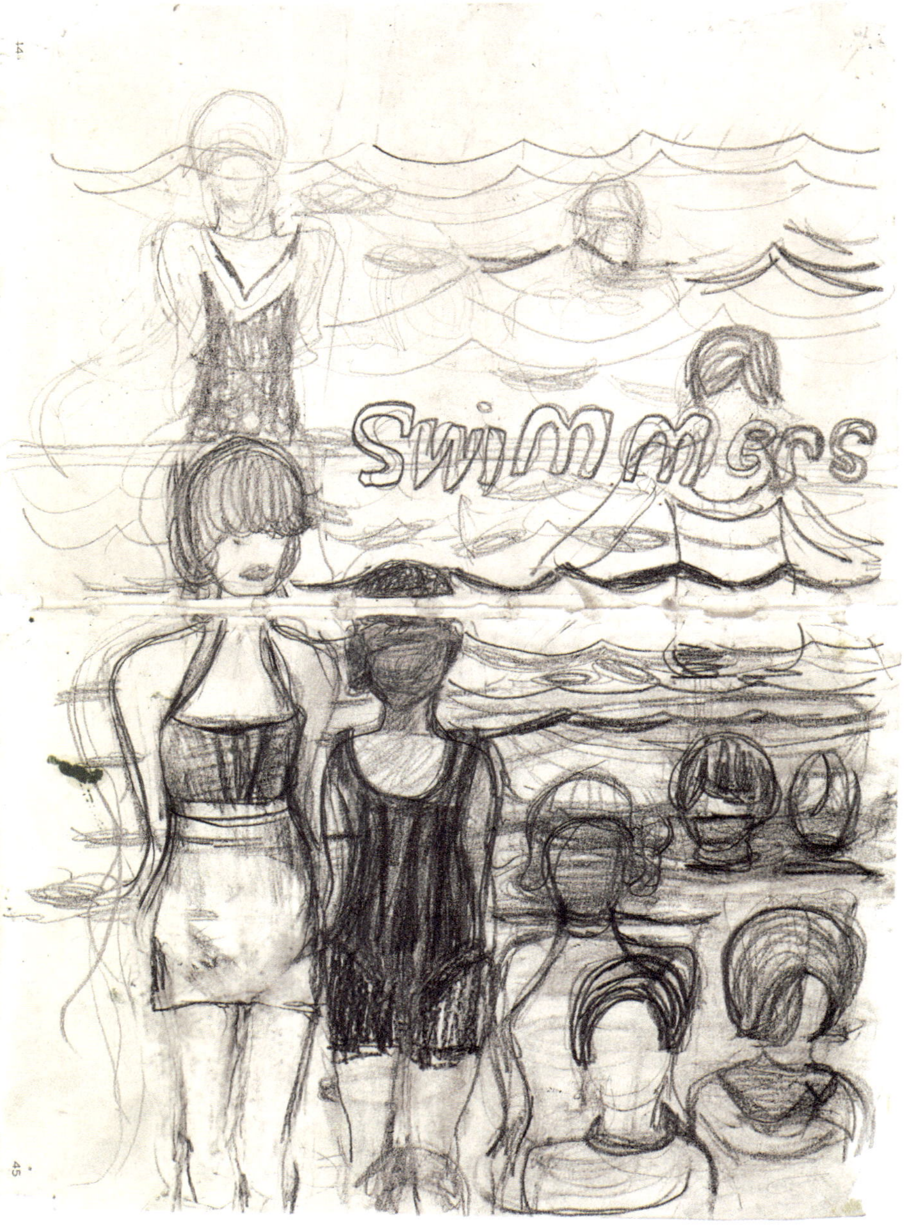


 *The swimmers*, 2020, pencil on paper, 28.7 x 20.5 cm

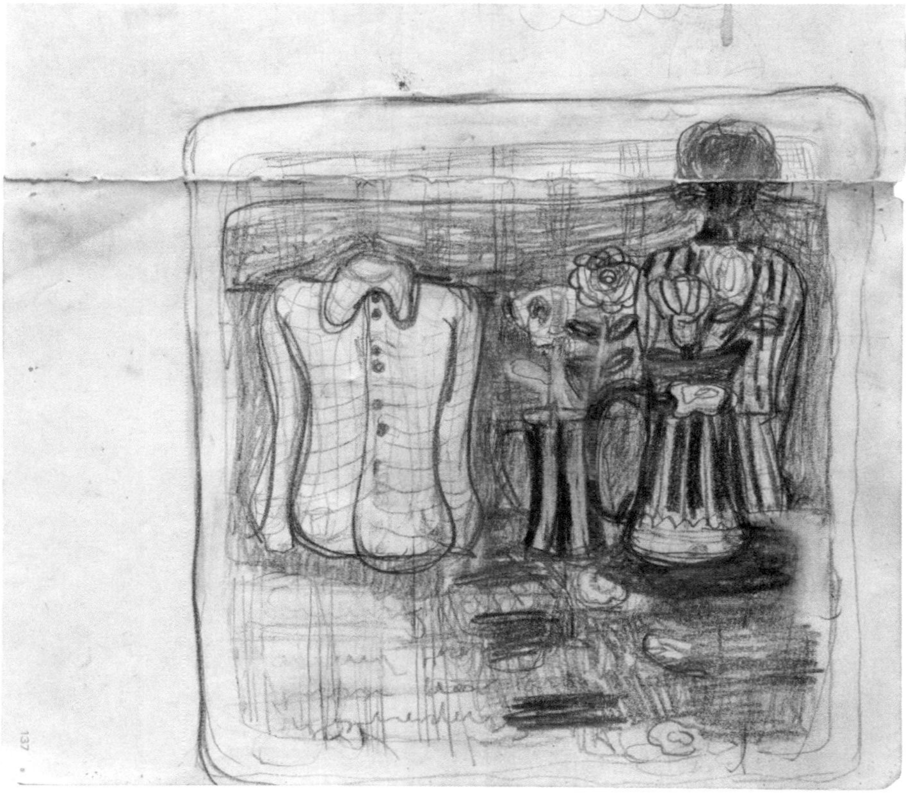

*Cul-de-sac*, 2018, pencil on paper, 18.3 x 20.5 cm 

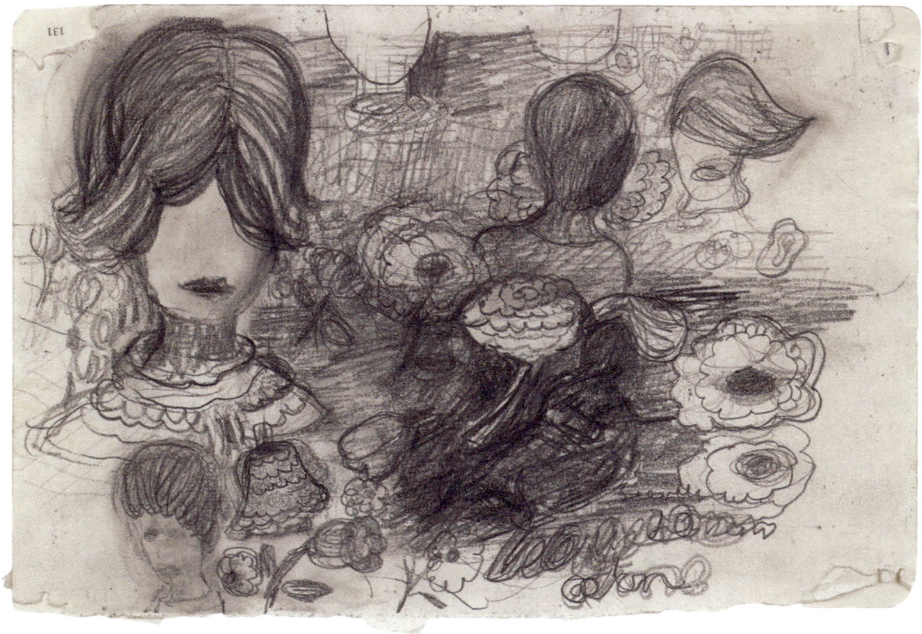

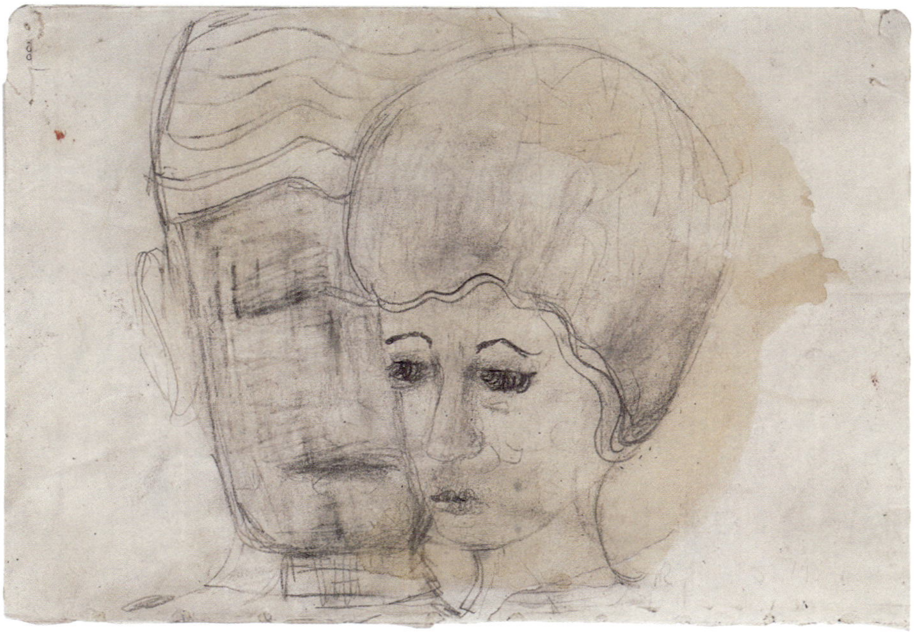

Above: *In the eves*, 2020, pencil on paper, 14.3 x 20.5 cm
Below: *Do you sleep on the right side or the left*, 2019, pencil and watercolour on paper, 14.3 x 20.5 cm

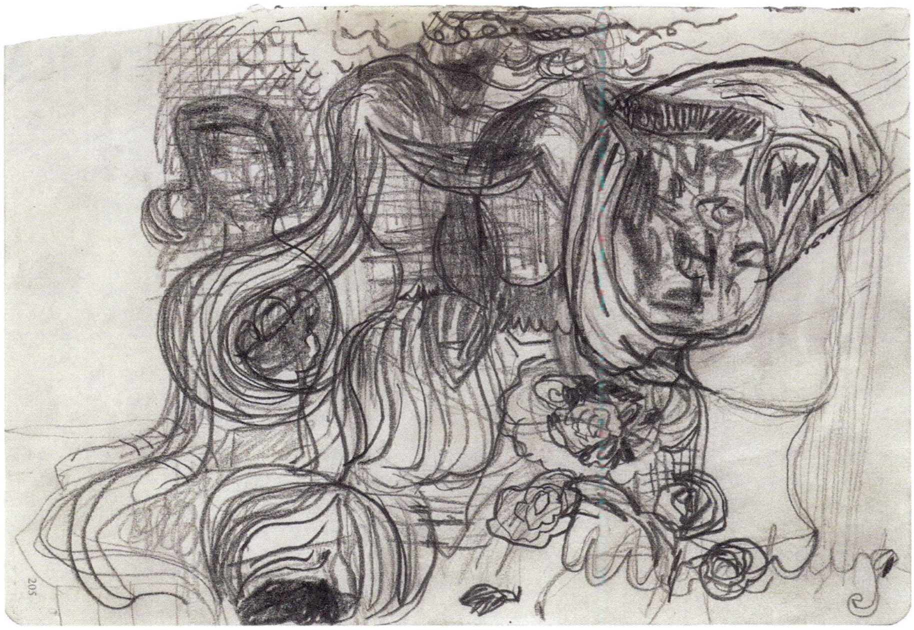

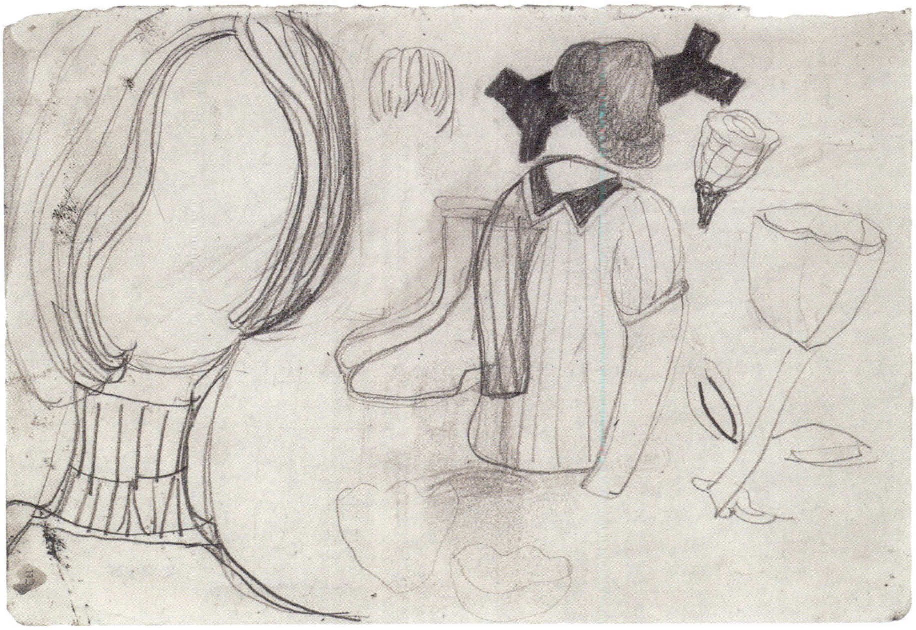

Above: *Milly Molly Mandy*, 2020, pencil on paper, 14.3 x 20.5 cm
Below: *Her clothes, her hair, her shoes*, 2017, pencil on paper, 14.3 x 20.5 cm

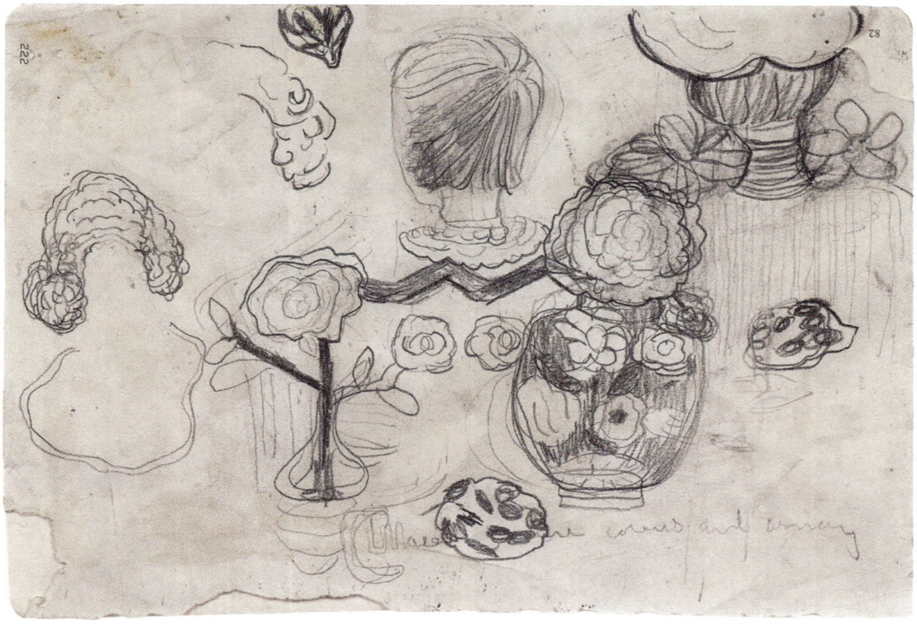

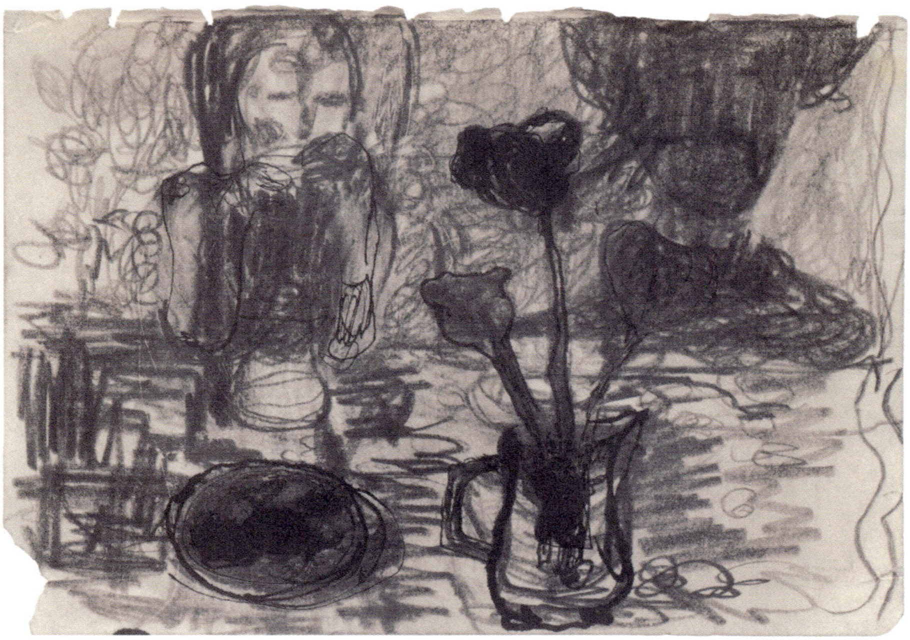

Above: *In half an hour*, 2018, pencil on paper, 14.3 x 20.5 cm
Below: *A winter drawing*, 2019, pencil and ink on paper, 12.4 x 17.4 cm

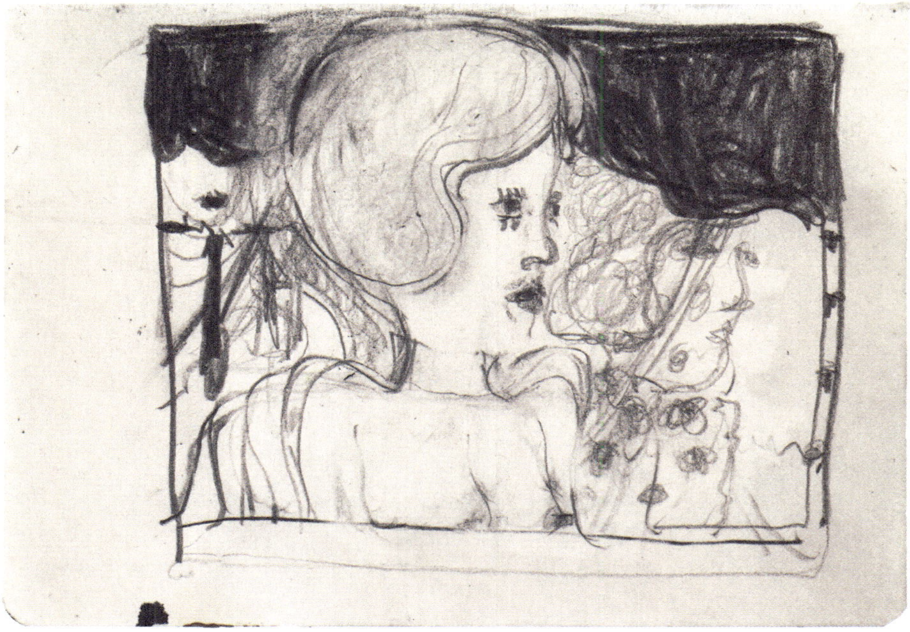

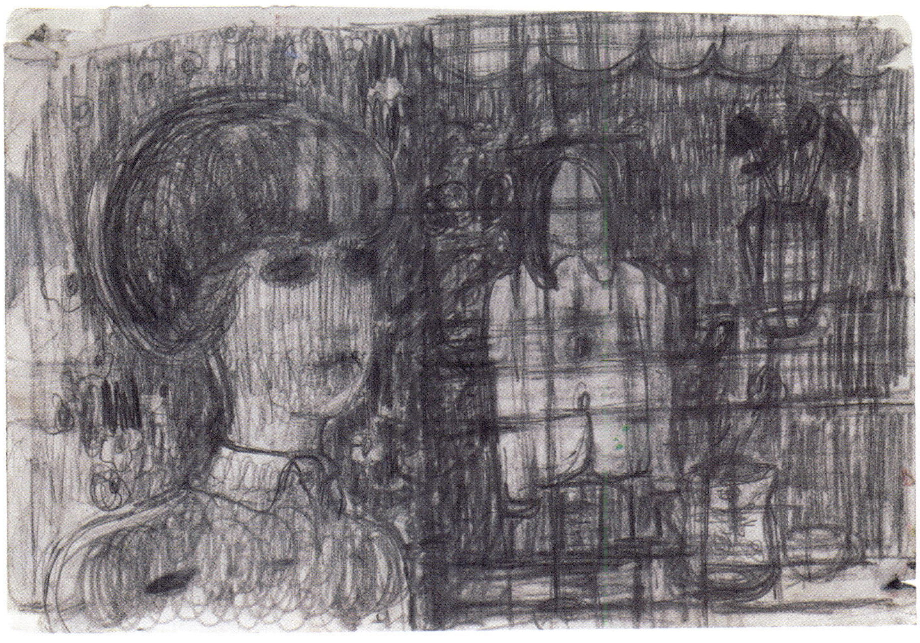

Above: *Duet*, 2020, pencil on paper, 12.7 x 17.5 cm
Below: *In a boring town*, 2019, pencil on paper, 20.7 x 29.4 cm 

## MIKEY CUDDIHY

Mikey Cuddihy is an artist and writer living in East Sussex. Born in New York, she was educated at Summerhill School, Edinburgh College of Art, and Central Saint Martins in London. She lived and worked in London for over three decades, where she co-founded the Beck Road Arts Trust – a live work community of artists in Hackney. In 2014 Atlantic Books published her memoir *A Conversation About Happiness*, about her childhood and early years as an artist.

## HETTIE JUDAH

Hettie Judah is the chief critic on the daily newspaper *The i*, a columnist for *Apollo* magazine, a contributing editor to *The Plant*, and writes regularly for the *Guardian*, *Vogue*, *Frieze* and the *New York Times*. Recent and upcoming books include *Lapidarium* (John Murray/Penguin, 2022), *How Not to Exclude Artist Mothers (and other parents)* (Lund Humphries, 2022), *Frida Kahlo* (Laurence King, 2020) and *Art London* (ACC Art Books, 2019). She is currently working on a Hayward Touring exhibition and book on art and motherhood.

## LORNA ROBERTSON

Lorna Robertson was born in Ayr on the west coast of Scotland in 1967. She studied at Duncan of Jordanstone College of Art in Dundee and currently lives and works in Glasgow. Recent exhibitions include *Faces in the Water* (with Andrew Cranston) at Cromwell Place in 2021 and at Kingsgate Project Space (with Robert MacBryde) in 2019; *thoughts, meals, days* is her first exhibition at Ingleby.

## LIST OF WORKS

### LARGE PAINTINGS



### SMALLER PAINTINGS



### WORKS ON PAPER

## DRAWINGS

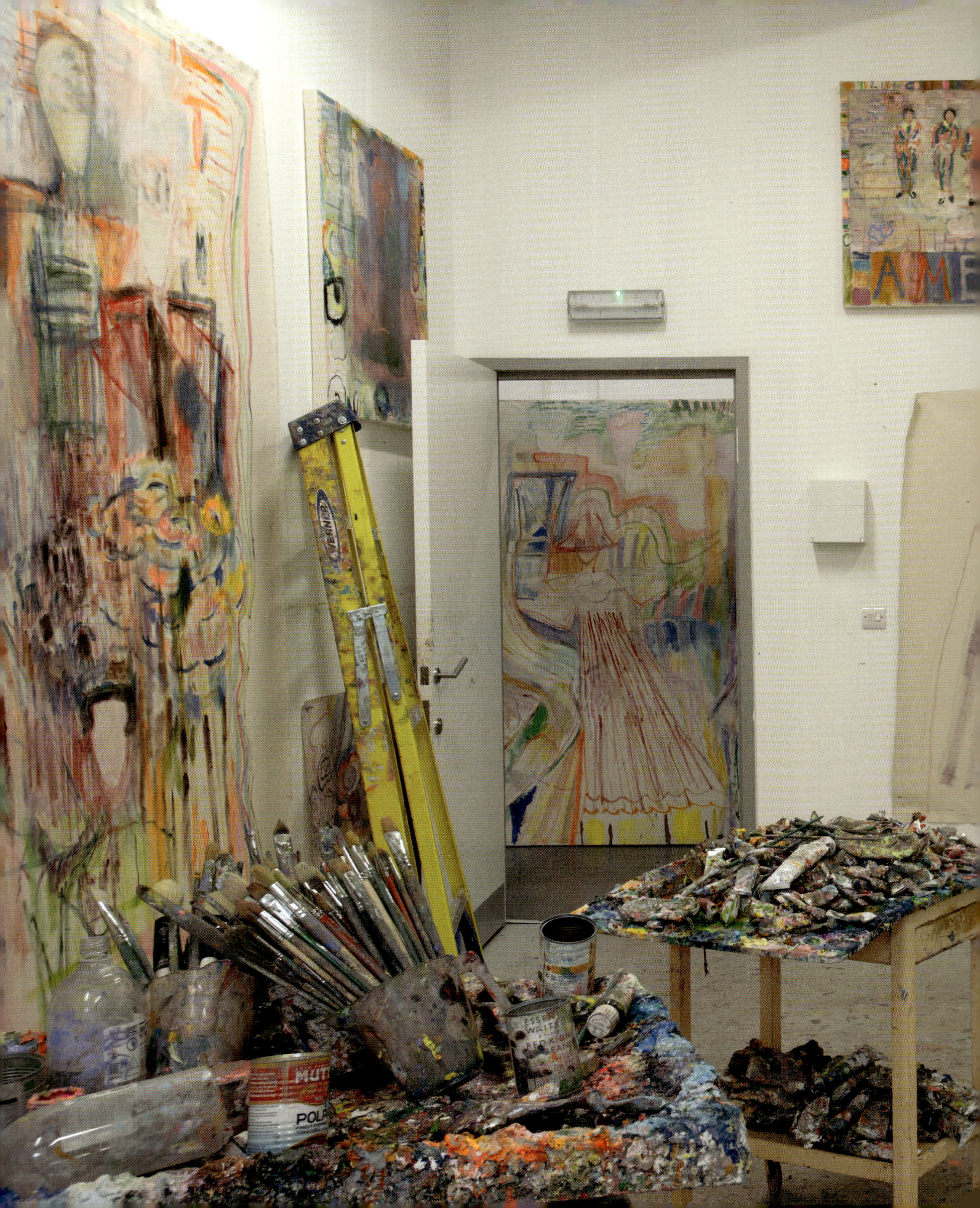

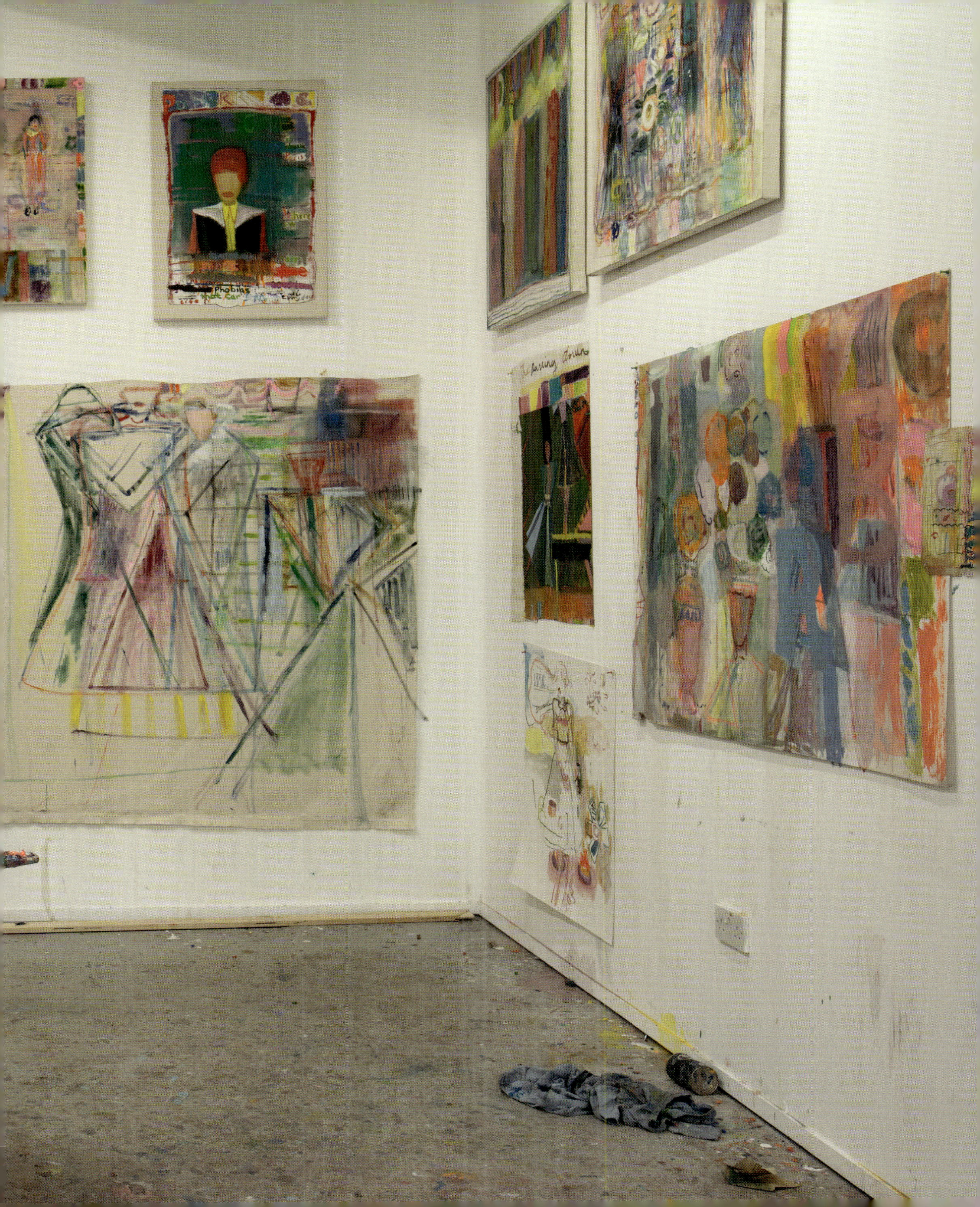

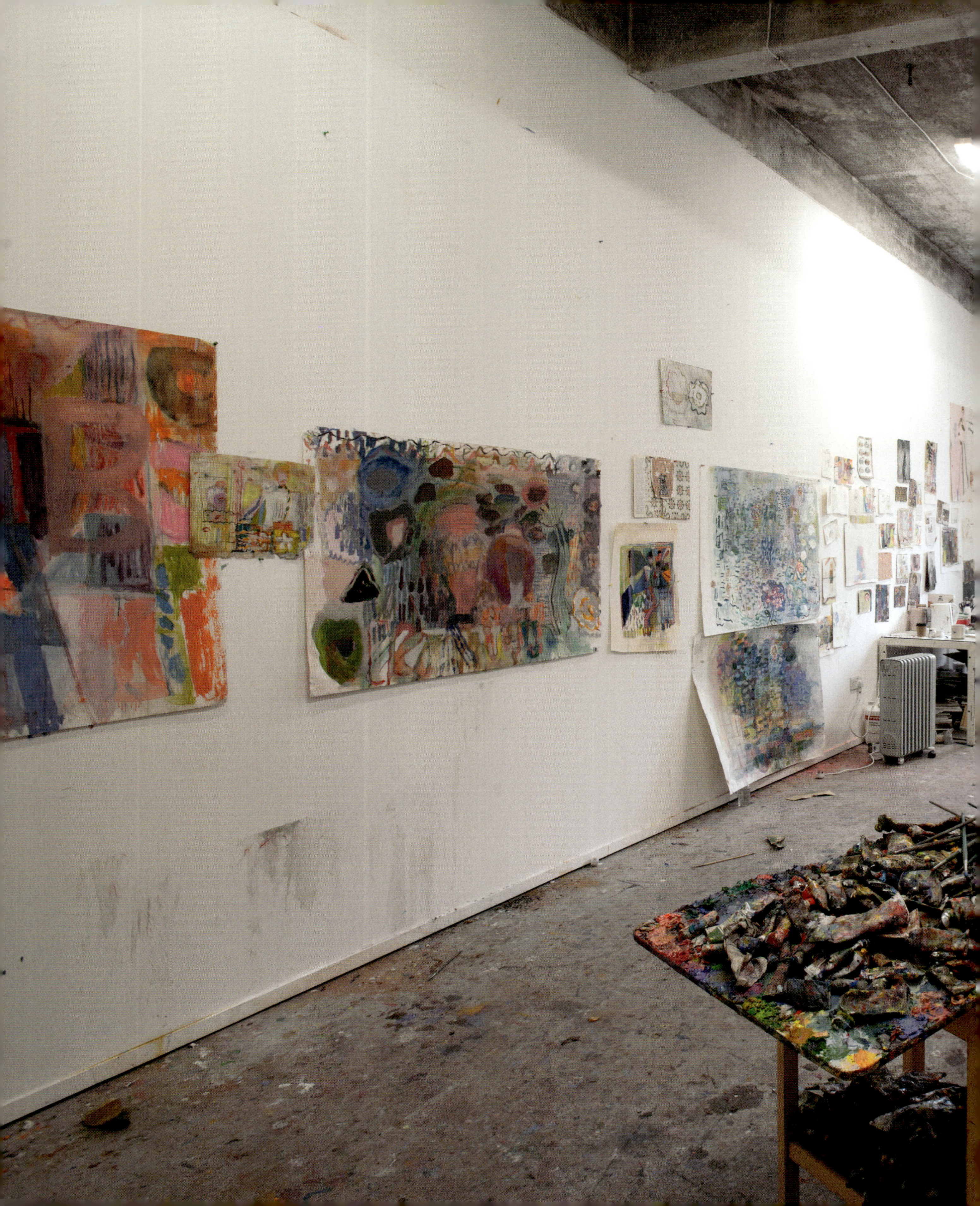

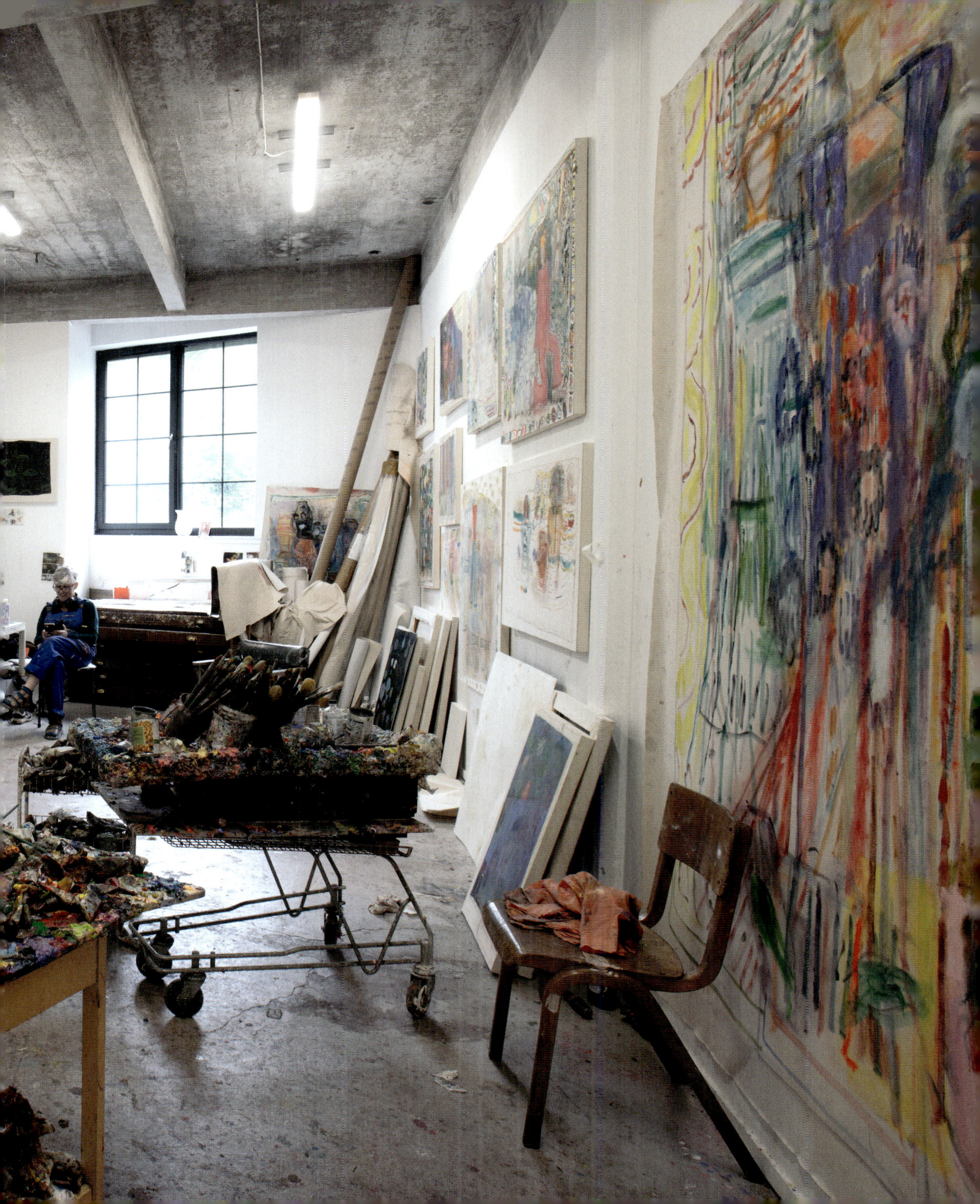

ACKNOWLEDGEMENTS

I'd like to thank Florence and Richard Ingleby and all the staff at Ingleby.

Hettie Judah, Mikey Cuddihy, Dan Howard-Birt, Marie McQuade,
Peter Chalmers, David McDiarmid, Stuart Noble, Jon Nicolson.

Andy, Lewis, Jude and Joseph.

First published in 2022 by Ingleby, Edinburgh,
and Anomie Publishing, London

Printed in an edition of 750 copies

ISBN 978-1-910221-42-6

All works © Lorna Robertson
All words © the authors

All rights reserved. No part of this publication may be reproduced, stored or transmitted in any form or by any means without the written permission of the copyright holders and of the publishers.

Design by Joanna Deans, Identity
Studio installation photography by Alan Dimmick
Artwork photography by John McKenzie
Printed by Albe De Coker, Antwerp
Distributed by Casemate Art

Cover image: *The swimmer*, 2020, oil and collage on paper, 37.2 x 54.4 cm

INGLEBY
33 Barony Street
Edinburgh
EH3 6NX

www.inglebygallery.com

INGLEBY **Anomie**

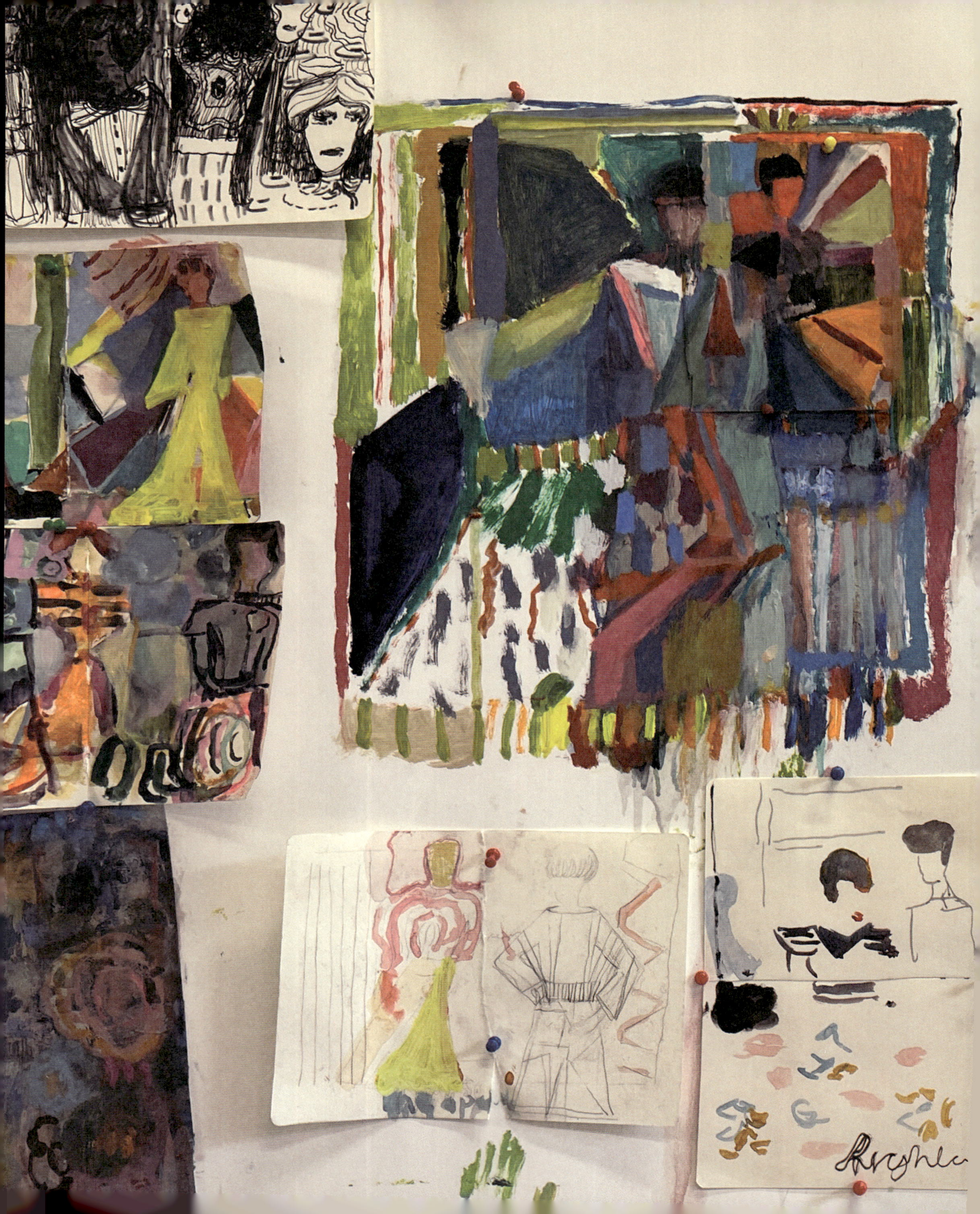